THE WAR 1941–45

ILYA EHRENBURG

The War 1941-45

Volume V of
MEN, YEARS – LIFE

*

Translated by
TATIANA SHEBUNINA
in collaboration with
YVONNE KAPP

LONDON
MACGIBBON & KEE
1964

FIRST PUBLISHED 1964 BY MACGIBBON & KEE LTD
ENGLISH TRANSLATION © MACGIBBON & KEE LTD 1964
PRINTED IN GREAT BRITAIN BY
COX AND WYMAN LTD
LONDON, READING AND FAKENHAM

TRANSLATORS' NOTE

All quotations from foreign authors are translated from the
Russian of Ehrenburg's text, save for certain passages in
Chapter 18 which we have translated from *Destin du Siècle*
by Jean-Richard Bloch (Les Editions Rieder, Paris, 1931).
The footnotes are ours.

ILLUSTRATIONS
between pages 96–97

1

I NOW come to the years which are engraved on the memory of every one of us. Viktor Nekrassov, Emmanuil Kazakevich, Vassily Grossman, Vera Panova, Olga Bergholtz and Alexander Bek – to mention but a few – have devoted excellent books to those years. So the reader must not be surprised if I make only brief references to outstanding events or omit them altogether: there is no need to repeat what others have already said so well.

As I have had occasion to remark before, in peacetime each man follows his own course, has his own joys and sorrows, whereas war not only clothes everything in protective colouring but allows no room for spiritual diversity: age, individual traits of character, everything that goes to make up a distinctive personal life gives way before its demands. During the war years I thought and felt like all my compatriots.

I am as reluctant to repeat myself as to repeat others, but that, I am afraid, is inevitable. In my long novel, *The Storm*, many encounters, conversations, pictures, emotions and experiences are drawn from personal memories. I recall the two houses in Rzhev – christened respectively 'Colonel' and 'Lieutenant-Colonel' – at which Raya, one of the heroines of the novel, often gazed; I met Osip in Minsk when the houses mined by the Germans were blown up and collapsed; I was with Sergey in the Ros cemetery in Vilnius and, like Doctor Krylov in Shchigry, I spent a night in the house of a young woman who had lived with a German officer. What I would like to do is not so much retell the events as try to look at them with my eyes of today.

The first months of the war leap to my mind. As time passed people grew accustomed to things, a wartime way of life evolved, but in the summer and autumn of 1941 the towns were storm-tossed, splitting, crashing down like trees. Everything was new and bewildering: the mobilization depots, the partings, the defiant songs, the word 'encirclement' – as terrible as plague or pestilence; the roads crowded with refugees, the rising alarm. In my notebook there are dates and towns: 27th June – Minsk; 1st July – Riga; 10th July – Ostrov; 14th July

9

– Pskov; 17th July – Vitebsk; 20th July – Smolensk; 14th August – Krivoy Rog; 20th August – Novgorod, Gomel, Kherson; 26th August – Dnepropetrovsk; 1st September – Gatchina, Kakhovka; 13th September – Chernigov, Romny; 20th September – Kiev. (I took down what I learnt from *Red Star*; the communiqués generally used the phrase 'in the direction of'.) In three months' time we lost territory far greater in extent than the whole of France. Today that has become so many pages of history, but in those days it spelt mortal anguish. We waited for each communiqué with bated breath. Private radio sets were shortly commandeered and there remained only the 'plates' (public and community loudspeakers); twice a day the 'plate' hoarsely informed us that Sergeant Vassilyev's unit had destroyed three enemy tanks, that the prisoners captured said the German army's morale was deteriorating, that Greek or Dutch patriots sent greetings to the Red Army, and that we were retreating, retreating, forever retreating.

'What news?' I would ask Colonel Karpov at the office. 'It's in the Vyazma direction,' he would reply. 'But we've already left Vyazma.' It was impossible to understand anything; all we could do was to have faith and, in common with everyone else, I believed implicitly: despite the communiqués, despite the refugees, despite the women with bundles who thronged the streets of Moscow.

I talked to many people, both old friends and strangers, who came to the *Red Star* office, I visited military hospitals and airfields, travelled to the front, met generals and soldiers. I could remember the First World War, I had lived through the Spanish experience, I had witnessed the French collapse and so in a sense I was steeled, but I must confess that at times I felt despair. As for the younger people, they asked in utter bewilderment: 'But why is it like this?' for they had been told that if the enemy poked his snout into our garden he would be met with a shattering blow and that the war would be fought on enemy territory; yet now they had watched the fascists sweep almost unhindered from Brest-Litovsk to Smolensk. The words 'superior enemy forces' explained a great deal, but they did not explain the main thing: how was it that the Germans had so many more tanks and planes than we?

On 3rd July, early in the morning, we listened to Stalin's speech: he was evidently greatly moved (one could hear him pause to take a drink of water), and he began in an unusual way, calling us 'brothers and sisters', 'friends'. Stalin ascribed the military reverses to the suddenness of the attack; he spoke of Hitler's 'treachery'. At the same time he repeated that, thanks to the Soviet–German Non-Aggression Pact, we had gained time and had been able to prepare our defences. People listened in silence. During the day I wandered about the city. Moscow was very hot. Everyone was standing about and talking in the streets, in the public gardens, at their front doors. In Pushkin Square a large map was displayed in the window of the *Izvestia* office. The Muscovites looked at it gloomily and then went off home.

It is impossible to assess the confusion, bitterness and alarm felt by each one of us. But we had no time for historical appraisals: the fascists were straining towards Moscow.

Home Guards shuffled along the alleys of the Zamoskvorechye, breathing heavily, weighed down by age and ill-health. But in those days few people gave any thought to military bearing.

Like everybody else, I was filled with anxiety and, like everybody else, I was liberated from doubts by the sheer demands of the situation. Never in my life have I worked so hard: every day I wrote three or four articles; at home I sat at my typewriter, in the evening I went to the *Red Star* office, prepared an article for the next issue, read German documents and intercepted radio messages, edited translations and wrote captions for photographs. Later on I shall have more to say about *Red Star*, but at the moment all I am trying to do is to convey what I felt. I found arguments to prove that we were bound to win. I believed in victory, not because I relied on our resources or on the Second Front, but because I needed to believe: for me in those days, as for all other Soviet citizens, there was no alternative.

Telegrams began to arrive from abroad. Various newspapers wanted me to write for them: the *Daily Herald*, the *New York Post*, *La France*, Swedish papers, the United Press of America. It was not just a matter of using a different language; different formulations were needed for the Red Army men from those needed for the Swedes. Practically every day I broadcast to Soviet listeners, to the French, the Czechs, the Poles, the Norwegians, the Yugoslavs.

Lozovsky told me that Stalin attached great importance to the material for England and America. The Sovinformburo began to organize radio conferences, mainly for America: Slav conferences, Jewish conferences, Women's and Young People's conferences. I took part in the Jewish conference. Other speakers were Mikhoëls, Eisenstein, Peretz Markisch, Bergelson, the architect Yofan, as well as Peter

Kapitza and others. (Several of those who spoke at the meeting or signed the appeal were arrested eight years later simply because they had been members of the Jewish Anti-Fascist Committee.)

On that same day my old friend the poet Broniewski came to see me; he had been released from prison a short while before. He was in a black mood as he proceeded to tell me what he had felt and thought about in prison; he was deeply angered by many things. I kept telling him that the fascists had to be defeated, at which he smiled wryly: 'I realized that long before you did'. He said he knew it was his lot to be imprisoned. If the Germans were defeated and Poland liberated, he would be put in prison there. But he would far rather be gaoled in Poland, not because it would be better, but because he was a Pole.

Broniewski was a passionate and honest Communist. I had first met him in Warsaw in the days of Pilsudski and had immediately thought: here's a true internationalist. Something had changed in the world; at the time I had been unable to formulate it but I had vaguely felt it and understood Broniewski. We had both been nurtured on nineteenth-century ideas, we hated national exclusiveness and believed that frontiers would soon become a thing of the past. I had been stunned by the happenings of the First World War. I had sought the answer in Descartes, but history has never studied logic. In Spain I had understood the people's grief, but there it had been a case of civil war; the exploits of the International Brigade were in some sort a continuation of the Commune, of Dombrowski, of Garibaldi. Then one day, suddenly, I became aware of something vital and gripping – one's native land. I was sitting on a bench in a Moscow boulevard. Next to me sat a woman with a child, homely, sad, with infinitely familiar features. She kept saying: 'Now Petyenka, don't be naughty, I've got enough worries'. It came to me that she was my kin, that one could die for Petyenka. Ideas are all very fine, but there is this factor too.

At the end of July the bombing of Moscow began. After Madrid and Barcelona it seemed pretty feeble to me – the anti-aircraft defences were effective. But for the Muscovites it was a new experience. People behaved according to their individual nature: there were those who remained calm, others who were frightened at first, and some who lugged bags with their belongings to the shelters. The air-raids usually took place when I was at the *Red Star* office. We carried on our work in the cellars of a mansion in the Malaya Dmitrovka (we jokingly called these cellars 'contempt for death'). When I emerged early in the morning and walked along Gorky Street I rejoiced: all the houses were still standing as usual. I had never thought much of the architecture of these houses, but I looked at them with affection as at dear friends who had come out of the fray alive.

One night, as I was coming back from the office, I was not allowed through to Lavrushensky Lane: our house was cordoned off. Firemen were at work. It gave me a fright: what had happened to Lyuba, to Irina? I soon found them in a side-street. It appeared that a small bomb had hit our block of flats and all the tenants had been evacuated.

On 26th July the bombing caught me at home: I was in the midst of writing an article. The poet Selvinsky was injured by the blast; I can still hear him scream. The bomb had exploded quite close, in the Yakimanka.

One day I was at a press conference: Lozovsky was showing foreign journalists German documents on the plans for chemical warfare. The sirens began to wail and I found myself in the air-raid shelter with the American writer Erskine Caldwell and his wife. We fell into conversation and several hours passed without our noticing it. When the all-clear sounded I went home with Yevgeny Petrov. Walking along Nikolskaya Street we saw dead bodies being dragged out from under the debris. The orange reflection of fires blazed in the distance.

In the very early days of the war Lozovsky called the writers together and spoke to them about the importance of newspaper work. Several of them told him at the time that stock phrases should be dropped and that writers should be allowed to speak to readers in their own voices. Lozovsky was very clear-sighted but his scope was limited: Shcherbakov was the man who made the decisions. Several lines in my notebook are devoted to a long and uncomfortable talk with him. (This was on 3rd September.) When I said that people took no interest in reading stereotyped articles, Shcherbakov replied: 'They were having too easy a time before the war'. Then the conversation passed on to the Allies. Shcherbakov said that I ought to write every day for the west, upon which I remarked that my articles were cut or not released at all by the Sovinformburo. This angered him: 'Well then you shouldn't try to be original'.

At any other time a conversation of this sort would probably have discouraged me, but I went on working: I had no time for doubts. I am sure there were many others in those days who lived through like moments – some in the rear, others at the front – when they came up against muddle, narrow-mindedness and injustice. Yet no one paused to dwell on these shortcomings or ceased to work, to struggle: people sacrificed everything in every way. One can hardly imagine more grievous times, yet those who went through them recall them with pride.

For a long time writers (naturally not of their own free will) passed over the first months of the war in silence, beginning their narrative with the counter-offensive of December 1941. Yet everything was decided precisely in those first few months when the people showed its spiritual strength.

There were of course both confusion and panic. Many a time I heard the cruel words: 'We've asked for it'. One day I happened to be in the village of Afonino which for a short time was recaptured from the Germans. A collective farm woman was giving the soldiers water and was earnestly trying to convince them that it was foolish to resist: the Germans were well organized, they arrived in cars, they were neatly dressed, even the common soldiers were issued with chocolate. One of our men swore. But there were also those who sighed in sympathy.

In October the corn stood unreaped. Often the evacuation was badly carried out. German tanks broke through the gaps and swept on to the east. Sometimes the local authorities said lightly: 'No need to panic', but a few hours later were on their way. The organization was cumbersome, with 'wheels within wheels'; in peacetime it worked – more or less – but in the autumn of 1941 something different was needed: initiative, a feeling of personal responsibility, civic inspiration.

I recall Stalin's speech on 7th November 1941. I was shocked by his words about 'frightened little intellectuals'. Of course among the intelligentsia, too, there were some who had lost their bearings, but no more so than among other sections of the population. I do not know why Stalin had once again to make a scapegoat of our intelligentsia. The intellectuals were at one with the people; they fought at the front, they worked in the field-hospitals, in the factories. I should like to remind people that from the very first day almost all the writers did what they could. Gaidar, Krymov, Lapin, Hatzrevin, Petrov, Stavsky, Utkin, Vishnevsky, Grossman, Simonov, Tvardovsky, Kirsanov, Surkov, Lidin, Gabrilovich and many others left at once for the front. The anguish we endured was not only owing to the fact that Hitler's army was indeed strong, but also because we saw how gravely our defences had been weakened in the pre-war years: by the boasting, the incense, the bullying, the red tape and, above all, by the terrible losses inflicted on the cadres of the Red Army and on the 'little intellectuals'.

I have looked through the files of old newspapers from July to November 1941: Stalin's name was hardly ever mentioned. For the first time in many years there were neither portraits of him nor rapturous epithets; the smoke of nearby explosions had driven out that of the incense-burners. (This could only mean that Stalin had woken up to the fact that he had to make room for others.) Though some knew that they were defending the October Revolution from ruthless, brutal Fascism, while others thought only of their own cosy little nest, the people as a whole stood firm and fought, and the Soviet intelligentsia went into battle with the rest of the people.

Foreigners were puzzled by the steadfastness of the Russians. What did it spring from? Some of them explained it by such cant phrases as 'Russian mysticism', 'long-suffering', 'oriental fatalism'. After the Moscow counter-offensive an American journalist said to me: 'It's no puzzle at all – it's the size of your territory that saved you'. At first sight this seemed convincing enough, but it did not convince me. I remembered how in Spain the fascists had marched almost without a halt from Cadiz to the outskirts of Madrid and then, suddenly, to their great surprise, had met with furious resistance. Had Moscow been nearer Brest-Litovsk the December days might have taken place in September or October.

A conversation I had with Caldwell during an air-raid comes back to my mind. Trying to understand, he asked me a lot of questions and said that apparently there was a great feeling for our native soil. I said that we were attached both to our Russian soil and to the Soviet régime, even though life was not easy. (At the time I could not tell Caldwell about all our difficulties, my pride would not let me. But though our people knew a lot they did not go out to face death because they were ordered to – for when death is close at hand discipline alone is not enough: self-sacrifice is needed.)

From a military historian's point of view the first months of the war look decidedly black; the limited successes of our forces at Yelnia and Briansk could not outweigh the German victories, the occupation of a vast territory, the encirclement of large formations of our troops. But I did not lose hope. At Briansk I came to see both our weak and our strong points. There was a good deal of confusion, communications left much to be desired and in the air the enemy was also far superior. But the men fought, even when they knew they were doomed, and the Germans suffered heavy losses.

At Briansk I met General Yeremenko. He was addressing the newly arrived reinforcements – youths untested by fire; he spoke well, in a human way, admitting that at first everybody felt fear, that one had to take hold of oneself; he told the men that in his childhood he had been a shepherd.

There, too, I met one of the 'Spaniards', General Petrov of the Tanks. He grinned: 'D'you remember? The same kind of picture. Only here, I think, we'll hold out'. We were sitting in a peasant's house. The work-worn peasant woman hushed her child: 'Be quiet, the General is thinking'.

Carts creaked along the road. The Germans dive-bombed and once again I saw a mother wailing over a boy who had been killed. There was plenty of grief, terrible grief, but, strangely enough, in those months people were kinder to one another. I do not want to idealize anything, I am stating the honest truth: people who had squabbled in peacetime in their communal flats over a displaced saucepan, or at shop counters over a length of material, now shared a piece of bread and helped each other to carry the children.

On the Volga I met an elderly engine-driver; he had been on the footplate for seventy-two hours without a break and told me that when he felt sleepy he stopped the train and rubbed his face with snow. My surprise seemed to surprise him: 'What else could I do? There's no other way in these times'. An old Jewish woman from Vinnitsa came to see me at the *Red Star* office and told me how she had managed to escape, covering sixty miles on foot; then she was picked up by a lorry, and she had brought with her somebody else's child whose parents had been killed by the Germans. When Turgenev's museum was being evacuated from Orel, the curator had to appeal at every station for the van carrying the museum material not to be uncoupled. People got angry: 'Who wants all this old rubbish?' An ancient threadbare sofa stood inside the van. For the hundredth time the curator explained that this was the famous *samoson* ('self-sleep') sofa, as Turgenev used to call it. The objectors relented: 'All right, all right, take it along'. All this is rather incoherent. I have written *The Storm*, a book with a plan and a story. But now, as I recall those months, there is a catch in my throat: it was so terribly hard for the people; truly, they had not deserved it.

The Germans were rapidly advancing on Moscow. The prevalent sense of anxiety deepened. A small girl said to her mother: 'Mummy, please make me unborn again'.

Red Star was transferred to the basement of the Red Army Theatre because it was said to be quieter there, underground. All around the theatre there were pot-holes and ditches. The nights were dark, I fell and hurt myself, but all the same I got my article written for the next issue.

Why conceal the fact that the general mood was appalling? But people need to laugh, and on one occasion we owed a good laugh to Peter Bogatyrev, a Slavonic scholar. I had made friends with him long ago in Prague, during the twenties. He was far more at home with ancient Czech folklore than with maps of military operations. His tread was loud, like a hedgehog's – tap-tap. He came in one morning in a very cheerful frame of mind, saying that the Germans would soon be smashed. Lyuba asked him where he had picked up this optimistic news. Bogatyrev explained: 'I was on my way here and someone – not just anyone but a military chap – said that Guderian's army was approaching Moscow. Lots of tanks. This means the Germans'll be driven off'. Bogatyrev thought that Guderian was an Armenian.[1] We laughed heartily but Bogatyrev was upset: 'If that's the case there's nothing to laugh about'.

Towards the middle of October there were few people left in our house in Lavrushensky. I did not want to leave. Petrov suddenly rang me up: Shcherbakov's orders were to evacuate the Informburo and the group of writers attached to it. In the excited confusion of the first months they had forgotten to put me down as a member of the staff of *Red Star*, though the editor regarded me as one of his men. But Shcherbakov said that I must work for foreign consumption, it was of prime importance that I should send articles through the Informburo. Shcherbakov was secretary of the Central Committee and there was no question of arguing with him.

What went on at Kazan Station defies description. However, the plague is the plague wherever it breaks out, and I had already witnessed Barcelona and Paris. I lost my small suitcase containing the MS of the third part of *The Fall of Paris*. Later on I felt very sorry about it, but at the time my thoughts were on anything but literature and I was more worried by the loss of my razor – how was I going to shave? We

[1] Most Armenian surnames have this ending.

17

travelled in a suburban railway-coach; it was so overcrowded that there was scarcely room to move and the journey to Kuibyshev took five days. The train was a long one; the diplomats travelled in a sleeper, another coach was occupied by members of the Comintern (I remember Dolores Ibarruri and Raymond Guyot). At the stops the diplomats took the buffet by storm. Yaroslavsky's wife alternately wept and cursed as she looked at the unreaped corn. Petrov tried to joke, but even his jokes fell flat. Afinogenov kept telling himself out loud that everything was all right. At some station or other, crammed with refugees, we heard the communiqué: the enemy had broken through our defences and was approaching Moscow.

We spent the first night in Kuibyshev at the house of the editor of the *Volga Commune*; then we lived for several days in the staff quarters of the Grand Hotel until we were turned out: the British had demanded rooms for the embassy servants.

Suritz put me up for the night. We talked till nearly morning. He let himself go, saying that Stalin had been warned over and over again of the impending attack, that he knew nothing of how the country lived and that he was being misled. Then he took a Rodin drawing out of his suitcase, set it up against the headboard of the bed and, oblivious to everything else, exacted my admiration of it.

I wrote my articles in a corridor of the building which housed the People's Commissariat for Foreign Affairs and the Sovinformburo, with my typewriter on a packing-case.

Some time later we were given a room. The one next to ours was occupied by Grossman and Gabrilovich who had just come back from the front. I put my typewriter on a suitcase and went on hammering away.

Foreign correspondents badgered me to death with their complaints: why were they not allowed to go to the front, why had they been brought to Kuibyshev and told to dateline their cables Moscow? They lived at the Grand Hotel, drank a lot and occasionally treated Petrov and me to whisky or vodka. They were sure that in a month or two Hitler would conquer the whole of Russia, and sometimes comforted themselves and us with the thought that the struggle would continue in Egypt or India. When the news came of the Japanese attack on Pearl Harbour, the Americans in the Grand Hotel came to blows with the Japanese journalists. Afinogenov was summoned to Moscow, and soon after was killed in an air-raid. We did not know how to break the news to his wife Jenny.

Umansky described America to us, and what he said made us feel uncomfortable. Before leaving for Washington Litvinov had good-humouredly remarked to me at dinner: 'I'm afraid it's going to be pretty bad'. He did not explain why; when all is said and done, he was a far better diplomat than Suritz: he knew when to hold his tongue.

Early in December, in the vicinity of Saratov, I was present at the review of General Anders' army recruited from Polish prisoners of war. Sikorski arrived accompanied by Vyshinsky. I do not know why the choice had fallen on Vyshinsky for this occasion. It may have been because of his Polish origin. But I remembered him in the role of prosecutor at one of the trials. He clinked glasses with Sikorski, smiling very sweetly. Among the Poles there were many grim-looking men, full of resentment at what they had been through; some of them could not refrain from admitting that they hated us. I felt that they would never be able to put the past behind them. Sikorski and Vyshinsky called each other 'allies' but hostility made itself felt behind the cordial words.

The Moscow Art Theatre was performing in Saratov. They were producing *Three Sisters*. On the stage Vershinin said: 'In two hundred, three hundred years' time life on earth will be unimaginably beautiful, wonderful'. Everybody listened and sighed.

I kept on pleading to be allowed to go back to Moscow. Lozovsky replied: 'In a week's time the situation will be clear. In the meantime one's got to work'.

I sat and wrote five articles a day.

The editor of *Red Star*, General Ortenberg (also known as Vadimov), decided immediately to put me on his paper; he said that the men at the front liked my articles. One day (this was still in July) he told me that I must write the leader. I raised objections: this was not the sort of thing I knew how to do. He said: 'In wartime one must know how to do everything'. Two hours later I brought him my article; he began to read it and burst out laughing, though he seldom laughed and, besides, there was nothing funny in the article. 'This isn't a leader at all. From the very first sentence one can tell who's written it.' Leaders, it appeared, had to be written so that every word was familiar. Vadimov put my name to the article: 'It'll have to go into the third column'.

Perhaps the reason why the men at the front liked my articles was precisely because they were unlike leaders. Or it may have been because

I managed to express something of what people were feeling at the time. War inevitably brings with it the censor's scissors, but in Russia during the first eighteen months of the war writers felt much freer than they had done before.

Here are some passages from my articles of those days: 'The enemy is advancing. The enemy is threatening Moscow. We must have one single aim – to hold out' . . . 'We shall probably be able to remedy our shortcomings, but even with our shortcomings we shall be able to hold out. Perhaps the enemy will succeed in driving deeper into our country. We are prepared for this. We shall not surrender. We have ceased to live by the minute-hand, from the morning communiqué to the evening one. We have regulated our breath to a different tempo. We boldly look ahead: to where grief is – and victory' . . . 'Many of us have grown accustomed to letting someone else do our thinking for us. This is no time for it. Today everyone must take upon himself the full burden of responsibility . . . Do not say that someone is thinking for you. Do not expect someone else to rescue you' . . . 'Badly or well, we have still been living in our own home. The Germans bring death to all' . . . 'There was a lot that we did not understand. We had grey-haired people with infants' minds. Now even our children understand everything. We have grown older by a century'.

I cannot see why Shcherbakov accused me of trying to be 'original'. The passages I have quoted show that my articles did not contain any original ideas. But the men at the front apparently enjoyed them: every day I received a number of letters from soldiers and officers.

I said at the time in *Literatura i Iskusstvo* (Literature and Art): 'The day will come for a *War and Peace,* but at present we have war without inverted commas – not a novel, but life itself . . . An author must know how to write not only for the coming centuries but also for the brief moment if during that moment the fate of his people is being decided'.

In peacetime every writer is like a composer, he listens for something which others cannot yet hear. He does not always succeed, and more often than not he finds himself playing the part of a musician committed to some particular musical instrument. There are times, however, when the writer is himself only an instrument – a trumpet or a reed-pipe – which is picked up by the roadside and which gives out sound only by virtue of the breath of others.

2

On 16th September I read Lapin's and Hatzrevin's dispatch telephoned from Kiev to the newspaper office. They said that the Germans had advanced almost up to the city but that the Kiev people had not lost heart: 'The Kreshchatik (Kiev's main street) is as crowded and noisy as usual. In the morning they water it with hoses, wash it and scrub it . . . Lessons have started in the schools . . . There are barricades in all the side-streets . . . There is a queue at the circus booking-office'. Four days later the Germans were marching along the Kreshchatik.

Lapin and Hatzrevin had left for the front as far back as June. In August they came to Moscow. Hatzrevin fell ill. The editor of *Red Star* wanted to hasten their departure, and a week later they left again for Kiev. At the beginning of September Lapin made a call from Kiev, joking and saying that we should probably meet soon.

In 1932 I had first met many young writers: Lapin, Slavin, Boris Levin, Gabrilovich, Hatzrevin. We talked about new forms, the role of the essay, romanticism, the trends of our literature. Lapin gave me his book *Pacific Ocean Diary*, which I admired as much for its freshness as for its craftsmanship. The personality of the author interested me too: he looked like an unassuming young scholar, a thoroughly bookish fellow, whereas in reality he travelled all over the world, readily exchanging his desk for a ship's deck, a tent of animal skins, the barracks of a frontier guard.

Each of Lapin's books represented a search for a new genre; he presented fantastic stories as historical chronicles, wrote essays like short novels, trying to blur the line that separates a dry report from poetry. This was part and parcel of Lapin's spiritual make up: he read the works of historians and economists, philologists and botanists, but best of all he loved reading poetry.

In one of the earlier parts of these memoirs I have related how Irina informed me that she and Lapin were married. I was in Spain when we were allotted a flat in the Writers' House in Lavrushensky Lane. They lived with us for six months in 1937–8 and again, for a while, during the last year before the war. It was not long, but it was a time when people seemed to eat the proverbial *pood* of salt[1] at one sitting. I came to know and to love Boris Lapin.

He was twelve years old when the Revolution broke out. His father, a doctor, took his son with him when he left for the front line in the Civil War (the mother had gone abroad). At the age of seventeen Lapin published a volume of poems, provocative and extravagant, reflecting the author's age and the contradictions of the times. He took a passionate interest in the old German romantic writers and in the Chinese Revolution, in the cosmos and in word-formations; he frequented stormy literary gatherings and dreamt about India. Soon he passed on to prose, but poetry continued to attract him. He included poems in various books he wrote, claiming that they were translations from ancient Tajik poets, Chukotka incantations, Japanese *tankas*, American folksongs.

Irina has in her possession an old document: 'The holder of the present certificate of identity is in truth Comrade Buri, son of Mustafa Quli, native of the Ajaristan vilayet, who arrived in 1927 on 11th May at the order of the Soviet State to carry out a general census and in the course of nine days set down on paper the entire population of the Yazgulozh community, and is now making his own way back, for which purpose Comrade Buri, son of Mustafa Quli, has been issued with this certificate of identity'. Comrade Buri, son of Mustafa Quli, was twenty-two-year-old Boris Matveyevich Lapin who, on horseback or in a cart, moved from one Pamir village to another, clad in a colourful padded robe and pointed Afghan slippers. He was studying the Tajik language and had forgotten Hoffmann in his enthusiasm for Persian poetry.

A year later Lapin set off for Chukotka and took a job at a fur depot; he lived among the Chukchi, learning their language; the Chukchi called him affectionately *tindlilakka* which means 'the little bespectacled fellow'. He went to Alaska and the Kurile Islands and then returned to Moscow to write a book. He might have settled down as an ordinary urban man of letters, but he availed himself of every opportunity to see new lands and new people. He went off to Central Asia with a geological expedition and to the Crimea with an archaeological one; he signed on as navigation officer in the steamer *Chicherin* and visited

---

[1] Russian saying:' To get to know a man you must have eaten a *pood* (36 lbs.) of salt with him'.

22

Turkey and Alexandria. Twice he was sent to Mongolia. In 1939 he worked with Hatzrevin as war-correspondent of the *Red Star* at Khalkhin-Gol.

This list of varied travels and professions may be misread as the biography of an adventurer. But there was nothing in Lapin of the tourist's insatiable thirst for the exotic. He immersed himself in the day-to-day life of the Pamir or of Chukotka, accepted any kind of job, quickly learnt to speak the language of the local inhabitants and found something congenial and homely in their character and customs.

Languages came easily to him. He had a true linguist's passion. He read German and Persian, English and the languages of the people of the North; he knew hundreds of Chinese ideographs. Before the war we used to sit of an evening in adjoining rooms listening to the radio. Sometimes if I got home late I would look in on him and ask what news had been broadcast from London. It would turn out that he had been completely carried away listening to broadcasts in unfamiliar languages, pleased because he had understood a lot of the news in Serbian or Norwegian. He delighted in the etymology of words, and in this he remained a poet.

Despite the habits of his vagrant life he had a tremendous capacity for work. I can see him now at his desk; he could sit for hours on end over a blank page trying to find the exact simile or the essential word. Occasionally he would write a scenario or a feature article in collaboration with his friend Hatzrevin, whom we called Hatz. Hatzrevin had written a fine book called *Teheran*; he had great imaginative talents but was prone to indolence. He would stretch out on the bed, saying now and then: 'That's not quite right', or: 'Here we must introduce a description of scenery', while Lapin would be busily scribbling away.

Boris Lapin belonged to the first generation of the intelligentsia to grow up in Soviet times. Much of what surprised, delighted or repelled me seemed perfectly natural to him. When the year 1937 came, my contemporaries – Mandelstam, Paustovsky, Pasternak, Fedin and Babel – were over fifty; we had had time to write quite a lot and, what is more, to think a great deal. Lapin and the writers of his generation were caught entirely unawares by the events; they had only just said good-bye to youth and were barely on the threshold of adult writing. It was much harder for them than for us, their elders.

Boris Lapin was a courageous man. I remember General Vadimov saying as he sharply criticized some of the newspaper staff: 'As for

Lapin and Hatzrevin, I'm easy in my mind; they won't dig themselves in at Staff HQ. I've seen them at Khalkhin-Gol'. Yes, Lapin welcomed danger. But when, in 1937, friends, comrades and acquaintances began to vanish without trace, he withdrew into himself. By nature sociable and full of curiosity, he found it hard to master the new art: he learnt not to ask questions and not to answer them. He had always spoken in a quiet voice, but in those days it dropped lower. Now and again he would joke with Irina and me, but when he took off his glasses I could see the pain and bewilderment in his eyes.

One day, early in 1938, I came into his room when he was writing. Something started us talking about literature, about what writers ought to be doing now. Boris said with a smile: 'I'm writing about the Gobi Desert. When I wrote *Pacific Ocean Diary* and *The Exploit*, I chose my own subjects. I wrote the way I lived. Today it's different. I should very much like to write about another desert, but that's impossible. All the same one's got to go on working, otherwise it's even harder'.

The time of which I am speaking was particularly painful for Lapin: he could not bear the deterioration in personal relationships. As a man of exceptional loyalty, he was most deeply wounded by mistrust, by the disregard for friendship, by the vain efforts of those who tried to save themselves at any price.

Almost every evening Hatzrevin, a charming and unpredictable fellow, came to see Lapin. He was nice looking and women found him attractive, but he was afraid of them and lived entirely alone. What particularly struck me about him was his mildness, his dreaminess, his preoccupation with his health. For some reason he concealed from everyone, even from Lapin, that he suffered from epilepsy. In August Lapin tried to persuade him to stay in Moscow for a month or two, but Hatzrevin was in a hurry to return to the front.

I have already described how Lapin and I spent one of our last evenings together in Peredelkino reading Hemingway's novel. Anti-aircraft guns were barking in the distance. Now and then we would lay the pages of the manuscript aside and Boris would tell me about what he had seen at the front; the heroism, the muddle, the courage, the confusion: he had experienced the retreat of the first weeks. Somehow we started to recall the year 1938. Lapin said: 'You know, when all's said and done, it's easier now; things have somehow shaken down'. Then we would go on reading again. I glanced at him and realized that, almost without being aware of it, I had grown fond of him. And as we were on our way back to Moscow, he said: 'When the war's over, I'm sure a lot of people will write real books. Like Hemingway'.

But he never had the chance to write the book he had in mind.

Lapin and Hatzrevin left Kiev for Darnitsa with the army; they reached Borispol. The Germans surrounded our forces. Some succeeded in breaking out of the encirclement. It is from them that we later learnt the fate of Lapin and Hatzrevin. There was not a minute to be lost but Hatzrevin was lying on the ground in an epileptic fit. Lapin refused to abandon his friend. 'Hurry up! The Germans are quite close,' a correspondent shouted to him. Boris answered: 'I've got my revolver'. Those, to my knowledge, are the last words he uttered.

For a long time Irina lived in the hope of some miracle. During the war myths are invariably born: people used to turn up claiming to have seen Lapin on one front or another.

Before he left for Kiev Lapin had copied out his old poems. It may be that at Borispol he had still listened to the sound of words, of unfinished strophes: he was a poet, a modest man – a 'little bespectacled fellow' in the words of the Chukchi – who did not betray his feelings, indulgent to everyone except himself. Some lines of the tenth century Tajik poet Rudaki, translated long ago by Lapin, have just come to my mind: 'And many deserts have been turned into richly flowering gardens, but often you will find a desert where once a golden garden bloomed'.

On 9th May 1945 there was a festival: the desert of the war had come to an end. But in the lives of almost every one of us there was a new desert, a desert that will never blossom: the memory of our dear ones.

3

TALKING TO soldiers in the first months of the war I was sometimes filled with pride and at others driven to despair. Of course we had every right to be proud of the fact that Soviet teachers had been educating children and young people in the spirit of brotherhood. But here we were, giving up one town after another, and yet I heard more than one Red Army man say that it was the capitalists and landlords who had driven the soldiers into battle against us, that there was another Germany besides Hitler's Germany, and that if they were only told the truth the German workers and peasants would lay down their arms. Many sincerely believed this, while others readily fell in with it: the Germans were swiftly forging ahead and people will always clutch at any straw.

The men defending Smolensk or Briansk repeated what they had heard first at school and later at political meetings, or read in the newspapers: in Germany the working class was strong, it was a leading industrial country; true, the fascists, supported by the Ruhr magnates and the social-traitors, had seized power, but the German people were in opposition and were carrying on the struggle. 'Naturally,' the Red Army men said, 'the officers are fascists, and of course there must be misguided men among the rank and file, but millions of soldiers advance only because otherwise they'd be shot.' During the first months of the war our soldiers did not feel any real hatred for the German army.

On the second day of the war I was summoned to the PUR (the Political Department of the Armed Forces) and asked to write a leaflet intended for German soldiers; I was told that the fascist army was held together by deceit and iron discipline. In those days quite a number of military commanders pinned their hopes on leaflets and loudspeakers.

I, too, might have shared these illusions if during the pre-war years I had lived in Moscow and listened to lectures on the international situation. But I remembered Berlin in 1932, the workers at fascist gatherings; I had talked to German airmen in Spain and spent six weeks in occupied Paris. I put no trust in leaflets and loudspeakers.

The few prisoners (mainly Tank Corps men) whom I saw in the first months of the war behaved with complete self-assurance, firm in the belief that what had happened to them was a temporary unpleasantness and that any day they would be liberated by their advancing troops. There was even one man who suggested to the commander of the regiment that he should surrender to Hitler's mercy: 'I guarantee your men's lives and good conditions in a prisoner-of-war camp. By Christmas the war will be over and you'll return to your homes'. Among these prisoners there were also some workers. It is true that after the defeat at Moscow I heard frightened prisoners say 'Hitler *kaput*', but in the summer of 1942, when the Germans were driving towards the Caucasus, the men were once again confident of their invincibility. During interrogation the prisoners were on their guard, fearing both the Russians and their own comrades. And if one did find among them soldiers who were genuinely critical of Hitler, they were for the most part peasants from remote Bavarian villages, Catholics, good family men. The real change of feeling did not occur until after Stalingrad, and even then, up to the summer of 1944, the hundreds of millions of leaflets distributed to the enemy brought over only an insignificant number of deserters.

It was not merely that at the beginning of the war our men did not feel any hatred for the enemy, they even felt a certain respect for the Germans, born of esteem for the outward signs of civilization. This, too, was a result of their education. In the twenties and thirties every Soviet schoolboy had been taught that the cultural standards of this nation or that was expressed in mileage of railway lines, numbers of cars, the existence of a technically advanced industry, the spread of education and of social hygiene. On all these counts Germany was among the leading nations. In the prisoners' kitbags the Red Army men found books and diaries and patent razors, in their pockets there were photographs, fancy cigarette-lighters and fountain pens. 'That's culture!' our men, Penza collective farmers, would say with admiration and not without a certain wistfulness as they showed me a lighter shaped like a tiny revolver.

I remember a depressing conversation with gunners in the front line. The battery-commander had received orders to shell the highway. The men did not move. I was enraged. One of them said to me: 'We can't just shell the road and then retreat. We must let the Germans approach and try to explain to them that it's time for them to come to their senses and rise against Hitler, and that we'll help them to do it'. The others feelingly supported him. A young and intelligent-looking artillery man said: 'Who are we shooting? Workers and peasants. They think we're against them, we don't leave them any choice'.

There is no doubt that the most terrible thing of all in those months was the Germans' superiority in military equipment: the Red Army men attacked tanks with 'bottles'. But I was no less terrified by the good-natured attitude, the naïvety, the muddleheadedness.

I remembered the 'phony war', the solemn burial of a German airman, the blare of loudspeakers. War is a terrible, a hateful business, but it was not we who had begun it, and the enemy was strong and vicious. I knew that my duty lay in showing the true face of the fascist soldier, who, with an excellent fountain pen, recorded in a neat diary blood-thirsty, superstitious nonsense about his racial superiority, evil and ferocious things that would have shamed a primitive savage. I had to warn our soldiers that it was futile to rely on the solidarity of the German workers, to hope to awaken the conscience of Hitler's soldiers, that this was no time for trying to find 'good Germans' among the advancing enemy troops who were bringing death and destruction to our towns and villages. I wrote: 'Kill the German!'

In an article which I entitled *The Justification of Hatred* and which was written at a very difficult moment – the summer of 1942 – I said: 'This war is unlike former wars. For the first time our people face not men but cruel and vile monsters, savages equipped with every technically perfected weapon, scum acting according to rule and quoting science, who have turned the massacre of babies into the last word of State wisdom. Hatred has not come easily to us. We have paid for it with towns and regions, with hundreds of thousands of human lives. But now we have realized that we and the Fascists cannot live together on the earth. Naturally there are both good and bad men among the Germans, but it is not a matter of the character of one Nazi or another. They murder because they believe that only people of German blood are worthy to live on this earth. We hate the Nazis because we love our country, the people, humanity. In this lies the strength of our hatred and also its justification. When we encounter the Fascists we realize how blind hatred has laid waste the soul of Germany. That kind of hatred is alien to us. We hate every Nazi for being the representative of a man-hating principle, we hate him for the widows' tears, for the crippled childhood of the orphans, for the pitiable hordes of refugees, for the trampled fields, for the annihilation of millions of lives. We are fighting not men but automata in human likeness. Our hatred of them is the stronger because outwardly they appear to be men, because they can laugh and pat a dog or a horse, because in their diaries they indulge in self-analysis, because they are disguised as human beings, as civilized Europeans. It is not of vengeance that our soldiers dream. We have not brought up our young men to degenerate to the level of the Fascists. Red Army men will never kill German children, burn down Goethe's house in Weimar or the library of Marburg. Vengeance is repayment in the same coin, a retort in the same language. But we have no common language with the Fascists. We rejoice in the diversity and complexity of life, in the individuality of nations and of men. There will be room for all peoples on this earth. The German people will also live, once purged of the hideous crimes of the Nazi decade. But there are limits to tolerance: at the moment I do not want to speak or think about the future happiness of a Germany delivered from Hitler; such words and thoughts are out of place, nor would they be sincere so long as millions of Germans are committing outrages in our country'.

Every day I read German newspapers, army orders, and diaries and letters belonging to German soldiers: what I had to do was to show up the spiritual degradation of the fascists and to do so irrefutably, with documentary proof.

A man in the firing line likes to smile now and again, and I not only denounced Hitler's soldiers but also ridiculed them. I believe I was one of the first to coin the collective nickname 'Fritz'. Here are the titles of some short articles (I wrote one every day): *Fritz as a Philosopher*, *Fritz the Narcissus*, *Fritz the Lecher*, *Fritz in 'Shmolengs'*, *Fritz as a Mystic*, *Fritz as a Man of Letters*, etc. – dozens, hundreds of them.

The first time that I saw real hatred for the enemy was during the counter-offensive outside Moscow when our troops reoccupied villages burnt down by the Germans. Women and children were warming themselves at the smouldering ruins. The Red Army men swore or were grimly silent. One of them began talking to me; he said that he could not understand it at all: he had thought that towns were bombed because they housed government offices, garrisons, the press. But why did the Germans burn down peasants' dwellings? They housed women and children. And it was cold out of doors. In Volokolamsk I gazed for a long time at a gallows erected by the fascists. The soldiers also looked at it. Thus a new emotion came into being, and it played an important part in deciding the future.

The war unleashed by Fascist Germany was unlike previous wars: it not only destroyed and maimed bodies, it also distorted the spiritual world of men and nations. The Nazis succeeded in imbuing millions of Germans with contempt for men of different birth, in depriving their soldiers of moral brakes, in transforming respectable, honest, industrious citizens into 'torch-bearers' who burnt down villages and rounded up old men and children. In the past there were sadists and marauders to be found in any army, for war is no school of morality. But what Hitler did was to incite into committing mass atrocities not only SS and Gestapo men but the whole of his army, binding millions of Germans together by complicity in crime. I recall a sandy-haired, amiable-looking German; before the war he had worked in Düsseldorf where he had a family; he had thrown a Russian baby into a well because he suffered from insomnia, had taken several sleeping-tablets and the child had prevented him from falling asleep. I have held in my hand a cake of soap stamped with the legend 'pure Jewish soap', prepared from the corpses of people who had been destroyed. But there is no need to speak of these things: thousands of books have been written about them.

The Russian is by nature mild; he has to be very badly hurt to be goaded to fury; in anger he is terrible but he quickly cools down. One day I was driving in a jeep to the front line – I had been asked to pick out the Alsatians among the prisoners. The driver was a Byelorussian; he had only recently learnt that his family had been wiped out by the Germans. On the road we met a party of prisoners. The driver seized his tommy-gun and I had barely time to stop him. I spent quite a while talking to the prisoners. On our way back to HQ the driver asked me for some tobacco. Tobacco was scarce at the time and, as I had managed to get two packets the day before at Divisional HQ, I had given him one. 'But where's yours then?' He said nothing at first but finally had to confess: 'While you were talking to your Frenchies the Fritzes crowded round me. I asked if there were any drivers among them. There were two and I gave them some smokes. Then all the others started begging. It's either one thing or another: either you kill the lot or, if you can't, well, a man's got to have a smoke after all.' This was in 1943, and a year later, in Trostiantsy, near Minsk, where the Nazis had been murdering women and children, I once again witnessed the goodheartedness of our people. Our men were cursing, saying that no prisoners should be taken. A group of Germans was holding out in a small wood nearby. A captured infantryman was brought in. The Major asked me to interpret. When the prisoner was asked whether there were many soldiers in the wood he said he had difficulty in speaking because he was tortured by thirst. Someone brought him a mug of water. He made a wry face, said that the mug was dirty and wiped the rim with his handkerchief. This annoyed me: when a man is tortured by thirst he is not finicky. But the soldiers who had started shouting that it was no use talking to him, the brute ought to be shot, had cooled down by then, and half an hour later one of them brought him a bowl of soup: 'Eat, you swine!'

(I behaved the same way myself: many a time, seeing prisoners who were afraid of being killed, I wrote on scraps of paper which I signed that they were Alsatians or that they were 'good Germans'. In other words, although I hated Fascism I saved disarmed fascists. I believe that anyone would have acted in the same way in similar circumstances.)

Goebbels needed a bogey, so he spread the legend about the Jew Ilya Ehrenburg who thirsted to exterminate the German people.

I still possess cuttings from German newspapers, intercepted broadcasts, leaflets. The Nazis often wrote about me, saying that I was fat, cross-eyed, with a hooked nose; that I was bloodthirsty; that in Spain I had stolen museum pieces to the value of fifteen million marks and sold them in Switzerland; that I employed the same stockbroker as Queen Wilhelmina of Holland; that my capital was invested in various Brazilian banks; that I visited Stalin daily and had drawn up for him a plan for the annihilation of Europe, calling it 'Trust D.E.'; that I wanted to turn the lands lying between the Oder and the Rhine into a desert; that I called for the raping of German women and the killing of German children.

In an order dated 1st January 1945 Hitler himself condescended to mention me: 'Stalin's court lackey, Ilya Ehrenburg, declares that the German people must be exterminated'.

Propaganda did its work: the Germans regarded me as a fiend incarnate. At the beginning of 1945 I was in Bartenstein, an East Prussian town that had just been occupied by our troops. The Soviet Commandant asked me to go to the German hospital and explain that nothing threatened either the German medical staff or the wounded. I kept reassuring the doctor in charge; finally he said: 'That's all very well, but what about Ilya Ehrenburg?' I was tired of talking to him, so I replied: 'Don't worry, Ilya Ehrenburg isn't here, he's in Moscow'. The doctor then calmed down a bit.

The incident amused me, but at the same time I found it repellent. I hated the Germans who had invaded our country, not because they lived 'between the Oder and the Rhine', not because they spoke the same language as Heine, one of the poets nearest my heart, but because they were Fascists. Already in my childhood I had come up against racial and national arrogance and had suffered more than a little from it throughout my life; I believed in the brotherhood of nations and then, all of a sudden, I had seen the birth of Fascism. In my Utopian novel *Trust D.E.* Europe perishes through the madness of European Fascists backed by greedy American businessmen. Of course I had been very wide of the mark: when I was writing the book, French occupation forces were stationed in the Ruhr and the hope of a revolution in Germany was still, if feebly, alive. In the novel, Germany, Poland and part of the Soviet Union are devastated by France, at the head of which stands the fascist Brandevaux. The pattern turned out to be different: France, Poland and part of the Soviet Union were devastated by German fascists and Brandevaux was none other than Adolf Hitler.

I am now going to relate an incident which concerns me but which falls outside the limits of an autobiography. In 1944 the Commander of the 'Nord' Army group, wishing to raise the morale of his men discouraged by the retreat, issued the following Order of the Day: 'Ilya Ehrenburg is urging the Asiatic peoples to drink the blood of German women. Ilya Ehrenburg insists that Asiatics should enjoy our women. "Take the flaxen-haired women, they are your prey", he says. Ehrenburg is arousing the lowest instincts of the steppe. He who retreats is a blackguard, for German soldiers are now defending their wives'. On learning of this Order I immediately wrote in *Red Star*: 'At one time the Germans used to forge documents of State importance. Now they have reached the stage of forging my articles. The quotations that the German general attributes to me betray their authorship'.

The legend created by Hitler's general outlived the collapse of the Third Reich, the Nuremberg trial and much else.

Not so long ago, Kindler, the publisher of the German translation of my memoirs *Men, Years – Life*, who lives in Munich, passed on to me some rather interesting photostats. It appeared that in 1950 a certain

Jürgen Thorwald had published in Stuttgart a history of the war in which he wrote: 'For three years Ilya Ehrenburg freely, openly, breathing hatred, told the Red Army men that German women were their legitimate prey'. It turned out that Jürgen Thorwald was none other than Heinz Bongartz who in 1941 had published a book extolling Hitler and had dedicated it to the war criminal Admiral Raeder.

In 1962 the Munich newspaper *Soldatenzeitung* launched a campaign against the publication of my memoirs in West Germany. Naturally the newspaper recalled the fictitious leaflet on the raping of German women; it threatened the publisher and referred to me as 'the greatest criminal in history'. Some writers, such as Ernst Junger, supported the newspaper. Others, however, were disgusted. Kindler proved that Thorwald had simply been repeating Goebbels' lie; and yet to this day the neo-Nazis go on talking about 'the memoirs of the murderer and rapist'.

I repeat: it is not I who matter. But among the fifty million victims of the Second World War one is absent: Fascism. It survived May 1945; for a time it sickened, it moped, but it is still alive.

During the war years I went on saying day after day: we must advance into Germany to destroy Fascism. I was afraid that all the sacrifices, the great deeds of the Soviet people, the courage displayed by the Polish, Yugoslav and French partisans, the grief and pride of London, the incinerators of Auschwitz, the rivers of blood, that all, all might disappear like a brief Bengal fire of victory, remaining as no more than an historical episode, if base, unclean politics were once again to get the upper hand.

In 1944 I wrote: 'The French writer Georges Bernanos, a militant Catholic, indignantly rejecting the attempts of certain democrats to defend Fascism, writes in *La Marseillaise*: "Before the war a considerable section of public opinion in England, America and France justified, supported and extolled Fascism. I repeat, it not only accepted Fascism but aided and abetted it in the hope – a stupid one, I may say – of controlling this pestilence, of turning it against its opponents and competitors ... Munich was not merely a piece of folly, it was the shameful outcome of business speculation" ... Unfortunately there are men to this day who want to keep the pestilence in cold storage, merely slightly diluting the culture-medium in which the plague bacteria are bred. We must remember that Fascism was born of the greed and stupidity of some and of the perfidy and cowardice of others.

If humanity wants to put an end to the bloody nightmare of those years, it must do away with Fascism. If Fascism is allowed to breed anywhere, then in another ten or twenty years rivers of blood will flow again. Fascism is a frightful cancerous growth, it cannot be treated at a health resort, it must be excised. I do not believe in the kind hearts of people who weep over executioners; these "kind" men are preparing death for millions of innocents'.

Looking at the pages of old newspapers I feel perturbed. Indeed, it has all come to pass as I foresaw. Fascists were left to breed. The cadres of the *Reichswehr* have been kept in reserve. They want the German army to have atomic weapons; they feed the fever of revenge; what the late Bernanos called a 'business speculation' goes on, but the stakes are no longer conventional 'powder-kegs', not tanks or bombers, but rockets and hydrogen bombs. In truth, one's whole being revolts against it.

I have run twenty years ahead. Let me return now to the first winter of the war. We were driving along the Warsaw road to Maloyaroslavets, round which battles were still raging; we drove past villages laid waste by fire. The bodies of dead Germans lay on the ground or here and there stood propped up against trees. It was bitterly cold; the sun looked like a frozen blood-clot, the snow shone blue. In the frosty air the faces of the dead men were flushed and seemed alive. The officer who was with me cried in happy excitement: 'Look what a lot have been done for! *They'll* never see Moscow'. I have to confess that I shared his joy.

One might say that this was an evil and heartless emotion. Quite true. Hatred had not come to me any more easily than to others; it is a horrible feeling, it freezes the soul. I knew this even then and I wrote in the war years: 'Europe had been dreaming of the stratosphere, yet today it is forced to live like a mole in air-raid shelters and dugouts. Hitler and his followers have brought about an eclipse of the century. We hate the Germans for the vile and brutal murder of our children, but we also hate them because we are obliged to kill them, because out of the whole treasury of words in man's possession we have been left with only one: "Kill!" We hate the Germans for despoiling life'. I wrote this in a newspaper article but might just as easily have written it in my diary or in a letter to an intimate friend. The young will hardly be able to understand what we went through. Years of universal blackout, years of hatred: a plundered, mutilated life.

34

4

THE ADVANCE was swift though the snow was deep. A signpost 'Pokrovskoye' stuck out above the blackened snowdrifts, but there was no village: the German 'torch-bearers' had destroyed it. Perhaps the Red Army men had thought that if they hurried they would prevent the village from being burnt down. After all, in Byelousovo all the houses had remained intact, and the Germans had even left their belongings behind as they fled; while in Balabanovo, taken by surprise during the night, they had rushed out of the houses in their underwear.

Tired Red Army men furiously struck their spades into the deeply frozen earth: they were digging up the bodies of German soldiers buried in the main square of Maloyaroslavets.

The Germans buried their dead with infinite pains. (This was perhaps the only thing about them which I envied.) Later I came across many cemeteries with orderly rows of birchwood crosses bearing neatly inscribed names. But in the first year of the war in Russia for some reason they buried their men in the town squares. Perhaps it was easier to do this, or perhaps they wanted to show that they had come to stay. It made the Red Army men very indignant. There was little left now of the former tolerance: war was being waged even on the dead.

The collective farmers were also stung to fury. One old man said to me: 'I thought the German was an educated man, that he'd leave us alone, but the parasite took my cow and fouled up all our pots and pans, washing his damned feet in them. Yesterday four of them came to the house asking to be let in because they were frozen stiff. The women came rushing out and battered them to death'.

The frosts were exceptionally severe, but the Red Army Siberians grumbled: 'Now if a real frost set in, that'd kill them off at once'. One Ukrainian said: 'When I saw the Germans on the run, my heart leapt with joy'.

Victory seemed to come as a surprise to everyone. Collective farm women confessed: 'We never thought we'd see our own people again'. The soldiers smoked Bulgarian cigarettes found at some abandoned HQ and indulged in day-dreams: 'We'll get it over by the spring'.

35

General Golubev said with a smile: 'I've graduated from two academies. This is the third one and the course is a bit more rigorous'. He told us that he had been caught in an encirclement and had made his way out of it in his general's uniform but wearing peasants' bast shoes. 'What is a pincer movement? All the theories ought to be revised.' He said that his army had been given a great deal of help from the old factory workers in Podolsk: the factory had been evacuated but the old men had remained and gone on making ammunition for the mortars.

All this was new to me: the songs, the pepper-vodka which burnt the palate, a certain Mashenka who was a telephone operator or perhaps the commander's wife, the long conversations about the past and the future. Tongues were loosened; bureaucrats were severely criticized; one officer said angrily: 'What was there for our prosecutor to boast of? The number of convictions – he was overfulfilling the plan'. Another remarked thoughtfully: 'Good men were destroyed'. And yet everybody realized that it was not only their homes that they were defending, but the Soviet State itself, dear to them despite the offences, the shortcomings; they realized that it was precisely the Soviet workers of Podolsk who had helped the army, that the words 'our cause is just' were no mere current slogan but the plain truth. The people were voting, not spurred on by agitators and not with ballot papers, but with their blood.

Two emotions mingled in me: the first victory had gone to my head but I tried to tell myself that the German army was still very strong, that the war was just beginning. It was difficult, however, to think soberly: after all, only a short time ago the Germans had been confidently announcing that they would celebrate Christmas in Moscow, yet here they were being driven to the west. Even the appearance of the prisoners was significant: frozen, their heads wrapped in shawls and rags, frightened to death, snivelling, they reminded one of Napoleon's soldiers in 1812, with the inevitable icicle at the tip of the nose, as depicted by our painters.

Medyn had been taken, now there was talk of Vyazma and even of Smolensk. Everybody wanted to believe that the turning-point had been reached. I, too, believed. (I never became a prophet.) On the day of the winter solstice I wrote: 'The sun is set for summer, the winter is set for frost, the war is set for victory'.

Yes, in January I still thought that our offensive would not be halted. On 18th January I was with General Govorov. I liked him from the first. In this part of my memoirs I shall have many occasions to speak of meetings with generals. Like writers or, for that matter, men of any profession, the generals differed very much from one another; there were the innovators and the sticklers for routine, intelligent and narrow-minded ones, those who were unassuming and those who were vain. Leonid Alexandrovich Govorov was a true artilleryman, that is to say a man who made precise calculations, who had a sober and clear way of thinking. He told me that he had studied at the Petrograd Polytechnical Institute of Shipbuilding; the First World War was on and the young ensign was sent to the front. He loved Leningrad and had something of the typical Leningrader: reserve and latent passion. He said that in the battle for Moscow the artillery had played the main part: in the 5th Army he could not rely on the infantry, the losses had been tremendous and reinforcements were slow in coming up; he expounded a distinctive theory: in modern war, owing to the saturation with automatic weapons, the artillery must not limit its action to knocking out the enemy's guns and machine-gun nests, but must participate in every phase of the battle. He spoke with such enthusiasm that I was quite carried away. Although military science is more of an art than an exact science, it depends on technical equipment, and even the most up-to-date conceptions are soon rendered obsolete. (There is, incidentally, one art which also depends on technical equipment, and that is the cinema. The sculpture on the Acropolis still seems to us unsurpassed, whereas silent films make us smile today.) Of course Govorov could not foresee in 1942 the era of atomic weapons. I am recounting all this now only to try to convey the character of the man: in the icy cottage near Mozhaisk, it was not a bluff soldier whom I talked to but a mathematician and engineer, a good Russian intellectual. (Later I met Govorov several times at the front, in Moscow and also in Leningrad; I remember one evening in May 1945 when we talked about the beauty of the White Nights, about poetry, about the Admiralty spire.) For all his reserve and a certain tendency to scepticism, Govorov, like everybody else, was heartened by the successes, saying: 'Perhaps in a week's time we may take Mozhaisk'. But Mozhaisk was taken a few hours later. General Orlov disobeyed his CO and broke into the town that same night. Govorov laughed: 'Victors are not judged'.[1]

[1] Russian saying.

Once again I saw burnt-out villages, houses that had been blown up: Semenovskoye, Borodino. The soldiers were in a hurry but the German graves in the centre of the town were not allowed to remain there. The cold was growing more bitter – 35° C. below zero – and anger was growing more bitter too. An elderly woman looked with vacant eyes at the soldiers, at the snow, at the white sky. Her husband had been a teacher of mathematics, he was sixty-two; as he was walking along the street he had taken out his handkerchief and was shot 'for attempting to signal to the Russians'. On a wall I read orders about the 'normalization of life', threats that for aiding partisans or hiding Jews the inhabitants of the town would be hanged. On the next day I pushed on to Borodino. Before they went the Germans had set fire to the museum and it was still blazing. In two days the division had advanced twelve miles. General Orlov said jokingly: 'You'll soon be coming to my part of the world' (he was from Byelorussia). That night one of the majors got hold of some vodka and sausage and we made a feast of it. The major counted the stages, bending his large horny fingers, starting with: '9 miles to Gzhatsk, that'll take us two days'. But the distance to Gzhatsk proved to be four hundred and thirty days: ahead lay the terrible summer of 1942. We did not know it at the time.

(I was not alone in my hopes. Vassily Grossman who was then *Red Star* correspondent on the Southern Front wrote to me: 'The men seem to have changed: they are animated, full of initiative, bold. The roads are littered with hundreds of German cars, abandoned guns; clouds of staff documents and letters are blown across the steppes by the wind, German corpses lie about everywhere. This, of course, is not yet the retreat of Napoleon's army but there are indications that such a retreat is possible. It is a miracle, a marvellous miracle. The population of the liberated villages burns with hatred for the Germans. I have spoken to hundreds of peasants, old men, old women, who are ready to die themselves, to burn down their own houses if that would bring destruction to the Germans. Yes, a great change has taken place: it is as if the people had woken up. . . . Of course this is not the end, but it is the beginning of the end. I want to think so, there are plenty of grounds for thinking so'. Grossman was usually very circumspect in reaching conclusions, but even he did not foresee at the time the ordeals still in store for us.)

Shcherbakov remarked to me sarcastically: 'And you criticized our press, you said the Muscovites were nervous. They're worth their weight in gold'. Moscow was indeed losing the features of a front-line city. True, at night patrols stopped people every hundred yards, you had to carry your pass in your glove; but the 'hedgehogs' had been cleared off the streets, and there were also more people about. Even an exhibition of landscapes was held; it was cold in the gallery and the visitors went round the paintings wearing their military greatcoats or sheepskin jackets.

People resumed their administrative functions and former habits. The editor of *Izvestia* rang me up once in the night: 'You've written that Ribbentrop toured the capitals and was received everywhere as a gentleman. This could be taken the wrong way: he came here too. You'll have to alter that'. On another night, I was present at the *Pravda* offices during a lengthy discussion about Simonov's poem *Wait for Me*. The editor and another responsible comrade wanted to change the words about 'yellow rains': rain could not be yellow. But it was precisely the 'yellow rains' that I had liked above all in the poem, and I defended them as best I could by recalling the clayey soil and referring to Mayakovsky. Towards morning the editor decided to risk it, and the rains remained yellow. On one occasion a great commotion broke out at *Red Star*: 'We've been so absorbed by the war that we've forgotten our dates. Tomorrow's the fifth anniversary of Ordzhonikidze's death'.

It was very cold at the Writers' Club but people came there to drink vodka and nibble pickled mushrooms. Many writers were in uniform: from the front line one could reach Moscow in three or four hours. I remember seeing Petrov, Simonov, Svetlov, Margarita Aliger, Hecht, Gabrilovich, Katayev, Fadeyev, Lidin, Surkov, Stavsky and Slavin. One day the members of the presidium were treated to corned beef, after which the session began. A new style made itself felt in some of the speeches, a style that blossomed out five or six years later. Lydia Seyfullina could not contain herself: 'My father was a Russified Tatar, my mother was Russian. I've always felt myself Russian, but when I hear things like that I want to say that I'm a Tatar'. When we were leaving I embraced her. (There is so much of the fortuitous in life: for years on end you meet casual and even disagreeable acquaintances almost every day and very seldom come across people to whom you feel drawn. I had only three or four proper talks with Lydia Seyfullina, yet I liked her for her outstanding honesty. In the twenties her books played an important part in setting young Soviet literature on its feet. Their unmistakable sincerity impressed me at a time when writers were often leading a kind of double life. Lydia Seyfullina had made herself proof against lies. She received little attention and never pushed herself forward; what held her back was not only her great modesty but her complete sincerity. My memory has preserved the image of a small woman with kind, slanting Tatar eyes and that high moral integrity which, recalling the literature of the past century, we often call Russian.)

One evening the poet Dolmatovsky came to see me. He told me he had been caught in an encirclement by the Germans and had witnessed their atrocities. He said: 'I feel as if I were a corpse, or as if I had never been alive'. He had managed to escape. He recited his poem about water: how he yearned for a mouthful of water when they would not give him anything to drink. He described to me what had happened when he reached our lines: he was warmly welcomed, then taken to HQ and interrogated at length. He had to prove his identity, for encirclement is encirclement. He stayed with me till four in the morning. When I fell asleep I was immediately awakened by my own shouting: I had dreamt that I was being interrogated and could not prove that I was myself; but I cannot remember who was interrogating me.

Tikhonov, looking very emaciated, arrived from Leningrad. He described in detail the horrors of the blockade; he could not stop talking about the heroism of the people, the lack of food, the fact that all the dogs had been eaten, that the bodies of the dead lay in cold, unheated rooms because the living did not have the strength to remove and bury them.

I met Margarita Aliger for the first time. She recited a melancholy poem: the flame of a taper, pink and blue Kaluga. Her husband had been killed at the front. She looked like a small bird and had a thin little voice, but I could feel her strong inner power.

At the beginning of April Lyuba and Irina arrived from Kuibyshev. Vadimov gave out officially that Lapin and Hatzrevin were 'missing'. Irina bore herself with fortitude, only her eyes betrayed her; there were times when I had to look away.

It seemed as though everybody ought to die from a shell or a bomb and that natural death had become unnatural. But at the end of December the painter Lissitsky died. In March I learnt about the death of José Diaz.

Life went on. The food situation grew difficult; everybody began to talk about rations and ration cards. In January you could still get a meal at the Moskva Hotel. One day when I was lunching there with Lidin he said to me: 'We'll remember this liver one day'. True enough, a month later things were quite changed. The Central Art Workers' Club gave me one meal; it was always eaten by three, and sometimes by four people.

The foreign correspondents returned to Moscow from Kuibyshev. Some of them came to see me: Shapiro, Handler, Champenois and Werth. They were all agog for news, clamoured to be allowed to go to the front, took offence, grumbled. I continued to write articles for the foreign press: for the United Press, for *La Marseillaise* and for English and Swedish newspapers.

Almost every day I had to give talks: in hospitals to the wounded, on airfields to anti-aircraft and balloon-barrage crews. I saw a lot of grief and a great deal of courage. The people had somehow matured all at once; men fought, worked and died, conscious that they were dying with a purpose: the reed was thinking.

But there were other aspects as well. Lidin had been at the front since the first month of the war; he wrote many articles for the press, and then one day an article of his (*The Enemy*) angered someone. I read it several times but could not see what was wrong with it. Lidin talked to the editor of *Izvestia* and wrote to Shcherbakov, but it was no use: they stopped printing his articles. Petrov, too, incurred displeasure by a perfectly innocent piece called *The Trophy Sheepdog*. Umansky said: 'It's so depressing. The Germans are in Gzhatsk. They're bringing over divisions from France. I've been asked to write an article about atrocities. And now they're opening this second front – an offensive against Yevgeny Petrov'.

But why talk about them, the dogmatists, the puffed-up officials, those who played for safety? During the war years we had other worries and tried not to think about such people. Every day I received letters from readers at the fighting front and on the home front. I would like to quote a few letters from women: very little has been written about our women in wartime, and yet they were in a very real sense building victory. Here is a letter from a collective farm woman in the Kalinin region: 'From Semyonova, Yelizaveta Ivanovna. Complaint against the wicked enemy. When the enemy came to Kozitsino, they took my cow away from me before anybody else's. Then they took my geese. When I tried to prevent them, a man slapped my face. And he stamped his foot and said: "Go away!" The children saw him slap my face and they too shouted: "Go away! Let the enemy guzzle them!" The next day they came to take my last sheep. I cried and would not give it up. Then the German stamped his feet and shouted: "Go away, woman!" When I looked back he fired. I fell into the snow out of fright. And he took away my last sheep after all. When they were retreating from our place they burnt down my house, they burnt all my belongings, and I was left without anything, and my three children, in a stranger's house. I have two sons in the Red Army: Kruglov, Alexey Yegorich, and Kruglov, Georgy Yegorich. Sons, if you are alive, fight the enemy without mercy. And we shall help you as best we can'.

Here are some passages from the letter of a Siberian peasant woman sent to me by Red Army man Dedov: 'Greetings, dear brother Mitrosha. I send you my heartiest greetings and wish you all the best in your victories over the wicked enemy. My first duty is to tell you that Filya has died a hero's death in the struggle against the German Fascists. . . . When the notice of his death came Papa was summoned to the militia. He came home weeping bitterly. Mama asked: "What are you weeping for?" He did not say, but when at last he said that Filya had been killed, Mama was like someone dead. We cried a lot for two days. Now we shall never see him again or hear his voice. He used to reassure us, he kept writing: "Papa, Mama, do not worry about your son, I am living very well and my health is good" . . . Mitrosha, we have received the money you sent, thank you very much. But about Filya, Mitrosha, you must take your revenge on the Germans for your brother. Be a hero! . . . Mitrosha, we are feeling rather sad now, do write and say where you are at present. . . . Not so long ago we received a letter from Tanya and Natasha, they say that so far things are not too bad with them. Natasha is a team-leader on a collective farm. But now I shall tell you about my life. It is very hard for us, there is no bread, nothing to eat. The collective farm issues 20 pounds for seven people for five days. In our family it lasts one day, and the other days we live as we can. But that is nothing. We shall last out. They are taking on girls here for the front. Mitrosha, I would willingly go to avenge my beloved brother, he died for the happiness of the people'.

And here are some passages from the letter of O. Khitrova: 'One often hears that there is a war on and therefore our end will come soon, so it is not worth while working well. But is this true? I think it is the other way round. If there is a war on, one must work still better. And if you die before your death, you will not see victory. . . . I am working on road construction. We ask the superintendent of works what we have to do but he does not tell us and in general just lets things slide. Now why? That is no way to get things done. At the beginning of the war I, too, gave way to this mood; when I heard a bad communiqué in the morning, all through the day I could not get anything done. But now I have taken heart. When I hear from the communiqué that things are bad, I tell myself: just to spite them I'll tidy things up, I'll sew, I'll wash a Red Army man's pants and even darn them. I do not want to die before my death! If there is a spy about, let him see how we are holding out'.

And here are some passages from the letter of the Head of the Department of Western Literature in Kiev University, Edda Khalif evacuated to the village of Kotelnikovo: '. . . Then the day came when we had to leave the house. Every member of the family had a rucksack, only I, because of my "unsuitability", as they say in Kotelnikovo, was exempted from carrying one. Just before we left I went back to my room, burnt the photographs of my dear ones and letters, went up to the bookshelves and took down my own books: here was the work on the lexicography of the French language, it had taken me a whole year; here was the history of the French language in the nineteenth century – two years; a short introductory course to the study of Romance languages – four years' work. I looked at them, turned over a few pages and put them back on the shelf. I went away with empty hands. We left Kiev behind us, you know what this means . . . Somewhere on the way we boarded a train carrying our own Kiev people, there was one coach with the children and staff of the Spanish Children's Home. Some of the staff used to teach at our Faculty, and the children came to our New Year celebrations. Eight-year-old Octavio explained to my three-year-old niece Natasha that our airmen would soon drive the Fascists away and then Natasha would return to Kiev and he would go back to Bilbao. We were taken to Kotelnikovo. Here Natasha saw camels, not in a zoo but on the steppes. Many terrible things happened. I lost my father. News came from the front of the death of dear ones. At times I felt as though my heart would break. But it holds out. It appears that if grief and suffering are combined with burning hatred, you become strong, you want, as my friends from the front humorously say, "to stand up to the X-ray of war" . . . It is not easy: a new society, new surroundings, demand new standards of behaviour. Strangely enough, I found it difficult to change over from university work to that of secretary to the village Soviet. Everything here is simpler, more exposed to view, and this makes the situation difficult. . . . In order to stand up to the X-ray, to be able to look honestly into the eyes of one's comrades after the war, one has to mobilize all one's inner resources'.

Even now I am intensely moved on rereading the stack of letters, and in those days they put new heart into me. I, too, knew that one had to stand up to the 'X-ray of war'.

I lived in the Moskva Hotel (my flat had been damaged by bombs); it was like paradise and recalled the Knyazhi Dvor in 1920: warmth, light. Taking advantage of a lull at the front, I finished writing the last chapters of *The Fall of Paris* during January and February. Every day I met friends who were also living at the hotel – Petrov, Suritz and Umansky. Sometimes we began talking about the future. Petrov, being the optimist he was, believed that in the spring the Allies would open the Second Front, the Germans would be defeated and that after the war there would be many changes in our country. This irritated Suritz: 'Men don't change so easily'. And lowering his voice he added: '*He*, too, hasn't changed'. According to Umansky the Allies would start fighting only when the Germans had been bled white in the battles with us, and on post-war prospects he kept silent or would briefly let drop: 'It's better to expect the worst'.

Towards the end of January it became clear that our advance had been halted. On 23rd January I travelled with Pavlenko to GHQ on the Western Front. Zhukov, the general in command, described to us the course of the offensive: the battle for Moscow was over, on certain sectors it might be possible to gain ground, but the Germans had dug themselves in and to all intents and purposes the war would be of a positional character till the spring. Then to my surprise the general began to talk about Stalin; he did this without adopting the usual formulas – there was no mention of 'strategist of genius' – and in his tone, too, there was no trace of adoration; for that very reason what he said impressed me. He remarked more than once: 'That man has iron nerves'. He told us that he had said to Stalin over and over again: we must try to throw the enemy back, otherwise the Germans

44

will break through to Moscow. Twice a day he spoke to him by direct line. Stalin invariably answered: we must wait; in three days' time such-and-such a division will be coming up; in five days' time anti-tank guns will be moved up. (Stalin had a notebook in which were entered all the military units and technical equipment that were being brought up to Moscow.) Only when Zhukov told him that the Germans were bringing up their heavy artillery did Stalin give permission to open the offensive. On my return to Moscow I wrote this all down.

I am no military expert and, besides, I have no data that would enable me to form any estimate of Stalin's strategic talents. Only seven or eight years ago our historians ascribed the victory over Germany primarily to his 'genius'. The *Great Soviet Encyclopedia* illustrates its article on the Great Patriotic War with a coloured reproduction of an inferior painting that represents Stalin poring over military maps; in the chronological table enumerating nearly six hundred of the most important events, one hundred concern not military operations but Stalin's speeches, the conferring on him of various decorations, his welcomes and receptions. As for military operations, in 1944 the enemy was dealt 'ten Stalin blows' according to the encyclopedia. A photograph is attached: 'The telegraphic apparatus used by Joseph Vissarionovich Stalin to communicate with the front'. I can see this telegraphic apparatus, but what Stalin said to the various commanders I have no idea. Of course, while Stalin was alive the part he played in the victory over Germany was grossly exaggerated. But the story told us by the commander of the Western Front sounds true. We all know that Stalin stayed on in Moscow, made a speech on 7th November and said that the enemy would be halted.

(The success of our armies at the approaches to Moscow enhanced Stalin's prestige abroad. As for our soldiers, they fervently believed in him. On the walls of the ruins of Berlin I saw his photographs cut out of newspapers or the weekly *Ogonyok*. Tvardovsky's line: 'There's nothing here that one can add or take away', comes back to me.

They say that one should know when to die. Who can tell: had Stalin died in 1945 the war might have obliterated a great deal; people would have clung to the illusion that it was owing to Yagoda, Yezhov and Beria that millions of innocent people had perished, and the memory of those who took part in the war would have preserved the image of Stalin in a soldier's greatcoat symbolizing the arduous days of the battle of Moscow. Pushkin has said that a deceit which elevates us is more precious than 'a thousand lowly truths'. But there are also deceits that debase a man, and I often thank my stars that I have lived to see this day and to know the cruel truth.)

In December 1941 Hitler declared that the Germans had retreated from the approaches of Moscow of their own free will because they had decided to spend the winter in more convenient positions, and that, though some delay had occurred, this was owing to the exceptionally severe frosts, and the offensive would be resumed in the summer. This last assertion turned out to be true, but even the most credulous German could not believe what was said about the 'deliberate shortening of the front line'. At the gates of Moscow Germany was dealt a heavy blow, not so much to her fighting capacity as to her prestige. It was natural that along with many others I should have exaggerated the scale of our successes, but I was soon made to realize my mistake when the terrible summer of 1942 came and, in the space of two or three months, the Germans reached the Volga and the northern Caucasus. Nevertheless, the battle of Moscow was no mere military episode; it determined the issue of many events to come.

No one will accuse the German soldier of lack of courage; the technical equipment of the *Wehrmacht* was of a high order; their officers were well versed in military science and had experience. All this is beyond question, but in the winter of 1941–2 the Achilles' heel of the fascist army was revealed: it was good only when on the offensive and inspired by its sense of superiority; it was enough for Hitler's soldiers to meet with genuine resistance for them to lose much of their spirit. The battle before Moscow was Germany's foretaste of the eventual débâcle.

5

JUST NOW I have stopped for a moment to think about this book; the part I am writing is the last but one, so I am nearing the end. The reader may ask why it is that the *years* I have lived through are often shown as grim, while the *people* I have met are lovingly described and all that is best in them is brought out. Of course I did meet informers, mercenary turncoats and careerists, but they did not become my friends, not that I am particularly keen-sighted but simply because the Fates were kind to me. I did have some disappointments; occasionally I associated with people, without exactly making friends of them, who later turned out to be petty and heartless, but in evoking so many of my memories I have preferred to speak about the years and the circumstances which were conducive to moral corruption rather than about the people so corrupted; I have no desire to judge, the less so since I am not at all sure of being impartial.

Still, at this point in my recollections I have reached the incident of a brief meeting with a man who caused much harm, and it is a chapter I cannot omit.

On 5th March 1942 I drove to the front along the Volokolamsk highway. For the first time I saw the ruins of Istra, of the New Jerusalem monastery: everything had been burnt down or blown up by the Germans. For twelve years now I have been living near New Jerusalem. Istra has been rebuilt, but there are times when, as I drive past the new houses, the park, Chekhov's memorial, I see the snow and the blackness, the emptiness and death of that winter day long ago.

I passed through Volokolamsk. Close to Ludina Hill General A. A. Vlassov's command was quartered in a peasant's log house. I was struck first of all by the general's size – over six foot three – and then by his manner of addressing the men. His language was full of imagery, now and then deliberately coarse but at the same time hearty. My feelings were divided: I admired him but was also put off by something theatrical in his turns of phrase, his intonation and his gestures. That evening when Vlassov embarked on a long conversation with me I began to realize the source of his behaviour: for two hours he spoke about Suvorov, and in my notebook I set down among other things: 'Talks about Suvorov as if he were someone with whom he had lived for years'.

The next day the soldiers talked to me about the General with approval: 'He's got no side', 'He's brave', 'The sergeant was wounded, he wrapped him up in his own cloak', 'He can't half swear'.

At that time it was a war of position. Endless battles were going on for Bezymiannaya (Nameless) Hill, for the village of Petushki (Cockerels). There was nothing left of the village. A small hill would be attacked, taken, recaptured by the enemy. While I was with Vlassov in the dugout the Germans opened a heavy artillery barrage. He told me that there had been grave losses on both sides.

Some time after I saw a forest with every tree smashed to splinters and looking quite dead. The snow was still white, it even had a bluish tinge, but in the sun it went mushy and settled gently. An hour later our men went into the attack. The tanks flushed the Germans out of a small hollow.

We went into a dugout; it had evidently been occupied by German officers: there were two nickel-plated bedsteads, while illustrated magazines with pictures of Hitler and film-stars were strewn about. One soldier found a tin of Dutch cocoa. Stretcher-bearers were carrying out the wounded. Vlassov said: 'But we didn't reach Petushki. Those bloody *petushki*! However, it's just what's needed: we're gnawing through their defences'.

We drove back. The car kept skidding. It was freezing hard. At HQ a girl whom they called Marusya had made things cosy: the table was spread with a small cloth, a lamp with a green shade had been lit and vodka was served from a decanter. A bed was made up for me. We talked till three in the morning, or rather Vlassov did the talking, telling me things, discoursing endlessly. I took down some of his stories. He had been near Kiev when the armies were encircled; unfortunately he had caught a chill and could not move, so he had had to be carried to safety. He said that after that the men looked at him a bit suspiciously. 'But then Comrade Stalin telephoned and asked how I was, and everything changed immediately.' Several times during our conversation he returned to Stalin. 'Comrade Stalin entrusted an army to me. You know, we came here from Krasnaya Polyana: we started out practically from the last houses beyond Moscow and covered thirty-five miles without a halt. Comrade Stalin rang me up and thanked me personally.' He found much to criticize: 'Education's been faulty. I ask a Red Army man who's in command of his battalion and he says "a red-haired chap" – doesn't even know his name. The men haven't been taught respect. Now Suvorov knew how to make himself respected'. When he wanted to praise something he would use the phrase: 'That's cultured, that's good'. Telling me about a young girl hanged by the Germans, he swore: 'We'll get them yet'. A little later he said: 'We've got something to learn from them. Did you notice the beds in the dugout? Lugged out from the town. There's culture for you. Every one of their soldiers respects his commander, *they* wouldn't reply "a little red-haired chap"'. Speaking about the military operations he added: 'I tell my men: "You are not to be pitied but looked after". That's something they understand'.

During the night he was rather nervous: the Germans had lit up the sky with Very lights. 'They're bringing up reinforcements by air. Tomorrow they'll probably recapture the hollow.' He frequently interspersed his remarks with proverbs and odd sayings, some of which were new to me. One of these stuck in my memory: 'Every Jack uses his own excuses'. Another thing he said was that loyalty counted above all else; when he was in the encirclement he had been thinking about it: 'We'll hold out, loyalty will support us'.

Early in the morning he was rung up on the direct line. When he returned he was excited: 'Comrade Stalin has just given me proof that he places great confidence in me'. Vlassov had received a new appointment. His kit was immediately carried outside. The house was stripped. Marusya, in a padded coat, superintended the packing. Vlassov gave me a lift in his car, he was going to the front line to take leave of his men. There, under mortar fire, I parted from him. He went off to Moscow while I stayed behind with the officers who asked me to have lunch with them. It was night when I got back to Moscow. Anti-aircraft guns were blasting away. My thoughts were busy with Vlassov. He seemed to me an interesting character, ambitious but brave; what he had said about loyalty had touched me. In an article devoted to Bezymiannaya Hill I briefly described the army commander.

Colonel Karpov told me that Vlassov had taken over the command of the 2nd shock army which was to attempt to break through the Leningrad blockade, and my reaction was: well, it's not a bad choice.

Four months later, on 16th July to be exact, the Germans announced that they had captured an important Soviet General; he had been hiding in a peasant's hut and wearing private's uniform, but at the sight of the Germans had cried out that he was a General; when he was taken to HQ he proved that he was indeed General Vlassov, the commander of a special army.

Some time after, a Soviet officer who had escaped out of the encirclement told me that Vlassov had been lightly wounded in the leg, he had been hobbling along the verge of the road with a stick and swearing.

A month passed and the Germans announced that General Vlassov was recruiting prisoners of war for an army which would fight 'on Germany's side for the establishment in Russia of the New Order and of the National-Socialist regime'.

A leaflet picked up at the front was brought to me and I have still got it. It refers to me: 'The Jewish dog Ehrenburg is fuming', and is signed: 'Vlassov's men'. As I read it I remembered how six months ago the tall general in his Cossack cloak had kissed me three times as we said good-bye, and I swore (without much artistry – I am no Vlassov).

It is true that another man's heart, as the saying goes, is a dense forest; yet I shall hazard a few guesses. Vlassov was no Brutus and no Prince Kurbsky[1], it was all much simpler as I see it. Vlassov fully intended to carry out the task entrusted to him; he knew that Stalin would congratulate him again, that he would receive yet another decoration, would be promoted to a higher rank and would impress everybody with his ability to interlard quotations from Marx with sayings à la Suvorov. Things turned out differently: the Germans were stronger, the army was again encircled. In the hope of saving his skin Vlassov disguised himself. When he saw the Germans he was frightened: they might kill an ordinary soldier out of hand. Once a prisoner, he began to deliberate on what he should do. He was politically educated, he admired Stalin, but he had no convictions of his own, only ambitions. He realized that his military career was finished. If the Soviet Union was victorious, the best he could hope for was demotion. There remained only one solution: to accept the Germans' offer and do everything to bring about a German victory. Then he would become Commander-in-Chief or Minister of War in

[1] Prince Kurbsky abandoned his troops and fled to Poland, deserting Ivan the Terrible.

a truncated Russia under the aegis of a victorious Hitler. Naturally Vlassov never said anything of the kind to anyone; in his broadcasts he declared that he had long hated the Soviet regime, that he was eager 'to free Russia from the Bolsheviks'; but had he not quoted to me the saying: 'Every Jack uses his own excuses'?

Vlassov succeeded in forming several divisions from prisoners of war. Some joined because they were driven by hunger, others because they feared their own people. In battle the Vlassov men proved unreliable, so the Germans used them mainly for putting down the partisan movement. When I was in France after the war the inhabitants of the Limousin told me about the brutality with which Vlassov's men had dealt with the local population. There are evil men everywhere, regardless of the political regime and of upbringing.

In July 1942 when Vlassov took the decision to serve the enemies of his country, three machine-gunners and the Red Cross nurse Vera Stepanovna Badina were defending a hillock near the Bolshoy Dolzhik farm. A battalion surrounded them, they kept firing back. The Germans started to shell them. A shell killed two of the gunners; the third and the nurse were severely wounded. The Germans shot the machine-gunner Napivkov on the spot and, brandishing their revolvers, threatened the girl, covered with blood, to force her to plead for her life. Vera Badina did indeed plead with the German officer, not for her life, however, but for a revolver so that she might shoot herself. She was twenty-nine.

On the same day that the Vlassov leaflet was brought to me I received a letter accompanied by a note: 'Found on Sergeant Maltsev, Yakov Ilyich, killed at Stalingrad'. This is what Maltsev wrote: 'Dear Ilya Grigoryevich[1], I earnestly beg you to edit my clumsy communication and print it in the newspaper. Sergeant Lichkin, Ivan Georgyevich, is alive. They were going to recommend him for a decoration but our battalion was wiped out. Tomorrow or the day after I shall be going into action. Perhaps I shall be killed. In these last minutes I am desperately anxious for our people to know about Sergeant Lichkin's heroic deed'. The sergeant described how, in August 1941, the battalion had been encircled; several men lost courage and surrendered to the Germans, others were killed; three men remained alive, and Lichkin led them out of the encirclement, disabled a German tank and

[1] Ehrenburg.

captured two Germans. I carried out Maltsev's posthumous request. Going into battle and apparently realizing that death awaited him, he had been thinking that last night not about himself but about his comrade-in-arms.

Can one answer the question: what is man, of what is he capable? In truth of everything, absolutely everything. He can sink as low as Vlassov did and he can soar so high that it defies description. I often think about how different people are though they may have grown up on the same soil, gone to the same school, and talked in the same terms. This is precisely why I decided to tell the story of Vlassov. (He has been long forgotten by everyone, even by his hirelings who fled in good time to the American zone of occupation. What they glorify now is not National-Socialism but the 'free world'; it is awkward for them to remember that they were once Vlassov's men.)

Birds fly, reptiles crawl. And man is not only an omnivorous creature, he is truly adaptable to all elements; he soars to heaven but he can also crawl; this is common knowledge, yet one never gets used to it, and each time it shocks one, not only as a child but even as an old man who, one would have supposed, had lost the capacity to be shocked.

6

THERE IS a snapshot before me: the *Red Star* editor's office at night.
I have just come in with my latest article, Captain Kopylyov is sitting
at the table, beside him stands Moran; the lamp throws its light on the
rough pulls.

I worked for *Red Star* from the first days of the war till April 1945;
years of my life are bound up with it. For a long time this paper gave
a fuller and clearer picture of what was going on at the front than
any other. I remember a weary soldier, one of the footsloggers,
grey with dust, stubbornly repeating: 'No, give me my little *Star*'. I
have kept a letter from a woman in Tomsk: 'I wish you would give me
the chance to read *Red Star* even if only now and then. I know that
I have no right to it but I have three sons at the front, the fourth was
killed in the very first days'. In October 1941 two American journalists
came to blows in Kuibyshev over the current issue of *Red Star*. It is of
course quite natural that during the war the army newspaper should
attract attention, but the success of *Red Star* must be attributed to its
staff.

From 1941 to 1943 the editor of the newspaper was D. I. Ortenberg-
Vadimov. He was a gifted newspaper man though, so far as I remember,
he never wrote anything. He spared neither himself nor others. I was
with him at Briansk. One of the paper's correspondents, R. D. Moran,
had been wounded and was lying in a field-hospital. We went to see
him. Vadimov asked: 'How were you wounded?' Moran replied: 'A
mortar'. Vadimov gave a satisfied smile: 'Good man!' The fact that
he feared neither bombs nor machine-guns does not need to be mentioned; he was sufficiently tested by fire. But as an editor he also
displayed courage. In the forties the expression 'flea-catching' was
used in journalists' jargon: when all the articles had been sub-edited and
approved, the editor carefully went over the proofs searching for a
word, and sometimes even a comma, that might incur the displeasure
of someone high up. But if General Vadimov 'caught fleas' he did so
without the aid of a magnifying glass; he often passed things which
someone else would have cut out. I knew, of course, that when he said

'this must be copied out on good quality paper' it meant that he had doubts and wanted to send the article to Stalin, though this happened very seldom. One day a feature article about the war was submitted by Avdeyenko who had been expelled from the Writers' Union on Stalin's orders. Vadimov sent the piece to Stalin with an accompanying letter in which he said that Avdeyenko had 'redeemed himself by his actions on the battlefield'. It was printed. Two or three times my articles were re-typed on good quality paper. I have no complaints against Vadimov; he was annoyed with me at times but nevertheless printed my stuff. One day he summoned Moran (the most erudite man on the staff) to verify whether the Erinnyes had really existed; in a way he was right: the men at the front were not required to be familiar with Greek mythology; he also protested against the word *reptilii* ('reptiles') – a word borrowed from abroad – and a reference to Tyutchev, but though he protested he nevertheless printed them. Kopylyov told me the other day that, on learning accidentally that Lyuba and I were provided by the Central Art Workers' Club with only one meagre meal between us, he had informed the editor. General Vadimov would not believe him at first, then was enraged and went off to see no less a person than the commander of all the rear areas of the Red Army, Lieutenant-General Khrulyov, with the request that I should be given army rations. Of all the staff Vadimov liked Simonov best; the occasional Kipling flavour that slipped into the articles and poems of the young Simonov probably found a natural response in him.

At the end of June 1943 I returned to Moscow from the neighbour-hood of Orel. General Vadimov questioned me about the situation at the front; he told me that news of Mussolini's resignation had just come through. Two hours later I brought him my article but his room was empty. 'He's rushed off,' Kopylyov explained. 'He rang up just now asking whether everything was all right. In other words, he's been removed. Shcherbakov can't stand him.'

Vadimov soon left for the front to join General Moskalenko's army. I sent him a volume of my collected articles. In his acknowledgment he wrote: 'You will never guess what a tremendous help a firm and friendly hand stretched out in days of cruel storms can be'.

About a fortnight later I met a quiet, very courteous General at the office; this was N. A. Talensky, the new editor of *Red Star*. I worked with him for a year and we never had a brush. After he left I had some very bad times, but fortunately this was only a short while before the end of the war. As for General Talensky, I travelled with him in 1962 to Brussels to a Round Table conference on disarmament, and once again recognized how easy it was to work with him.

Whenever I had a leisure hour I discussed poetry with Moran. I do not know how he came to work for an army paper. He loved poetry, and today he translates it and also writes verse of his own, but in those days he often wrote the leaders: Vadimov, as he paced the floor, limping, would explain to Moran exactly what he should write. Moran was a nice and extremely modest fellow. When the war ended he went to work for *Izvestia*, was arrested as a 'cosmopolitan', and I saw him again only in 1955.

Another member of the staff was Mikhail Romanovich Galaktionov, a man who had had a military education but for some reason had incurred displeasure and held no military rank. He was treated as a raw youngster, although he was the same age as I, and was even shouted at. Then one day suddenly everything changed, some high up individual remembered the existence of a certain Galaktionov, and Mikhail Romanovich appeared in a general's uniform. People started addressing him politely, but he went on doing his job as unobtrusively and conscientiously as before. In 1946 we travelled together to America, and in the last part of these memoirs I shall have have more to say about him and his subsequent fate.

Vadimov had succeeded in attaching good writers to the staff. Grossman stayed in Stalingrad throughout the most difficult months; it was there that he wrote his essays *The Direction of the Main Blow* and *Seeing Through Chekhov's Eyes*, which I still find admirable. I well remember Simonov's reportage from the Northern Front. Petrov wrote for *Izvestia* at the beginning of the war, but his last essays on Sevastopol appeared in *Red Star*. Among the war correspondents on the paper were other writers too: Pavlenko, Surkov and Gabrilovich. Colonel Karpov managed to persuade Alexey Tolstoy to sit down and write an article on the spot. As for myself, I often did routine editorial work, wrote informative notes and translated items from the foreign press; in short I did what I could.

I should like to say something now about the war correspondents. Their job was not an easy or rewarding one: they had to write their stuff hurriedly, between two air-raids, often by the light of a 'smoky' (a wick stuck in an oil-filled shell-case), then to 'push' the article through, that is, to induce the signals men to pass it on by cable, or to try and find someone who would be going to Moscow; sometimes the information was stale when it arrived and Vadimov or Karpov would throw the telegram into the office wastepaper basket.

In his play *The Front* Korneichuk presents an unpleasant journalist, Krikun (the Shouter). (As luck would have it, a journalist of that name happened to be on the staff of one of the front-line papers. He told me that the play made everybody poke fun at him.) Such types as the hero of this comedy did, of course, crop up among the war correspondents, but not very frequently. On the contrary, I was struck rather by the modesty of most of these men. I happen to have kept a letter from S. Borzenko: 'I am enclosing with this note a dispatch for *Red Star* about the latest battle of our Guards Division. I took part in the fighting and have tried to describe faithfully all I saw. Will you please take this dispatch, read it and, if you like it, tell the editor what you think of it. There is snow in it but do not let this put you off: it is 30th March today and 20° C. below zero'. Borzenko was made a Hero of the Soviet Union, and his heroism became public knowledge.

But who remembers gentle Lev Ish, the newspaper's general bottle-washer, who did not write himself but edited other people's articles? One day, in the autumn of 1941, as he was working on the dispatch from the Western Front, he suddenly let out a cry: the dispatch reported his father's brutal killing in Yelnia. He insisted on being sent to the front as a war correspondent. He wrote articles and suffered torments. In 1942 he wrote from besieged Sevastopol: '... I look enviously at the others who are shooting Germans and who can do this not once a month but every day'. (Lev Ish went out on many reconnaissance expeditions.) The end came; the last defenders of Sevastopol were fighting on the promontory and Lev Ish was among those who perished in the battle.

At the office I read articles by Colonel Donskoy. During the autumn of 1943 in Slobodka, across the river from Kiev which was still held by the Germans, I met this Colonel. His real name was Ollender. His articles always gave a good clear analysis of military operations; he taught the young officers a lot. But when we fell into talk it was less about the war than about life and art. Ollender recited Blok and Bagritsky, and then we went on to speak about loyalty, white cottages, separation. Ollender looked like a romantic boy, and I said to him:

56

'If I were younger, or you older, or, most important of all, if the century were a different one, we should be sitting in some Rotonde talking not about a strategic road, or pontoons, but about something very different, as we did today'. We parted like old friends though we had spent only a few hours together. In 1944 Ollender died a soldier's death from a bullet.

On the Dnieper I met Grossman and Dolmatovsky; on the Sozh, Simonov; at Mozhaisk, Stavsky; in Byelorussia, Tvardovsky; in Vilnius, Pavlenko. We never had time to discuss literature; there were more important things to do.

I recall the late forties. It is difficult to realize that during the war we lived like soldiers serving in the same regiment. I have been looking through a file of letters written during the war years. Of course I remembered that my old friends Tairov, Konchalovsky, Alexey Tolstoy, Anna Akhmatova and Alexey Ignatyev wrote to me. But there are many letters from writers whom I had never known until then and whom I rarely met after the war. In those days we had a common enemy; we knew well enough what German tanks were and Germans armed with tommy-guns. I have just re-read one of the letters written in those years. A young poet wrote to me from the front: '... What is the point of all these trashy verses about the soldier who goes into battle singing about his beloved and things of that kind? What are the innumerable variants of the *Blue Kerchief*[1] worth? Is it possible to believe that no bold authoritative voice in defence of Russian poetry will ring out in opposition to the vulgarity which – like the mud on the soldiers' boots – looks as though it will stick to us as we march on to the very day of victory? And in any case vulgarity floats to the surface, it is easier to skim it off; but what can one do about the endless flow of vapid, flashy and meaningless verse in which, however hard you try, you cannot find a trace of original first-hand feeling?' Further on the writer asks me to read the enclosed poems and explains why he is sending this letter to me: 'Why precisely to you? The reason is, and I say this without any flattering intention and quite sincerely, because at all times, including at the most difficult moments, your voice has been with us, because the soldiers at the front trust you. Besides, your authority and your devotion to Russian literature are a guarantee of the honesty and sharpness of your judg-

[1] Popular wartime song.

ment – the best qualities in a critic'. The letter was signed Nikolay Gribachev.

To be quite candid, in those years even flashy poems did not worry me. (This strikes me as odd. Probably the voice of war drowned all other sounds.) Looking through notebooks that have survived, I find military news, field-post addresses and the names of German prisoners I talked to. I collected many new friends who were neither writers nor even journalists, but gunners, airmen, sappers. I kept up a correspondence with many men at the front and shall have more to say about them later on.

In his reminiscences of the battle of Stalingrad General P. I. Batov recounts how his troops captured the 'Twelve Commandments', an instruction signed by Hitler on the way the Germans ought to treat the Russians. Batov writes: 'The political instructor of the 65th Army made good use of the "Commandments" in his talks to the troops. If I remember rightly, the talk with the Chebotayev men was given personally by the CO of the regiment. There was angry laughter. Resolution: "1. We swear to smash the Germans without mercy and be the first to reach the Volga. 2. Send the 'Commandments' to Comrade Ehrenburg and ask him to tear the Fritzes to pieces in *Red Star*".' I received hundreds of such requests. I wrote about the Fritzes, I wrote about the war, I wrote about our own people.

I called one of my 1942 articles *To live for One Thing Only*. To devote one's life to a single purpose is very difficult; it is possible only for a revolutionary working in illegality, for a dedicated believer in the catacombs and also, perhaps, for a scholar. Man is a complex creature: neither fish nor bird, he lives in various elements, for various things and in various ways. But it appears that almost everyone must undergo at least once in a lifetime the experience of being divorced from himself, from his accustomed meditations and doubts, from his circle of friends, from his inner theme. It was so with me in 1941–5, the years of *Red Star*.

7

IT WAS one of the first days of spring. In the morning someone knocked at my door. I saw a tall, sad-eyed youth in soldier's uniform. Many men from the front used to come asking me to write about their dead comrades or the exploits of their company, bringing me notebooks taken from prisoners, asking why there was a lull and who would start the offensive, we or the Germans.

'Sit down,' I said to the young man. He sat down but at once jumped up again and announced: 'I want to read you some poems'. I prepared myself for the usual ordeal: who in those days did not write verses about tanks, German atrocities, Gastello[1] or the partisans?

The young man recited in so loud a voice that he might have been in the front line with guns roaring rather than in a small hotel bedroom. I kept saying: 'More . . . more . . .'

Later on people said to me: 'You've discovered a poet'. No, that morning it was Semyon Gudzenko who had discovered to me much of what until then I had only vaguely felt. And he was no more than twenty; he did not know what to do with his long arms, and he had a timid smile.

One of the first poems he recited to me is now well known: 'Men may shed tears before the battle, for the most terrible hour is that of waiting, but when they go out to face death, they sing . . . My turn is coming soon. The hunt is up for me alone. O cursed year of forty-one – you infantrymen congealed in snow. It seems as though I were a magnet, as though mines were attracted to me. A burst and the lieutenant gasps. Death has passed me by yet once again . . . The battle was short and after it we swilled icy vodka while with a knife I scraped another's blood out of my fingernails'.

I repeat, I had witnessed the First World War, I had been through the events in Spain, I was familiar with many novels and poems – some in a romantic strain, others an indictment – about battles, and trenches, and life closely intertwined with death: Stendhal and Tolstoy,

[1] Famous pilot who died ramming a German bomber.

Hugo and Kipling, Denis Davydov and Mayakovsky, Zola and Hemingway. In 1941 our poets had written quite a few good poems. They did not watch the war from the sidelines; many of them were in daily peril of their lives, but none of them had scraped enemy blood from under his fingernails with a knife. The bayonet was still a bayonet, the lyre still a lyre. Perhaps this lent a slightly literary character even to the best verse of the poets whom I had known before the war. But Gudzenko felt no need to try and prove something, to convince somebody. He had gone to the war as a volunteer; he had fought behind the enemy lines and had been wounded. For him Sukhinichi, Duminichi, Ludinovo were not just jottings in the notebook of some Moscow or army press correspondent, they were part of the day's work. (At our first meeting he said to me: 'I read about your going to see Rokossovsky and that you were in Maklaki. That's where I was wounded. That, of course, was before you went there'.)

That morning he also read me his *Ballad on Friendship*. The word 'ballad' derived from traditional romanticism but the poem was far from romantic. The soldier knows that either he or his friend, one of the two, must perish in carrying out their task. 'I desperately wanted to live, even in separation, even without friendship. Oh well, all right, let me be the one to go, let him remain alive.'

I have said that Gudzenko revealed a great deal to me. The war we were living through was cruel, terrifying; nevertheless we were firm in our knowledge that the fascists must be defeated. Not for us now were those former honest curses or those new, no less honest, glorifications: 'Two yards of human flesh turned into mincemeat'. No, it was not only the scale of things that had changed, it was also the perception of them. A sacred war? The words jarred. And then I heard Gudzenko's verses.

I asked him no questions that morning, but just listened to his poetry; all I learnt about him was that he came from Kiev, that his mother was still alive, that he had studied at the Institute of Philology, Literature and History and had heard my poems about Paris 1940.

(Gudzenko seemed to me every inch a poet, a youngster who had not yet learnt to think in any way other than through poetry. He for his part entered in his diary at the time: 'Ilya Ehrenburg was with us yesterday. Like almost all the other poets he is very remote from deep social roots'. This often happens at first meetings: we did not know one another and each saw the other according to his own inner mood.)

60

I read Gudzenko's poems to everyone: to Tolstoy, Seyfullina, Petrov, Grossman, Suritz, Umansky, Moran; I rang up the Writers' Club and various editorial offices; I wanted to share this unexpected joy with everybody.

He came again, we got to know each other. I grew to like him.

His poems were published. Then a poetry-reading was organized by the Writers' Club; he took his place in literature. It was wartime: a man was quickly taken up, quickly acknowledged and as quickly dropped and forgotten.

He was bold and entirely unsophisticated; he did not flinch in face of death, but in literary circles he seemed like an embarrassed adolescent. There is a story about two of the lines which I have quoted above: 'O cursed year of forty-one – you infantrymen congealed in snow'. The editor insisted that the wording should be changed. Gudzenko meekly altered it to: 'The sky demands rockets, so do the infantrymen congealed in snow.' I asked him what the devil the sky had to do with it; he smiled sheepishly: 'What could I do?' Fifteen years went by. Gudzenko died, and in the 1957 edition a new variant appeared, as silly as the other: 'The hard year forty-one and the infantrymen congealed in snow' – as if the soldier who feels he is acting as a magnet to mines is academically reflecting: it's a hard year. Only in 1961, after the poetry congealed in snow had thawed out, was the original text restored.

In February 1945 he wrote to me from the front: 'I am sending you five poems, some printable and some not. I am writing a lot the whole time, my notebooks are full, but heaven knows what will come of it all. If there are some poems that can be printed, it would be very nice ... I have added variants in ink for publication. Censorship has taught me a lesson since my first poem'.

In 1942 Gudzenko talked grimly, but with assurance, of the future. Like all his comrades-in-arms and most of his compatriots, he believed that after victory life would be better, sounder, more just.

He had barely recovered from a severe wound when he was knocked down by a car in a Moscow street. After that he stayed at the rear for a long time; then he worked in Stalingrad with the mobile printing press of *Komsomolskaya Pravda*. From there he sent me his poems on Stalingrad, one of which struck me like a discovery: '... And at long last, like the reservists' troop-train, total silence has come. It lies, monstrously large, on shell-cases and fallen rubble, deafening you with

61

such heartbeats that you fall asleep on your feet'. In September 1943 he wrote to me: 'I am planning to leave for the Ukraine. Kiev does not let me rest. I shall soon be there. I can no longer write about the rear. I am writing about the front again. What will be the outcome?'

In November Gudzenko came to see me, happy to be off to the front and to be seeing Kiev again soon, but at the same time a shadow, like that of a passing cloud, would suddenly flit across his face. I do not quite know what made me note: 'Gudzenko asked me why separate education for boys and girls had been introduced and school uniforms were made compulsory; he told me about a Kiev Jew who had been hurt. He has grown up a lot in the last year'.

Gudzenko advanced with the army to the west. People do not need reminding that great poetry has always been born in times of great travail. In 1942 Gudzenko wrote: 'Everyone remembers in his own way, differently, Sukhinichi, and Duminichi, and the forest path to Ludinovo – scorched, deserted'. In 1945 not only did the names of towns where fighting was going on change, but the whole attitude of mind changed too. Gudzenko listened less to the beating of his heart than to ringing words, to rhymes: 'We've taken Dezh, we've taken Kluh, we've taken Kimpulung . . . There are no hopes. Only silence. So weeps the Nibelung'.

Shortly before the victory he wrote to me: 'On our sector the war is still very much a fact. Everything repeats itself. A few days ago I was caught by a heavy bombing at the crossing of the Morava . . . I lay there for a long time, it was nerve-racking. I should hate to die in 1945'.

The war ended. Those who had come out of it alive were demobilized. I saw Gudzenko in civilian clothes. But at heart he was still wearing out his old faded uniform. The subjects of his poems naturally changed: he described the villages of the Transcarpathian Ukraine, collective farms, the life of a peaceful garrison. He knew that there were great deeds in great capital cities, but he knew too that 'every poet has a province of his own' and confessed: 'I too have my province, always the same and unique, not marked on any map, harsh and open, a distant region – War'.

His notebook contains the following entry: 'Recited at the machine-tool factory named after Ordzhonikidze. The people listened. I was bored by my own verses'.

There are many novels, films and poems about the veteran's nostalgia after his return to peacetime life. Gudzenko did not refer to it, but no matter what he wrote about there was always something of the front-line soldier's nostalgia in his poems. On the surface all seemed well: he had found happiness, or the illusion of happiness, he talked loudly, had a smiling face, travelled about the country, worked hard and was regarded as an optimist. (I recall his youthful admission: 'The eternal companions of happiness are forty doubts and melancholy'.) One day he said casually: 'I've learnt to write now, but I don't write so well. Still, that's easily explained'. I did not contradict him, though perhaps he expected me to; I cannot say.

He appeared to be in good health, more adult and even seemed heavier in build. In 1946 he wrote: 'We shall not die of old age, we shall die of old wounds. So fill the mugs with rum, with captured russet rum . . .' This sounded like an ordinary army song. Then in 1952 I was told that Gudzenko was ill: the delayed after-effects of shell-shock. He underwent trepanning but the doctors were not sure that he would survive. I suddenly recalled the mug of russet rum.

While he was struggling with death Gudzenko wrote three poems. Once again he soared, as in his early poems of 1942. He was dying in his dear and distant region, dying as his comrades-in-arms had died. 'Oh, how I want to live now, as if I had again come back from the war.'

A few months before his death he came to see me. We talked for a long time but we did not seem to get anywhere; perhaps it was because he had brought a poet friend with him, or it may have been my own fault. In any case the times were not particularly favourable for heart-to-heart talks. Two or three days later he looked in for a moment on the pretext of having forgotten to write a dedication in his book; he lingered, smiled a little, and only when we were saying good-bye, remarked: 'A lot's turned out wrong somehow. But we'll meet soon and have a good talk'. I never saw him again.

Yes, a lot turned out differently from what we had expected in 1942. The atom bomb age set in. No one knew what would happen on the morrow. Innocent people were arrested: once more, again and again the shooting was aimed at our people. And Gudzenko died in a cold month, in February, the wintry, chill, dark February of 1953, shortly before the first thaw.

For me he has remained a poet of the generation which began its life at Sukhinichi, Rzhev and Stalingrad. Many of his contemporaries never came back from the war. I vaguely remember some young poets such as Kulchitsky and Kogan, who recited their verses on the eve of the war. Later I read their poems; they had died too soon, and their best poetry was written before the fighting. But Gudzenko was able to raise his voice above the din of battle, to express a great deal for himself and for others. In a poem which he called *My Generation* one line echoes persistently: 'We must not be pitied, for we should not have pitied anyone'. When he wrote that poem Gudzenko cherished the dream that his contemporaries would come home with victory and enjoy a full measure of happiness. In our dimly lit front hall as he was leaving in 1951 he had said to me: 'A lot's turned out wrong somehow'.

I am sorry about Gudzenko. He dwells in my memory as someone very young, just as he was on that distant morning of 1942 when he had come to see me for a moment and announced: 'I want to read you some poems ...'

8

ON 10TH MARCH 1942, the representative of the Free French, Roger Garreau, rang me up. I had to ask him to dinner and this was not too easy. After long discussions the director of the Metropole agreed to let me have a tiny room. (The washbasin was chastely hidden under a tablecloth.) The dinner we were given was excellent for those days; there was also vodka. Garreau turned out to be a lively Frenchman of short stature but full of spirit. He told me how difficult things were for de Gaulle in London: the English saw him as an *émigré* and nothing more. Garreau made plans: why not form French divisions in the Soviet Union? One could begin with the Air Force. He was rather gloomy about the situation in France: 'Almost everybody is disgusted with the Germans, but there you are, people cling to their money and their jobs, though I must say the workers behave better than the others'. He persisted in calling himself a 'Jacobin'.

Garreau invited me to spend an evening with him. Among the guests were the French general Petit, the journalist Champenois, the Turkish consul and the vicar of the Moscow Catholic church, Father Bron. Garreau fulminated: 'You'll see, the English and the Americans'll buy up the German factories for a song and then begin to defend "poor Germany." For them the war's a game of cricket'.

I spoke about what I had seen at the front, and Father Bron was aghast at the fascist atrocities. A few days later Shcherbakov told me that the Germans had sent Slovak troop units to the Eastern Front: 'Write a leaflet for them, you've been to Slovakia'. I immediately thought of Bron: among the Slovak peasants there were many Catholics and they would be impressed by an appeal coming from a Catholic priest. I went to see Father Bron who lived in a comfortable wing of the American embassy (the diplomats were still in Kuibyshev). He explained to me in a great many words that the Holy Father was strongly in favour of tolerance and that one could not take liberties with the Vatican. We talked about the dogmas of the church, about the situation at the front, about de Gaulle. Bron composed the leaflet but then he demanded that I should supply him with petrol for his car. I applied to the department for petrol allocations and was told that Bron was already receiving an extra allowance. He had written to say that he had to drive about a great deal in order to administer sacraments to the dying, and when his request was turned down he started threatening me not with torments in the next world but with a petty scandal.

In April, when I was awarded a Stalin prize for *The Fall of Paris*, Garreau handed me a telegram of congratulations from de Gaulle. And General Petit sent me a tremendously long tinder-wick for my lighter: unlike Father Bron, I had no worries about petrol all through the war.

In December, de Gaulle came to Moscow accompanied by General Juin and the Minister of Foreign Affairs, Bidault. The negotiations for a Franco-Soviet Pact reached deadlock: de Gaulle was not prepared to recognize the new Polish Government (the 'Lublin Committee'). I was invited to dine at the French embassy. There were no ladies present, and at table Lozovsky sat on one side of de Gaulle and I on the other. The general talked to me most of the time. He was out of humour and complained about the coldness of the Muscovites. I was later told that he had been taken to see the Metro, a visit to which formed part of the programme for all foreign guests. The Metro could have exceedingly little interest for de Gaulle since he is essentially a man of the seventeenth century, when there was no such thing as Fascism, nor yet a Metro or any other such innovation. As the carriages were packed, the section reserved for children was cleared for the French visitors. The passengers loudly expressed their indignation, while General de Gaulle took it into his head to address a formal speech of greeting to them. On hearing that the tall Frenchman was de Gaulle the grumblers were overawed. Complete silence fell in the carriage, and only one little old man, recalling the French he had learnt at school, said *merci* in a cracked voice. De Gaulle was annoyed and for a whole hour dinned it into me that the Moscow crowd reminded him of convicts. I saw him as a man of the Resistance movement, and I did my best to convince him of the Soviet people's genuine love for France.

General Juin seemed to me a bluff soldier. During a performance of *Giselle*, while Ulanova was dancing, he dozed off and then remarked: 'I hoped that at least you'd dropped all this rubbish about ghosts'. On the next day he saw the Red Army ensemble. When they were doing the Russian dance he jumped up and cried joyfully: 'Cossacks at last!' I believe this was the only thing he found to admire. It did not come as a surprise to me that he became an OAS sympathizer.

The last decisive night came. The French were invited to the Kremlin. Hospitality was on the usual scale. Garreau told me that early next morning he had gone to fetch Bidault whom he found with his head wrapped in a wet towel: '*Monsieur le Ministre*, put on your trousers, we've reached agreement, you've got to sign the documents'.

In 1942 everything was simple and clear. In those days the French paper *La Marseillaise* was published in London; de Kerillis was the editor. He asked me to send him articles, which I did. In October he replied to me with an article in his paper: 'For over a year Russia has been bearing the brunt of the war against the German army almost alone. Ehrenburg has been searching our paper for a response to his appeals. Today we are able to tell him . . . The French workers refuse to work for Germany. I know I shall incur criticism for comparing the stubborn refusal of the French worker with the valour of the defenders of Stalingrad. But you, Ehrenburg, know what day-by-day courage is needed when there are hungry children crying beside you, what courage it takes to strike under the threat of machine-guns'.

War leads to what we used to call 'feeling your neighbour's elbow'. In my room at the Moskva Hotel, at General Petit's on Kropotkin quay, at the French embassy men foregathered whom one could hardly suspect of sharing the same views: Maurice Thorez, Garreau, Jean-Richard Bloch, General Petit, the councillor of the embassy Schmittlein, Champenois, Gorse, Cathala. Our conversation was friendly. (In 1944 I brought back from Vilnius several bottles of old burgundy which had been given to me by Tank Corps men who said with disappointment: 'Ilya writes strong stuff but what he likes to drink is *kvass*'. The bottles bore the inscription in German: 'Only for the *Wehrmacht*. Sale forbidden'. I invited the Moscow Frenchmen to help me drink it. Garreau touched glasses with Thorez: 'To victory'; we drank the wine with special pleasure because it had been intended for German officers.)

At the end of 1942, at a very anxious moment, the first group of French airmen arrived in the Soviet Union: the *Normandie* squadron. They were billeted near the town of Ivanovo where they trained to pilot our fighter-planes. Champenois and I went to visit them bringing a present of a gramophone and some records. We arrived just in time for Christmas Eve, which everybody celebrates in France as we celebrate the New Year. To mark the festive occasion an airman who had been under arrest was released. His tale greatly amused us: in the

Ivanovo circus a girl had pressed a note into the French airman's hand making an assignation. The *Normandie* was quartered six miles outside the town. Snowdrifts had piled up everywhere. The French, unaccustomed to such winters, suffered terribly from the cold. But the airman who had got the note decided to take a chance and reach the address the girl had given him. He lost his way, got stuck in a snowdrift, and when he had been dug out of it the squadron-leader put him under arrest for a week. The released prisoner declared jauntily: 'I'll find her yet'. The French laid on a magnificent supper. When we had had a few drinks we all became rather sentimental and began to sing bawdy songs in chorus. One tune was so melancholy that one of the waitresses whispered to me: 'They're praying. They're going to be killed, and in a foreign country too'.

And in fact, of that first group of airmen who had arrived before the victory of Stalingrad, few survived. Commandant Tulasne, small and gay, whom the airmen familiarly called Tutu, was killed. After the death of Captain Littolff, the squadron-leader, General Zakharov, insisted that Tulasne should not take any risks: 'You're in command now, you've no right to'. But Tulasne was killed in the summer of 1943 at Orel. That remarkable man Lefèvre, who was posthumously awarded the title of Hero of the Soviet Union, was also killed. In the spring of 1944 near Vitebsk his plane caught fire. He was taken to Moscow with third-degree burns. I remember in the military hospital at Sokolniki a doctor saying sombrely: 'A very grave condition'. We buried him in the Nemetskoye cemetery (by a strange irony of fate the common grave of French soldiers who had perished during Napoleon's Russian campaign was close by). The hospital nurse wept. Among the killed were Littolff, de Tedesco, Derville, Genès, Denis, Joire, Durand, Foucaud, and many others. Two Heroes of the Soviet Union survived: Albert Durand, a former Renault worker, and an aristocrat, the Vicomte de la Poype. (One of his ancestors was a general in the French Revolution who fought the Chouans and, later, Suvorov in Italy.) *Normandie* became *Normandie-Niémen*, it chalked up three hundred German planes brought down. Ninety-five French airmen fought in our skies, and thirty-six of them survived.

I visited the *Normandie* airmen near Orel, then near Minsk; I met them in Moscow, in Tula, in Paris, and I would like to say that they were fine comrades, always in good heart, who adapted themselves easily to life in a strange country. Our own pilots, mechanics and interpreters grew to like them. I can never forget that Lieutenant de Seynes died rather than save himself and leave a Soviet mechanic behind. I can never forget that Captain Nazarian rescued Lieutenant de Geoffre in the Frisches Haff lagoon. In those days it was not at conferences that people expressed the brotherhood of nations. Blood proved thicker than water.

On 22nd August 1944, on returning from the front to Moscow, I read dispatches about the Paris rising. Garreau rang me up early in the morning: 'Paris has conquered'. I went to the French embassy. There I found General Petit, Garreau, Champenois, the embassy staff, some old women. A small gramophone was endlessly playing the *Marseillaise*. We were so gripped by emotion that we could not speak. Jean-Richard Bloch's eyes were filled with tears. Then we drank: to France, to the Red Army, to the Partisans, to the Paris Liberation Committee. I asked Garreau who was the Colonel Roly referred to in one of the telegrams as in command of the street fighting. Garreau said with some emotion: 'I don't think it's his real name. I believe he's a worker, a Communist. Whoever he is, he's a hero'.

De Gaulle's government awarded me the Cross of the Legion of Honour. The new ambassador, Catroux, ceremonially pinned the cross on my chest, embraced me and said that France would never forget those who had kept faith with her in the dark days.

When I was in Paris in the summer of 1946, an impressive gathering was organized one evening. The Salle Pleyel (where three years later the First World Peace Congress was to be held) was packed. Herriot, Langevin, Thorez and General Petit sat on the platform. They were waiting for Premier Bidault. He was late, the people in the hall were impatient and the proceedings began without him. While I was speaking Bidault arrived accompanied by two *flics* (that is the French equivalent of 'cops', whether in uniform or plain clothes). The chairman sent me a note: Bidault wanted to speak at once, he was in a hurry. As I walked away from the microphone Bidault came towards me. He tried to shake my hand but stumbled and nearly fell; I caught him up just in time; the people in the hall must have thought we were embracing one another. However, he made his speech, praising me highly.

In the spring of 1950, when Bidault once again headed the government, I had to travel from Brussels to Geneva; I had asked the French for a transit visa but was refused. At the Paris airport I had to change planes. A *flic* kept his eye on me in case I tried to slip away and he followed me until I boarded the Swiss plane; he obviously thought I was not going fast enough, for he gave me a shove as though I were a petty thief being taken to jug rather than a Légionnaire d'Honneur.

And so now I have reached the present day. As everybody knows, the generals of the former *Wehrmacht* are training on French soil the sons of those same soldiers whom I had seen in the Paris captured by the Germans. (Long ago Garreau had expressed the hope that all Hitler's generals would be hanged; they say that he has now changed, I have not met him in recent years.) Not long ago there was a military parade near Rheims with French soldiers marching side by side with German soldiers.

When I was a boy people danced the quadrille – there was no jazz in those days – a dance in which there are various figures; from time to time the leader would call: 'Change partners!' In my lifetime I have had to witness the figures of sinister quadrilles. In 1912 the Russian newspapers were full of the unity of the Slavs and the war of liberation against tyrannical Turkey. The Serbs, the Bulgarians and the Greeks defeated the Turks, signed a peace treaty, and a month later yesterday's allies came to blows among themselves; war broke out between Bulgaria on the one hand and Serbia and Greece on the other. Turkey in her turn attacked Bulgaria. At that time I was young and felt some surprise. Later I got used to that sort of thing. In 1915 Italy, a member of the Triple Alliance, launched a war against her former allies. The French press was full of admiration for the spirited behaviour of d'Annunzio and Mussolini. For a quarter of a century Italy became the 'Latin sister' of France. In 1940 the 'sister' attacked France. All this seems incomprehensible, or perhaps it is only too easy to understand.

Why, then, should the news of that Franco-German military parade have caused me pain? I know well enough that there is no relation between diplomacy and morality. The average man is often struck by details that seem rather trivial; I pointed this out when I related the story of the ill-starred telegram sent to Ribbentrop in December 1940. I now recalled Rheims in the years of the First World War, the mutilated cathedral, the school held in a wine-cellar; I recalled the story of the partisan, a native of Rheims, who was shot in 1943 – and I felt sick. It may be naïve, but I believe that the dead have their own rights, that blood is not wine at a political banquet, that man's conscience cannot always find itself in agreement with expediency, and that the ABC of morality is far more difficult to change than the orientation of foreign policy. (The parade was an *hors d'œuvre*. The politicians prepared the next dish: the alliance between France and the German militarists. I should not like to hazard a guess on what the dessert will be.)

Of course my feelings towards France could not be altered by the zigzags of one French government or another. In one of my poems I wrote the following lines: 'You say with jealousy and reproach that I have fallen silent. Paris is not a forest, and I am not a wolf, but life cannot be cancelled out of life. I have lived where a great city hums, grey and hoary like a stone forest, pale blue and dusted with the ashes of years. Forgive me for having lived in that forest, for having lived through it all and come out alive, for carrying with me to the grave the great twilight of Paris'.

Another poem contains the bitter question: 'Why did the devil tempt me to fall in love with a foreign country?'

But all that was said in anger: I could not and cannot regard France as a country alien to me; I have lived in Paris too long and have learnt too much there. I am often unjust in my way of thinking, and the reader will readily see why.

A short time ago the pioneers of Orel wrote to me saying that in their region they had discovered the graves of two French airmen. And my thoughts went back again to the gay and courageous Frenchmen who, when in 1943 the squadron had been quartered in a small birch wood, made it resound with their laughter, their songs and the *argot* of Belleville and Ménilmontant.

I know that to forget is a law of life; it is a rehearsal of death. The pain does not lie there. What hurts is the way in which relations between human beings become distorted by the pressure of events. In saying this I have in mind certain individuals whom I used to look upon as friends. You think that you are going your own sweet way, but it is an illusion; you march along but it is the platoon commander – called at solemn moments Time or History – who gives the orders: 'Left turn! Right turn! About turn! Forward march!' After which all you can do is to note discreetly: I do not meet so-and-so any more we have gone our different ways.

9

AFTER A LONG severe winter everybody greeted the spring with joy.
We basked in the sunshine and wondered what the summer would bring.
I recall Duminichi: before the war there had been a factory there
which made bathtubs. The town was burnt to the ground. Here and
there among the rubble bathtubs gleamed: all that was left of Duminichi. An elderly sergeant with grey stubble on his cheeks was lazily
philosophizing: 'Sanitation? What do those devils care? All they want
is to smash everything. I'd give a lot to go to a bath-house. Only I
don't think there'll be an end to it, we're sure to be fighting for another
year. They say we've got marvellous tanks. Now you ought to write
about that – and put some guts into it. The men are taking it hard.
Yesterday the political instructor said: "If the filthy brute tries it on
again, we'll shake him up so that his own *Frau* won't recognize him."
But who knows whether the enemy hasn't invented something new?
It's the men I'm sorry for. The bastards killed our Osipov. There was
a piece in the paper about him. Now can you tell me what makes those
parasites want to kill people?'

In Sukhinichi I met General Rokossovsky for the first time. Since
the battle outside Moscow his name had been on everybody's lips; he
was also very handsome. I think he was the most courteous of all the
generals I have ever met. I knew that he had not had an easy life by
any means. The poetess Olga Bergholtz told me that at the time when
she was arrested Rokossovsky was in the cell next to her. He was
wounded at Sukhinichi, a shell splinter grazed his liver. He could
hardly eat at all, the jolting of a car or any sudden movement brought
on pain, but he had such extraordinary self-discipline that almost no
one guessed there was anything wrong. Naturally I asked him what
would happen next. He answered quietly that the Germans were
making a big mistake in putting everything down to the Russian
winter; if anything, the winter had helped them by halting our offensive. He may have been saying this to hearten others or he may have
really believed it: though a chess player does not know his opponent's
plans, he can see the chessmen on the board, but all a commander

72

has to go on is the information picked up by reconnaissance, which does not always correspond to the true facts.

Two months later I heard military men say: 'We made the mistake of deploying our forces too widely – Yukhnov, Sukhinichi. And we didn't prepare our defences'. On this matter I can express no opinion. Mathematics is difficult to understand without special training, but once you have learnt its language it becomes quite clear to you that something is exactly so and could not be anything else. With history it is different: every event can be interpreted in more ways than one. Artists have depicted Urania, the Muse of geometry and astronomy, with compasses, but Clio, the Muse of history, with manuscript and pen. In the collection of Russian sayings published by Dahl a hundred years ago, several pages are devoted to the art of invention; there is even the saying: 'Was the Devil responsible for decreeing that Zakhar should hold office?'.

On 18th May the communiqué referred to our important successes 'in the direction of Kharkov'. I was sitting writing an article when Colonel Karpov came in and said with an air of mystery: 'Don't mention the Kharkov direction, we've had instructions'. A week later the Germans announced that three Soviet armies had been surrounded south of Kharkov. On 5th June Shcherbakov rang me up: 'Write articles for the foreign press about the Second Front'. Molotov left by air for London. On 10th June the Germans opened a big offensive on the Southern Front.

The bitter summer of 1942 set in. Names of new fronts occurred in the communiqués: the Voronezh front, the Don front, the Stalingrad front, the Transcaucasian front. It was horrible to think that a Düsseldorfer was strolling about Pyatigorsk, that Magdeburg *Burschen* were gaping at the sands of Kalmukia. It was all unbelievable.

I sat and wrote, wrote every day for *Red Star*, for *Pravda*, for the Political Department of the Armed Forces, for the English and American press. I wanted to go to the front, but the editors would not let me.

Army men used to come to the office with stories about the retreat. I remember a colonel who kept saying grimly: 'There's never been such a stampede'.

This latest retreat seemed more frightening than that of 1941, for what had happened then could be explained by the suddenness of the attack. Officers, political instructors, Red Army men sent me letters full of alarm and unhappy reflections. I did not know everything at the time, nor could I write about everything I knew; yet I did succeed during the summer of 1942 in putting into words some part of the truth; these disclosures would never have been printed either three years earlier or three years later. Here is a passage from an article in *Pravda*: 'I remember how some years ago I went into an office and walked slap into a table. "Everybody bumps into that table," the secretary said soothingly. "Then why don't you move it?" I asked. "The director hasn't given orders to move it. If I were to do it, I might be asked all of a sudden: 'What made you do it? What does it mean?' It's better to let it stay where it is, safer." We all of us carry the bruises from this symbolical table, from the narrow-mindedness, the indifference, the shirking of responsibility'. And here is a piece from an article in *Red Star*: 'Who can put into words what the men at the front are thinking, tensely, feverishly, insistently? They are thinking about the present and the past. They are thinking why yesterday's operation was unsuccessful and why there were so many things they had not been taught in the ten-year school. They think about the future, about the wonderful life the victors will build ... War is a severe test both of nations and of individuals. During the war many things have been thought over, reconsidered, reassessed ... People will live differently and they will work differently. The war has given us initiative, discipline and an inner freedom.'

There was great confusion at the front and also great and very moving heroism. The Germans were approaching Stalingrad, but the Red Army was approaching victory, though we did not know it at the time. What kept me going, like all my countrymen that summer, was a grim determination.

Moscow was in the deep rear and at the same time a front-line observation post. The Germans still held Gzhatsk, but on this sector they made no attempt at an offensive and Moscow experienced none of the fever of the previous autumn. Some wit composed a rhyme, parodying the old nursery song: 'Granny had a little grey mare, a story's a story but the Germans are near'. There were crowds of people in the streets, queues lined up, the trams ran packed to overflowing. The people were glum and silent. Everyone knew that the Germans had seized the wheat of the Kuban, the oil of Maikop, that they intended to cut Moscow off from the Urals and Siberia. The old Jacobin cry of warning appeared in the papers: 'The Motherland is in danger!'

74

I have still got the diary I kept that summer; the entries are brief and disconnected: dates of happenings, an occasional remark made by someone; the bits and pieces of life.

Selvinsky, arriving from Kerch, said: 'The men have caught on, but not the generals'. He described the panic, the German atrocities: they had driven the Jews and then the prisoners of war into the catacombs. Temin brought photographs from Sevastopol that spoke of the town's agony: ruined houses, Lenin's memorial, murdered children, a sailor in his blood-soaked striped singlet.

News of Petrov's death came through. I went to Katayev's place and found Stravsky there. We sat in silence.

I asked the British ambassador, Sir Archibald Clark Kerr, when the Second Front would be opened at last. Instead of replying he began to ask me about the kind of pipe Stalin preferred as he wanted to bring him the very best one available in London. I said that I did not know what kind of pipe Stalin smoked, I did not see him and, besides, it was of no importance: the time had come for the opening of the Second Front. Clark Kerr smiled discreetly and fell silent.

I was in my hotel room when I heard shouts in the corridor. I ran out and found that the poet Yanka Kupala had fallen down the staircase well from the top floor.

Shapiro, the United Press correspondent, came rushing in furious because the censorship had cut out the sentence 'It is five miles from Voronezh to the Don' in his report.

A woman was selling potatoes at twenty roubles a pound. She was killed. A lump of sugar cost ten roubles. There was a Frenchwoman, Annette, living in Moscow, who was the wife of a Soviet architect. She had a small baby. Her husband was far away. One day she rang up and announced with breathless excitement: 'Vanechka is home on leave, he's brought a bottle of oil'.

On 26th July there was a book bazaar at which the authors autographed copies. One woman asked indignantly: 'Why did you put a date on his and not on mine?' Nobody smiled.

Alexey Tolstoy puffed at his pipe and said: 'The Germans'll be beaten in the end. But what's it going to be like after the war? The people aren't what they used to be'.

On 29th July a decree was issued instituting three new military orders – the Suvorov, the Kutuzov and the Alexander Nevsky. At the same time Stalin's Order of the Day was read to the troops: it was not about decorations but about the undisciplined abandoning of Rostov and Novocherkassk, about confusion and panic; things could not go on like this, it was time everyone came to their senses: 'Not a step back'. Never before had Stalin spoken with such frankness and it created an enormous impression. A *Red Star* war correspondent said to me: 'A father tells his children: "We are ruined, we must learn to live differently now".' There was neither irony nor admiration in the way he uttered the word 'father', it sounded like a plain statement of fact.

The Germans, however, continued to advance towards the Northern Caucasus.

General Govorov arrived and said that he had been to see Stalin and had insisted on the evacuation of the civilian population from Leningrad.

At the office I read that the futurist Marinetti was on his way to Russia as he wanted to see how the Fascists were re-educating the *muzhiks*. This reminded me of a line written by Marinetti long ago: 'My heart is made of red sugar'.

I was handed the diary of Friedrich Schmidt, adjutant of the military police of the 626th Army Group. Here is his entry for 25th February: 'The Communist Yekaterina Skoroyedova knew about the Russians' attack several days beforehand. She spoke disparagingly of those Russians who co-operate with us. She was shot at 12.00. An old man, Savely Petrovich Stepanenko, and his wife, both from Samsonovka, were also shot. The four-year-old child of Goravilin's mistress was also liquidated. At about 16.00 four eighteen-year-old girls who had crossed over the ice from Yeysk were brought to me. The whip made them more submissive. All four are students and attractive pieces'. I published the diary and received a letter from a sergeant from Budenovka who had known the people who had been shot. It was hard to live knowing that there were such men as this Schmidt at close quarters.

A *People's Almanac, The Agriculturalist's Handbook*, published in Russian by the Germans for the occupied regions, was sent to me. At that time I was reading daily the most terrible reports of atrocities, of sadism, of the fascists' efforts not merely to ruin but in addition to humiliate our people. What could an idiotic handbook mean in the light of Hitler's methods? But there was one detail that nauseated me. I was so angry that I copied out these 'memorable dates': '*January*. 12th

– birthday of Goering and Rosenberg; 29th – Chekhov's birthday; *February*. 10th – Pushkin's death; 23rd – Horst Wessel's death; 24th – anniversary of Hitler's proclamation of the National Socialist Party programme; 26th – Shevchenko's death', and so on. Whenever it came to my mind I would mutter: 'Goering and Chekhov! Lovely!'

On 15th August there was a writers' meeting. The chairman said that times were difficult, people would have to pull themselves together, not grumble and not drink. On that day the Germans occupied Yelista.

A Kazakh, Askar Lekherov, wrote to me from the front: 'What is life? That is a very big question. Because everybody wants to live, but death is inevitable once in every lifetime. So one must die like a hero'.

The Germans reached Mozdok. Every day someone I knew would be notified of the death of a father, a son or a husband. I made several trips to the front. Exhausted women were mending the roads. Children worked in the factories and during breaks started to play games. War had made strange bedfellows of heroism and torpor, spiritual growth and daily hardship.

Since the opening of the German offensive everybody speculated about when the Allies would launch the Second Front at long last. Umansky said to me: 'Don't count on it, there's never going to be any Second Front'. I wrote sharp articles for the *News Chronicle*, the *Evening Standard* and the *Daily Herald*, saying what our people thought of the Allies' inaction. My articles were printed, I was even thanked for them, but of course they changed nothing. It is true that an MP, the Tory Sir William Davison, asked the Minister of Information a question in the House and referred to one of my articles, but English Ministers, even those of Information, are past masters in the art of leaving awkward questions unanswered.

I often met foreign correspondents. Leland Stowe was an optimist who kept saying: 'There'll soon be a landing in France or Holland'; his optimism was built in, like that of Petrov who, when he was leaving for Sevastopol, said to me: 'I'm certain that the Second Front will be opened in another week or two'. Hindus and Werth, on the contrary, were pessimistic. I shall have more to say about the foreign correspondents later on; I remember some amusing incidents, but during that summer there was little occasion for laughter. If at times we did laugh it was without gaiety. When they opened American tinned meat,

77

which they called *tushonka*, the men at the front said sardonically, 'Here goes, let's open the Second Front'.

Vast meetings were held in London and New York: the ordinary people called for a Second Front. On 12th August Churchill arrived in Moscow. We were very excited: would an agreement be reached or not? Shapiro came in hurriedly to say: 'Harriman isn't pleased with the results'. I passed this on to Umansky who smiled: 'Who's pleased? Nobody except perhaps Pétain'. The joint communiqué was vague.

After Churchill had left, news was received about the British landing at Dieppe. People gathered in the streets animatedly discussing it: 'That'll make the Germans sick'. I was asked where Dieppe was. I felt rather sceptical, but at the office that evening everybody said that this was the start of important operations, that Stalin had convinced Churchill, that the Germans would be forced immediately to move several divisions from our front. Vadimov telephoned Molotov: should there be a leader on the Dieppe landing?

Our illusions were short-lived: the Dieppe landing turned out to have been no more than a small raid. Perhaps the British government had wanted to throw a sop to public opinion? At the *Red Star* office Moran declaimed Polezhayev's verses: 'The British lord is proud and free, no patriot more staunch than he. Honour he loves and loves to eat, then on a steamer to retreat'.

I do not know how the British man in the street regarded the Dieppe raid, but our people were angry: they felt they had been tricked. Many finer feelings vanish in wartime; I often realized how much I myself had coarsened. But there is a feeling of generosity and a readiness for self-sacrifice that war brings into flower; our papers called it 'rescue in battle'. Gradually we began to be less impressed by stories of snipers who had accounted for fifty Germans and of infantrymen who had destroyed five tanks with 'Molotov Cocktails'; one can learn to take even extraordinary valour for granted. But there was one thing that never failed deeply to move me and all those whom I came across: self-sacrifice, the death of the soldier who gives up his life voluntarily to save his comrade. This is something you can never take for granted; each time it stops your breath, seems a miracle, and no matter how difficult things are, your confidence in life is restored.

There is such a thing as diplomacy which is the province of experts. There is also what is called foreign policy: this can be understood by anyone, but being closely bound up with expediency, with strategy

78

and tactics, its appeal is to the intellect. There is, however, another thing: conscience. It is dangerous to affront it. If I am to speak of what people lived through, I cannot pass over in silence the things we had to endure in that accursed summer. Of course I understand why the Allies opened their military campaign in the summer of 1944 and not in that of 1942. Wendell Willkie, and later Eden, told me that they were not well enough prepared for a landing and did not want to incur 'unnecessary sacrifices'. In their view Hitler's army had to be worn down on the Russian front. So the 'unnecessary sacrifices' fell to our lot. One can appreciate these calculations, for the reasoning is not all that complicated, but it is difficult to forget what took place: for practically every one of us it is spelt out in terms of personal bereavement.

10

In September General Vadimov allowed me to go to the neighbourhood of Rzhev where fierce battles had been taking place since August. In the history of the war these battles are described in the following way: 'The offensive action in the Rzhev region, which threatened the German military base of the "Centre" group, commanded by Colonel-General Model, pinned down large enemy forces, thus contributing to the defence of Stalingrad'. In the annals of many families Rzhev meant the loss of someone dear: the battles were fought at tremendous sacrifice. I never had the chance to visit Stalingrad, and all I know about the battle on the Volga comes from Grossman's articles, Nekrassov's novel, and what I was told by friends. But I shall never forget Rzhev. There may have been offensives that cost more human lives, but I do not think there have been any more tragic: for weeks on end there was fighting for five or six mutilated trees, for the wall of a shattered house or for a tiny hillock.

Rain set in; contrary to the views of *Pravda*'s editor, it looked yellow, even rust-coloured. What can be more melancholy in the autumn than the Tver swamps under a murky sky, with feverish spotted foliage and squelching mud on the roads? Cars stuck and, with desperate shouts of 'Heave!', the men tried to shove them on. Here and there the road was paved with felled tree-trunks, and the mud-splashed jeeps lurched and shuddered like wounded birds. It took us a long time to reach Rzhev. On the sites of what had been Torzhok and Staritsa – bombed and burnt by the German *Luftwaffe* – stood the charred, blackened shells of deserted houses. In the villages women were grubbing for potatoes which they clutched in their hands as if they were nuggets of gold.

Rzhev was visible from the top of a small hill; little of it remained, though from the distance it looked like a normal, populated town. Our forces had occupied the airfield, but the barracks were in the hands of the Germans; I could see two blocks of flats standing out: the taller one had been nicknamed 'Colonel' by the soldiers, and the other one 'Lieutenant-Colonel'. One part of a small wood on the outskirts of the town had been a battlefield; the trees blasted by shells and mines looked like stakes driven in at random. The earth was criss-crossed by trenches; dugouts bulged like blisters. One shell-hole gaped into the next.

Uzbeks in camouflage overalls, tall and handsome, looked like actors in some strange pantomime, while the patchy blobs of colour on their clothing reminded me of abstract painting.

Maps of the town divided into squares lay on the tables at Staff HQ, but in some places there was no trace left of the streets; the fighting went on for some minute patch of ground sprouting barbed wire and filled with shell-splinters, broken glass, empty tins and excrement. Several times I caught the sound of German singing or an occasional word: the enemy was moving about in similar trenches. The deep roar of guns and the furious bark of mortars were deafening, then sud-denly, during a lull of two or three minutes, the chatter of machine-guns would be heard.

The men lived in such close proximity, not only to the Germans, but to death itself that they had stopped noticing it; a way of life had been established. They wondered when they would be issued with their tot of vodka, and why Varya, who had moved into the battalion commander's dugout, had received a medal. By the poor light of the smoky oil-wick the soldiers quarrelled, wrote letters home, hunted lice (known as 'snipers'), and speculated on what things would be like when the war was over. No one wanted to talk about death; the men preferred to remember the past or to think about the future. When the Very lights went up someone would swear and then say evenly: 'There, he's put 'em up, the bastard. Now he'll begin'. Two hours later another would spit and say: 'The louse! He's dive-bombing'. At HQ decorations were handed out to those who had won them and lists of the missing were drawn up. In the field-hospitals they were giving blood-transfusions, amputating arms and legs. 'They won't let you get an hour's sleep,' an orderly complained. The girls on signal duty, those natural heroines of all war stories, the Marusyas, Katyas and Natashas, called: 'Oka, put me through to Star'.

According to a simple formula the regiments and battalions were alluded to as 'households' on the telephone. The commander shouted at Olga or Vera: 'Why do you keep getting in the way, damn you!' The girls evoked memories of school-leaving dances, of first love: almost all those I met at the front had come straight from school; they often winced nervously: there were too many men about with hungry eyes. At the divisional Press Centre a major dictated: 'Sergeant Kuzmichyov's gallant exploit. In carrying out the Commander's orders ...' Then he would share the news with his crony, the party membership organizer: 'They say Mekhlis'll be struck off, that'll be a fine thing!'

Behind all this, however, there was neither indifference nor preoccupation with trivial matters, but a ferocious bitterness. We were now in the second year of the war and it had long ceased to feel like a sudden catastrophe; it had settled down, and although everyone knew that terrible things were happening in the south, that the Germans had reached the banks of the Volga, there was a deep-rooted conviction that this war would last a long time, that many were doomed to die – some perhaps in a year's time, some within the hour – and that those who survived by a miracle would see victory. Every man believed that he personally was sure to survive, and every man superstitiously avoided speaking or even thinking about it.

There were times when things were quiet, and then again the fighting flared up. Colonel Gavalevsky succeeded in ousting the enemy from the northern bank of the Volga. For eight months the Germans had been fortifying their positions, laying minefields with great thoroughness. Junior-Lieutenant Rashevsky led his unit into the attack in defiance of orders, before the appointed time. This unit was made up of soldiers of various nationalities: Russians, Uzbeks, Tatars, Jews, Bashkirs. Rashevsky was wounded but remained in the fighting line. The Tatar Ibrahim Bagautdinov said: 'We tickled them up a bit'. The parents, wife and sisters of a collective farmer called Shumsky had stayed in one of the villages occupied by the Germans. 'I'm sorry for my old people,' he said, 'it makes me feel bad ...' He had a mild Russian face with ill-defined features but it was easy to see that he was eating his heart out; he kept muttering under his breath: 'Kill them!'

I remember the pale face of Daniil Alexeyevich Prytkov, formerly a Ural foundry worker. He fought like a man possessed. I found out that he had an old mother in the Urals and that the Germans had killed one of his comrades. Prytkov used to crawl at night to the German positions and bring back trophies: tommy-guns and snipers' rifles. 'Comrade Commander,' he would say to Lieutenant-Colonel Samosenko, 'let me have one of our own tommy-guns. I had sixteen German ones, but I gave them all away, I hate using them.' 'Take a day off,' said the lieutenant-colonel. Prytkov refused: 'If everyone did that who'd go in to the attack?' He lived for one purpose only. After he had been shell-shocked he became hard of hearing and would put his wristwatch to his ear: 'I've gone deaf. Never mind, I'll hear it there'. (Where 'there' was I never made out.) 'The devils, the devils!' he said over and over again. His eyes were burning, his lips moved, one could sense the feverish excitement that gripped him.

'They make one's heart wither,' said the soldier Ilya Gorev. And it was perfectly true; when I think back now to our feelings at that time, I realize it: we lived in such a state of hatred of the fascists, in such distress and anxiety, that the heart of every one of us was like the earth in times of drought: cracked, parched, burnt out. Yes, that summer of the year 1942 . . .

Sergeant Belyakov had been a staid elderly collective farmer. He got talking to me and spoke of his wife's hardships: she had three children, her health was poor, the collective farm was not prosperous; even before the war life had been far from easy and now it was worse. While the others joked, argued, exchanged war news, he sat in silence, occasionally smoking, which made him cough for a long time, though once, when a woman told him how, before leaving, the Germans had shot her cow, he lost his temper: 'They've got no conscience. A soldier, a child – it's all one to them. It's not enough to kill them. But what's to be done with them?' He fell silent again, shook a little home-grown tobacco into a scrap of newspaper (he did not care to read) and then added quietly: 'They used to tell us that they'd got fine shops, lots of goods. But what I want to know is, have people like that got a soul?'

Everybody made fun of Misha Savchenko; he wrote love poems and dedicated them to various girls: to Svetlana or to Lenochka. I took down some lines that I found amusing: 'At the front there is no rose, no Pegasus, and Fritz has planted his mines all over the place. But I am with you, my love, till the hour of attack! I shall fly with you into Berlin'. He felt hurt that not one of his poems had been printed in the divisional newspaper: 'They only accept clichés. If I wrote about the honour of the Guardsmen they'd put it in at once'. Yet when the Germans attacked, this Misha disabled a tank single-handed. General Chanchibadze pinned on him the Order of the Red Star and embraced him. Misha raised his already very high, thin eyebrows: 'D'you think I'd make way for a tank?' He dedicated a poem on his decoration to Grusha, but it was not printed.

Another man I remember was a small Jewish barber; I think the name was Fegel, it has got badly smudged in my notebook. Unlike the common run of barbers he cut people's hair and shaved them in silence. No one quite knew how he had managed to capture a prisoner for interrogation: he dragged in a tall German and was himself unable to explain it: 'I was fed up. And then I kept remembering things'. I did not attempt to find out what he had been remembering; some of his kin had probably stayed behind in occupied territory; he was from Minsk. I only asked: 'Were you frightened?' He shrugged: 'While I was crawling along I didn't feel anything. Or I may have felt something but I've forgotten what. But when I think of it now, I'm frightened'.

With the American journalist Leland Stowe I was once at the HQ of General Porfiry Georgyevich Chanchibadze, an impetuous, lively Georgian. That night the Germans kept up a heavy mortar fire, but Chanchibadze, quite unmoved, proposed flamboyant toasts and tried to drink the American under the table. Leland Stowe was a brave man, he had seen many different wars: in Spain, in Norway, in Libya; he could drink with the best but he had to give up: 'I can't drink any more'. Then the general poured out a full glass for himself and just enough to cover the bottom of a glass for the journalist, and said to me: 'Translate this to him: "This is how *our* people fight, and that's how the American's fight".' Stowe laughed: 'It's the first time I've felt glad that our people aren't fighting better'. The next night, on our way to army HQ, we came to a peasant's house. We knocked for a long time. At last a frightened woman's voice asked: 'Who's there?' 'Friends'. The woman let us in while keeping a mistrustful eye on us. 'I was already thinking you might be Hritzes'. (This was how she pronounced 'Fritzes'.) When she heard us talking to one another in a foreign language she burst into tears: 'Hritzes!' I explained to her that my companion was an American, upon which she said: 'Why are they sitting at home? Must we all die?' I translated her words to Stowe and he turned away: this was not the toast-master. A child woke up and began to cry; the woman rocked it in her arms.

Near Rzhev I unexpectedly met a 'Spaniard', Emma Lazarevna Wolff. She was working in counter-propaganda. We exchanged reminiscences of Madrid. We had been through all this before, and it seemed as though it would always be the same: field-telephones, mortars, death. But by now her son was grown up; she told me he was fighting at Rzhev, and also that our dear Gorev, the defender of Madrid, was no longer of this world. It was difficult to accept the idea that he had been killed by his own people.

'I had a comrade, a wonderful officer, who distinguished himself in the Finnish war, and he was imprisoned a month before the Germans attacked us,' said General Alexey Ivanovich Zygin, a very gallant and good man, one dark starry night on a quiet sector of the front. We were sitting in a tent on the river bank (Zygin said jokingly 'a small house on the Volga'). He was meditating aloud: 'When we get this lot over and done with, everything'll be different. There's a lot that stinks. Now they've published the play *The Front* in *Pravda*. All very true. Only why did they have to come to their senses so late? Think of all the innocent people they've destroyed. And the lickspittles in high places. They put fear into everyone. Here at the front I'm not frightened, but at that time I quaked in my shoes like everyone else. Do you think Stalin has the slightest idea what's been going on? I believe he doesn't know a thing, that they misled him, told him we were well prepared. And now he can't help seeing for himself. What he says is right. But who's to carry it out? The self-same men'.

General Zygin's thoughts were shared by many in those days. I want to be accurate; I am constantly afraid lest present judgments should affect my descriptions of the past. So let me quote from a letter I have kept which was written to me in September 1942 by a man at the front, Captain Shestopal: 'I have lost my wife and child (I say "lost" as if I were talking about objects – people in occupied territories are more lost than any object). My beloved blue-eyed Ukraine has been crucified by the vile Germans ... Never have I feared more for the fate of my country than now ... You hear nothing but that we have retreated to new defence lines, that our troops are hard-pressed by the enemy. Once the war is over, we shall wash our hands and sit in judgment on who did what to save the country, remembering those who ought to be remembered and those who should be mercilessly flogged for negligence and thieving ... It may well be that the press was genuinely trying to educate society by citing model conduct, but what it in fact produced was a picture of our social life free from all faults and blemishes. We are paying a high price for those lessons. Stalin has now sounded the alarm. The press will not fail to make a great hullabaloo about it and turn it into the latest campaign. To reassure themselves and others, even before the "historical" campaign ends.

For they used to shout: "Do not forget the wise historical words of the super-genius" (this is compulsory though not in the least necessary) "Stalin. But our frontier is safely locked, it is reliably defended by our faithful sentinels, etc." This is nothing short of suicide. The fact is we did lots of things badly and are now paying for it. In my opinion we shall not only make the Germans see sense but do the same for some of our own people. The war will teach us a lot'.

Zygin was killed in 1943. I do not know whether Captain Shestopal survived to our days. And there are many others about whom I know nothing. In those years I wrote: 'We are afraid of words, and yet, farewell! If by chance fate brings us together perhaps I shall not immediately recognize the grey passer-by in a travelling coat ... Any man you care to take is a strange creature: he passionately swears that he will love forever, and forgets when that was and to whom he swore it ... But even he will not be unfaithful to one thing: to the sparing word, to the warm hand, to the Rzhev forest and the sadness of Rzhev'.

A small shabby notebook; a great deal has got smudged, I am hard put to it to decipher my own scribbles. But here is a clear entry in a strange hand: 'Tell Kokorin's wife that he is alive and fighting', and a Moscow telephone number. I do not know what happened to Kokorin, I do not even remember where I met him: I think it was at the army newspaper's printing press, but we must have had a heart-to-heart talk near the Rzhev forest.

11

As early as the autumn of 1941 I began writing for the Swedish newspaper *Göteborgs Handelstidningen;* a year later I learnt from Alexandra Mikhailovna Kollontay, who was our ambassador to Sweden, that some of my articles made these normally placid and even phlegmatic Northerners fly into a rage. But first of all I should like to say something about Alexandra Kollontay.

I first saw her in Paris in 1909 at a lecture. I thought her handsome and, what was more, she was dressed in a very different style from that usually affected by Russian *émigrées* who stressed their contempt for femininity; even what she spoke about was bound to appeal to an eighteen-year-old: personal happiness, for which man was created, was unthinkable without universal happiness.

But it was only twenty years later that I made her acquaintance in Oslo where she was the Soviet Representative.

Although she was then in her late fifties I barely managed to keep up with her as she scrambled up steep rocks. There was a wonderful youthfulness, too, in her manner of arguing and her dreams about the future: this was in 1929, when it was still easy to argue and to dream. I was impressed by the popularity she enjoyed: many people in the street greeted her; when we went into a café the musicians recognized her and started to play Russian songs in her honour. Politicians spoke of her with respect, while artists and poets anxiously awaited her opinion on an exhibition or a book.

Alexandra Kollontay sometimes spoke to me about her past. She was the daughter of General Domontovich, her mother had been born in Finland. She was eighteen when she married the engineer Kollontay whom she soon left: domestic bliss was not to her taste. She was carried away by revolutionary ideas, travelled abroad, became a Social-Democrat, met Lenin, Plekhanov, Rosa Luxemburg, the Lafargues. In 1908 the Tsarist authorities prosecuted her: they had discovered a call to rebellion in her pamphlet on Finland. Alexandra Kollontay was forced to go abroad. (The Finns did not forget her struggle for the independence of Finland, and this facilitated personal relations in March 1940 when peace negotiations were opened. I was in Saltsjöbaden, at the country house of the Swedish actor Karl Gerhardt; he described to me the meeting of the representatives of the Finnish government and Alexandra Kollontay at his house: 'I've never met anyone of such high intelligence', he exclaimed. 'Usually strong convictions preclude broadmindedness and tolerance, but Madame Kollontay has immense tact.')

In 1914 Alexandra Kollontay was gaoled by the Germans for anti-militarist speeches. Afterwards she left for Sweden, but the neutral and, one would have thought, peaceable Swedish government also arrested and deported her. She went to Canada.

She had kept an article published in the organ of the Swedish Left Social-Democrats in July 1917 in which it said that friends had come to see Comrade Kollontay off when she went to Petrograd – to a Kerensky prison. And, in fact, Prince Beloselsky, a Commissar of the Provisional Government, was ready waiting for her at the frontier to send her forthwith to a women's convict prison. After the October Revolution she was appointed People's Commissar for Social Welfare; she organized crèches, fought to get milk for the children, drafted decrees on the care of mother and child. The first Soviet marriage law was drafted by her, and of course there were no 'unmarried mothers' or 'illegitimate children' in it. From 1924 to 1946 Alexandra Kollontay represented the Soviet Union in, successively, Norway, Mexico and Sweden.

I do not know why I have let myself be carried away by this record of service, the biography of a presumably well-known political personality. Alexandra Kollontay devoted sixty years to the struggle for the triumph of a Socialist society, yet little has been written about her, less than about many quite insignificant public figures.

I was attracted by her unaffected democratic manner. Always remaining herself, she talked easily both to the rather prim Swedish king and to ordinary miners. When she introduced me to her housekeeper she said: 'This is my personal assistant'. At the embassy everybody sat down at the same table: embassy officials, chauffeurs, the housekeeper. She had a great gift for education and many young people who worked under her guidance owe their spiritual development to her.

In 1929 she told me that art demanded modern forms, she was enthusiastic about the works of young Norwegians and Mexicans, and she admired Van Gogh. In 1933 we had a long talk about literature.

She expressed some astonishment: 'I have had two new novels sent me. Now what use are these good little boys? After Tolstoy, Dostoyevsky, Chekhov . . .'

In May 1938, passing through Stockholm on my way back to Spain from Moscow, I found Alexandra Kollontay aged and saddened. She invited Señora de Palencia, the ambassador of Republican Spain, to dinner, and grew very animated when Señora de Palencia talked about the new commanders who had emerged in the course of the fighting: 'I believe, too, that nothing is lost yet'. After this guest had gone Alexandra Kollontay asked: 'How are things at home?' and immediately added: 'You don't have to tell me, I know'. When I was taking leave of her she said: 'I wish you strength, you'll need twice as much as before, not only because you'll soon be in Barcelona, but also because you've just come from Moscow'.

I still have several letters which she sent me during the war; she wrote about my articles and made only passing references to herself: 'I work a lot, and great things are afoot'. She was like that.

In the last years of her life I often went to see her. She was partially paralysed but went on working. She was consulted by officials in the Ministry of Foreign Affairs. She was writing her memoirs that future historians might know what she had seen and experienced. She died at the age of eighty.

I must now return from reminiscences of this noble heart to petty politics. As everyone knows, Sweden remained neutral during the Second World War; her government, however, allowed Hitler to transport troops and war material across Swedish territory. Some Swedes approved of it, some grinned and bore it, but others were furious.

The *Göteborgs Handelstidningen* was pro-Ally and asked me to send them articles from Moscow. I realized that Sweden was in a difficult position and tried to write as tactfully as possible. Nevertheless my articles infuriated the Germans. The DNB (*Deutsches Nachrichten Bureau*) announced that at a press conference a representative of the Ministry of Foreign Affairs had warned the Swedes that 'Ehrenburg's articles in the Göteborg paper were incompatible with neutrality and could lead to unpleasant consequences for Sweden'.

Certain Swedish papers, such as the *Stockholms-Tidningen*, *Göteborgs Morganpost* and *Aftonbladet*, supported von Ribbentrop. *Dagposten* expressed itself most imaginatively: 'Ehrenburg has broken all records of intellectual sadism. There is no need to refute this swinish lying or to prove that Ehrenburg ascribes to the Germans things that are the usual practice of the Red Army men'.

Herr Tegner, the editor of the popular sports paper *Idrottsbladet*, bellowed as though he were at a football match. According to Hitler's various admirers, my writings were responsible for the sinking of Swedish ships in the Baltic, for the Russians' plans to seize Stockholm and other similar horrors.

Articles of mine published in the Göteborg paper found their way into the Norwegian and Danish illegal press. This naturally annoyed the Germans, and the *Frankfurter Zeitung* said that: 'All right-minded Swedes protest against the hospitality given to the bloodthirsty Moscow *provocateur*'. The newspaper quoted the explorer Sven Hedin on 'the ferocity of the Russian bear' and his approval of a Swede who had volunteered for the German army.

A man holding a responsible position as Chief of Posts and Telegraphs, Anders Orne, also had his say. He published an article entitled *Ilya Ehrenburg in Sweden* in which he said: 'We see an attempt to conquer Sweden from within in order to make it a part of the USSR'. This was in July 1942 when our army on the Don steppes was almost bleeding to death.

At the beginning of the year 1943 the Swedish journal *Folksvillen* said: 'We published Ilya Ehrenburg's comments on Hitler's latest speech. We omitted certain passages so that there should be nothing insulting to the head of the German State. No objections to the article were raised by the authorities in charge of press control. However, on the next day a cabinet meeting was held at which the decision was taken that all the copies of the issue carrying Ehrenburg's article should be confiscated. We think this is going too far'.

Professor Segerstedt, the editor of *Göteborgs Handelstidningen*, informed me that although he was obliged by the censorship to make occasional cuts in my articles, he was sincerely grateful to me and was glad to say that many readers had sent him letters expressing approval; Alexandra Kollontay wrote to me: 'You know, of course, that they like and appreciate you in Sweden'.

I sometimes went to see the Norwegian ambassador Rolf Andvord when I was in Moscow.

He was a friendly and hospitable man. We would recall our common Norwegian friends. He knew about the polemics in the Swedish press and would say to me: 'Don't pay any attention to the Chief of Posts and Telegraphs. He's a bureaucrat and nothing more, whereas the letters are written by ordinary Swedes. They're good people. They know about Norway's fate, and it causes them pain and sometimes makes them feel ashamed'.

Five years after the end of the war I happened to be in Sweden. I also went to Göteborg, and the *Göteborgs Handelstidningen* (Professor Segerstedt was no longer there) published a very unkind note about its wartime correspondent. I was not surprised: I had realized long before that when all attitudes are determined by politics, memory can be an unwelcome burden.

To make up for it I met people in Sweden who had supported us in the difficult years. I made closer acquaintance with Georg Branting whom I had met in Spain, with Meer and many others. I saw that the Norwegian ambassador had been right: there were many good people in Sweden. All of them remembered Alexandra Kollontay with affection.

So what does it all come down to? The life of a foreign country reminds one of a darkened theatre auditorium: only the stage is lit up. And on the stage actors appear and disappear – it all depends on the events, on the political situation, on the whims of the stage-manager known as History. When Hitler was nearing the Volga, when he was in Egypt and was opening the way to India, an inferior production of an inferior play was staged in the Swedish theatre. It was soon withdrawn: the Red Army men loosened the tongues of the Swedes. But what about the auditorium? There the ordinary spectators sit, they can clap or they whistle, but they have no chance to put in their word. And when at certain moments they burst on to the stage itself, then not only the scenery but the very theatre cracks asunder.

12

THE NEWS about the end of the battle of Stalingrad reached me on the road. I was with the staff photographer of *Red Star*, S. I. Loskutov, on my way to Kastornoye. I was in high spirits: it was clear that the turning-point had been reached; up till then one believed in victory as an act of faith, despite everything, but now there was no shadow of doubt: victory was assured.

It was freezing hard; February had come in with continuous snow-storms, with the sort of blizzards that lash one's face. But by the time we reached Kastornoye the night was cold and clear. The moon shone with a dead greenish light on the snow-covered fields, the shell-torn corpses, the battered tanks. We stood gazing at it for a moment and then went into a peasant's house.

In the morning I wandered round Kastornoye for a long time. Here the German divisions retreating from Voronezh had fallen into a trap and all at once an obscure village sprang into fame. Overturned lorries, jeeps buried in the snowdrifts, Opels, Citroëns, Fiats in which once upon a time honeymoon couples had driven to the seaside, Italian buses with their sides ripped open, staff documents, fragments of human limbs, field-kitchens, a bodiless head in a helmet, bottles of champagne, briefcases, dismembered hands, typewriters, machine-guns, a Paris mascot doll with huge eyelashes, and the heel of a naked foot that seemed to be sprouting up through the snow.

The sight of a killed man shatters one even in war; you cannot help wondering where he came from, what brought him here, whom he has left behind. This feeling has something human about it. But in Kas-tornoye no thought about the fate of any individual soldier could possibly arise. The winter sun came out for an hour, and in its light the corpses looked like waxworks, the snow-covered field with its scrap-iron, its broken bodies and severed limbs, its black pits, was like the stage model of some long extinct world.

A lieutenant gave me a drink of brandy. We were sitting in a dark peasant's house warmed by the animal heat of the human beings in it. Everyone was talking at once. The lieutenant told us how in one day they had covered seventeen miles over the snowy steppe. 'I fire and fall asleep on my feet.' I recall young Captain Tishchenko. Everything was in confusion and he found himself surrounded by Germans. 'What could I do? We were supposed to have encircled them, but in fact there were Fritzes all round me. I don't even know what put it into my head, it must have been sheer fright: I seized one of them by the hand and said: "Good fellow to surrender, *gut, sehr gut*". And they all put up their hands'.

I noted down: 'Sergeant Koryavtsev fell into icy water. The Company Commander said: "Go indoors somewhere, you'll catch a chill". But the sergeant answered: "I'm not cold, anger keeps me warm"'.

The soldier Neimark had a bandaged hand. Before the war he had been an accountant in Chernigov. Dirty, unshaven, with grey stubble. He was smiling: 'They speak of "Jewish luck", and you see what luck I've had: three fingers gone and two left, and it's just those two I need for my job. I must say, I'm longing to get to Chernigov'.

I also took down a long conversation I had with a German Intelligence Officer attached to the staff of the 13th Corps, Otto Zinsker. He was a middle-aged man and not unintelligent. He began by saying: 'I'm not dazzled by Hitler's greatness but I don't want to criticize him: he is what he is. He managed to awaken German national pride, that's to his credit. The pity is that the Nazis often get in the way of old experienced officers. Of course the eradication of Communism and the liquidation of the Jews are in the party programme. I'm not interested in politics, and a soldier doesn't have to spare the population of an enemy country: war is war. But, you see, violence and plunder can corrupt any army, even the German. Though when all's said and done that's not the most important thing either'. He fell silent, but an hour later, when he had warmed himself and smoked several cigarettes, he opened up: 'D'you think our Intelligence Service didn't know about your reserves? Why, our General not only knew the identity of your divisions but had all the data on their composition and equipment. It's an old story. When Intelligence supplied the information about the Russian divisions near Kotelnikovo it never went further than the Army Commander. General von Salmuth said that at Supreme Command HQ they didn't like receiving that sort of information: it was dangerous to report it to the Führer – the general's name would be associated with something unpleasant. There seems to be a law of association. So the information service ought to be renamed: our job is really to supply misinformation. Our Corps Commander deceives General von Salmuth, Salmuth deceives Keitel, Keitel deceives the Führer. It's a chain which is dragging Germany into the abyss'.

We wanted to push on further and got to Shchigry a few hours after our troops had broken into the town. We arrived late at night and knocked at doors for a long time without any result. Finally we were allowed into a house. Sergey Ivanovich Loskutov settled down with some delightful old people while I was taken into a room occupied by a young woman with her six or seven-year-old son. The boy woke up and began to whimper asking for jam. The mother took him into her bed while I slept on a small sofa. By the dim light of the lamp I took a good look at her: a nice Russian face, sad and tired. I felt bad at having alarmed her; I said that the horrors were now a thing of the past, that she would be able to rest and recover her peace of mind. She burst into tears: it was now eighteen months since she had heard from her husband; he was in the Air Force, the last letter from him had come at the beginning of the war; she asked me how she could trace him: the field-post number would have changed by now, of course, and she did not even know the name of his unit. I fell asleep and was awakened by the fretful voice of the boy who again demanded jam. At last I could see the object of his clamour – a tin of preserves with a French label. The mistress of the house gave me breakfast and explained: 'We have plenty of everything; the Germans left it all behind and we picked it up in the evening'. I asked her how the Germans had behaved. She said: 'You know yourself – they're not human. Fortunately I had nothing to do with them. They made their billets in good houses, and mine, as you can see, is a hovel. No German ever set foot in here'. The boy interrupted her: 'Mama, Uncle Otto used to come every day, he played with me, he played with you too'. The woman flushed painfully: 'Don't make up silly tales'. But the boy stubbornly repeated: 'I'm not making it up. Uncle Otto promised to bring a little chocolate house'. The woman gave me a scared look. 'Don't be afraid,' I said, 'I won't say anything about it,' and went out. (This scene remained in my memory; in the novel *The Storm* Doctor Krylov spends the night in a small town and hears a boy's story about 'Uncle Otto'.)

The colonel told me that a traitor, a *Polizei*, had been caught. In a small room sat a man of about thirty-five. He raised his head and looked at me with dull watery eyes. He had a large Adam's apple. He told me that the Germans had organized 'courses for policemen' in Shchigry. He was trained there. He had not really done anything wrong. He had merely written a letter of thanks to the Commandant, Pauling, in the name of the trainees who had been through the course. Now they were holding it against him. 'It's stupidity. I've never been very practical.' He began to snivel: 'I was frightened and now my own people have turned on me.' A few moments later he suddenly plucked up courage: 'After all, tell me, what wrong did I do? Why are they taking it out of me? They said "training courses", so I went. In my time I graduated from the ten-year school, I wanted to go on with my studies, but didn't have the chance. You can ask anyone here: before the war I held a responsible job, not a single penalty. The circumstances should be taken into account. I'm the first to rejoice that our people have come back. So why are they attacking me? I wasn't in Moscow; is it my fault that the Germans were masters here?'

All that remained of the town was the small wooden houses: the Germans had set fire to all the larger buildings before they left. In the town park I saw a German cemetery: long rows of crosses. The people told us what they had been through; when the partisans blew up a bridge the Germans had shot fifty hostages, and in the spring they had hanged six women in the public square for being in contact with the partisans. When they were led to execution the people had wept. One of the women caught sight of a girl with rouged cheeks and shouted: 'Shame on you, you German mattress'. (In *The Storm* I quoted a song written in one of the occupied towns at the time: 'You've done up your hair like German dolls, smeared paint on your faces, and spin and roll like tops. But your curls will not help you when our falcons return, and our lads will walk past you with nothing but scorn'.) The brothers Rusanov were tortured to death.

The colonel said that our forces were swiftly advancing towards Kursk and were sure to liberate the town in two or three days. We drove along the route indicated and were caught in a heavy air-raid in Kosorzha; we lay in the snow and when we got up again the fields were covered with large black patches.

A violent snowstorm blew up. The driver swore, stopping every hundred yards; we got out, not knowing which direction to take – the road had disappeared. After we had gone some five to ten miles the car got stuck. The light was beginning to fail, it was four o'clock. We had no food with us and we were freezing. The engine gave out. I

95

was rather insufficiently clothed: an army greatcoat, high boots, gloves instead of mittens. Night fell. At first I suffered a good deal from the cold, and then all of a sudden began to feel quite warm, even pleasantly so. Loskutov grumbled and said that as soon as it was light he would go in search of some human habitation. The driver and I said nothing. I was not asleep, only dozing, and I felt extraordinarily comfortable; the fact was I was beginning to freeze to death.

Several times in my life I have been very close to death. The most disagreeable way to die is by suffocation. On one occasion we were flying in a storm over the Alps: Korneichuk, Wanda Wassilewska, Fadeyev and I. The small aircraft rose to some thirteen thousand feet. Fadeyev went on reading. I glanced at Korneichuk and his face frightened me, it had turned green. I kept opening my mouth and realized that there was nothing to breathe. When the air-hostess brought me an oxygen mask I did not have the strength to draw a breath. It was horrible.

But it is with particular affection that I recall the night between Kosarzha and Zolotukhino. The dreams I had! I do not think that in all my life I have ever felt so blissful. The driver told me later that he, too, was slowly freezing to death and had also seen glorious visions. But Loskutov could not reconcile himself to such a fate and was determined to rescue us. As soon as the day broke he said: 'I'm off'. I said it was foolish, and then watched him flounder among the snow-drifts and went back to my dreams. I only vaguely remember a sledge drawing up. I was dragged out and covered with a sheepskin coat. Loskutov was grinning.

The major gave me a glass of vodka; I drank it and did not even know that it was vodka. The major shook his head and poured out another half-glass. Of course in ordinary circumstances if I had drunk as much as that on an empty stomach I should have fallen under the table; but now we had a snack and an hour later were sitting over a map with the officers of an artillery battalion discussing how to make our way to Kursk. Our car was towed to Zolotukhino, and from there we went on foot to Kursk along the railway track.

(A short time ago, after a meeting of the preparatory commission of the Disarmament Congress at which the representative of Kenya had explained to the pacifists that Mau-Mau was not a tribe but a party, my neighbour Nikolay Ivanovich Bazanov, an unassuming and wholly peace-loving man, suddenly asked me whether I remembered how

Right: Boris Lapin and Z. Hatzrevin near Kiev in the summer of 1941.
Below: Patrol in the Moscow streets, November 1941.

Above: 'Hedgehogs' in Moscow, November 1941. *Below:* Fifth Army G.H.Q. in 1941. From the left: General Govorov and General Ortenberg, editor of 'Red Star'; Ehrenburg on extreme right.

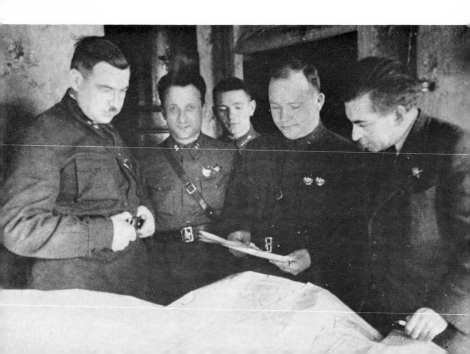

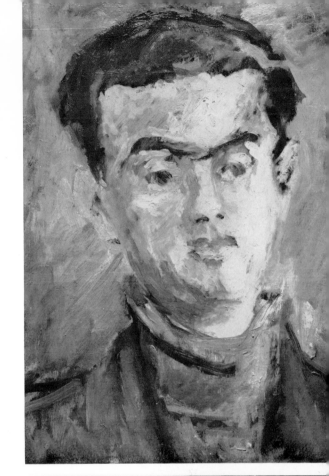

Right: The poet S. Gudzenko; portrait in oils painted by Lyuba Kozintseva (Mrs Ehrenburg) in 1944.
Below: 'Red Star' editorial office in 1943: left to right; Moran, Kopylyov (seated) and Ehrenburg.

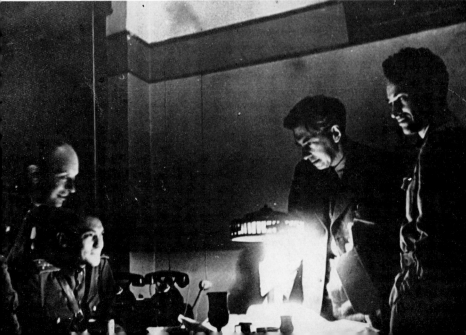

Above: With the commandant of the French air squadron 'Normandie-Niémen' on the Orel front in 1943. *Below:* fourth, from left, the author, fifth, General Rokossovsky.

Above: Ehrenburg with General Chernyakhovsky at the front in 1942.
Below: At the front with the 'Red Star' staff photographer Sergey Loskutov.

Above: With the Tatsin tankmen at the front in 1942. *Below:* Ehrenburg talking to Byelorussian peasants freed by the Red Army in 1943.

Above: The presidium of a meeting of Jewish representatives. From the left: Peretz Markisch, D. Bergelson, S. Mikhoëls and the author. *Below:* With a group of Jewish partisans in Vilnius in 1944.

Ina Konstantinova: photograph given to the author by Ina's parents

The funeral of Ina Konstantinova.

the gunners had thawed me out at Zolotukhino. I had met Bazanov several times before but never suspected that he was the major who had administered the vodka cure that far-off February morning.)

I have been presented with a folder bearing the label: 'On the time spent at the front by Ilya Ehrenburg. The file contains thirty-five numbered pages. Begun on 5th February 1943, ended 20th February 1943'. First there are telegrams signed by myself and by Major Loskutov. 'Arrived at "Topaz", leaving to join troops'; 'Arrived at "Searchlight"'; 'Left for Chernyakhovsky's place'. The telegrams are addressed to 'Velvet' which was the name used for Moscow. 'Searchlight', 'Tempering', 'Topaz', 'Cadmium' were the various Army HQs. After 6th February we did not give any signs of life and General Vadimov was worried; he sent telegrams to the chief of the political department on the Briansk front, General Pigurnov, to Generals Chernyakhovsky and Pukhov, to the *Red Star* correspondents Colonel Krainov and Major Smirnov, and telephoned to them on the direct line. Major Smirnov replied reasonably: 'Ehrenburg has evidently got stuck on the way, there's been a heavy snowstorm for the last four days, the roads are impassable'. But General Vadimov insisted that I must be found at once and even filled Lyuba with alarm, only calming down when he received the telegram: 'Arrived at Kursk 60th Army HQ'.

In Kursk I sat down to write an article: for the first time since the beginning of the war my name had not appeared in the press for three weeks.

The Germans had stayed in Kursk for fifteen months. There I saw for myself what the 'New Order' as described by the *Kurskiye Izvestia*, published under the occupation, had meant. I saw people either benumbed or else slightly hysterical and unable to stop talking. There were all kinds among them: heroes, cowards, petty bourgeois who adjusted themselves to looting, speculation, shootings, drunken orgies. The stories I heard built up a picture of feverish, incoherent and meaningless life. A portrait of Hitler hung in the hall where the Town Soviet had held its meetings. A certain Smyalkovsky had been appointed as mayor. I looked through his reports to the Town Commandant, General Marcel; the mayor quailed, grovelled and did his best to show that he was devoted to the Führer.

Several industries had been started: a knitted-goods factory, a tanning factory, a mill. Second-hand shops flourished, but the heart of the town was the market-place. Here people traded in sugar, drugs stolen from the Germans, Italian stockings and home-distilled vodka. A house porter had made a lot of money: he had reported that two old Jewesses were hiding in a cellar, thus winning favour with the Gestapo, was given a fine flat and was living in clover. A doctor sold sulphonamides in the market-place, and when in his cups was heard to say: 'When I come to think of it, I'm not sorry I stayed here. Of course the Germans are bandits, but could I ever have imagined that I should drink French brandy every night and make presents of stockings to the girls?'

I came across one girl, formerly a student at the Pedagogical Institute, who cried as she opened her heart to me: 'I feel I can trust you: I've read your novel about love, I don't remember the name, it's about some Frenchwoman. I don't know whether I was really in love or just carried away because I felt so wretched. He didn't pester me, just kissed my hand. He played the piano beautifully and talked about his feelings. I'd never heard words like that before. It melted me. And now I've got to pay for it'. She looked at me appealingly, seeking comfort. I said nothing. Many years later I saw the film *Hiroshima mon amour*: during the occupation a young Frenchwoman falls in love with a German soldier; the Germans are driven out, the girl is pilloried, her head shaved, she becomes like a small hunted animal. I have given much thought to the 'mysterious ways of love'. Why then could I feel no pity for the young girl in Kursk? It was all still too fresh. Only just before I had been talking to a Ukrainian schoolmistress; she had been ordered to dig ditches, a German officer had struck her across the face. I met another teacher, Privalova, whose son had been killed by the Germans. I talked to the only Jew who had survived. He had been lying in the typhus isolation ward and the nurses had told the Germans that he had died. The others were murdered in the suburb of Shchetinki. Babies in arms had had their heads smashed against rocks. I felt as hard as stone inside. Of course, the German with whom the student had fallen in love could have felt remorse, he may even have suffered, who knows? But at the time I had no feelings to spare for the 'mysterious ways of love'.

When I met another student from the Pedagogical Institute, Zoya Yemelyanova, who had smuggled arms to the partisans, it made me as happy as if she were the water of life; I made a note: 'Zoya – a true Komsomol!' (Later I sometimes received letters from her, our talk had lasted only an hour, but in my memory she had remained as someone near and dear to me.)

I met other brave and noble people, but I must confess that I felt heavy-hearted. I realized that the population had plumbed the full depths of suffering: there was no comparison between the fascists' behaviour in the occupied towns of France, Holland and Belgium and the methods used in the Soviet territory which the Nazis had seized. Yet in spite of the brutal repressions the people remained undaunted, and perhaps for that very reason all signs of well-being seemed unbearable. We were all torn with grief, resentment, wrath. There went a smart woman. How had she got that jumper? In what had that pink-cheeked, sandy-whiskered citizen traded? Dried eggs or boots taken from the feet of those hanged? Later I saw many liberated towns, saw tears of joy, the graves of heroes and the servile smiles of those who had accommodated themselves. I realized that life under the occupation was ghostlike. There were hardly any young men, all were away fighting in the ranks of our armed forces. Those who refused to submit were murdered or deported to work in Germany. 'Skimmed milk is never thick,' an old woman said to me in Orel. (She modestly said nothing about having kept a wounded Red Army man hidden in her cellar; I was told about it later at the Town Soviet.) Kursk remained firmly etched in my memory because it was the first liberated town I had seen.

It was in Kursk that I met General Ivan Danilovich Chernyakhovsky. I was struck by his youth; he was thirty-six, but impulsive, gay and tall, he looked even younger. During our very first talk he struck me as unlike other generals. He told me that the Germans were now complaining about the 'paradoxical situation': 'The Russians are striking from the west, and sometimes we are forced to press to the east'. Chernyakhovsky said: 'It looks as though they've forgotten their own theory of "pincer movements". We've learnt something from them'. Although he was a tank-man he said: 'Today the tanks seem like the beginning of a military era, but really they're the end. I don't know where the innovations will come from, but I'm more inclined to believe in Wells's Utopian novels than in the ideas of de Gaulle, Guderian or our own tank-men. You learn, you learn, and then you find that life overturns well-established truths'. At our next meeting he touched on the role played by chance: 'I don't know what part Napoleon's cold in the head played in a decisive battle. There's

99

been too much written about it. But there's a lot that's purely fortuitous and it alters circumstances. It's just the same as with the role of the individual in history: the decision rests on economics, of course, on fundamentals, but for all that a Napoleon may or may not turn up'.

A few months later, when I met him again near Glukhov, he talked of Stalin: 'Here you have a dialectical process, not in theory, but as a living example. It's impossible to understand him. All you can do is to have faith. I never visualized that instead of precision instruments, instead of accurate analysis, there would be such a jumble of contradictions'.

To go by words like these one could have supposed that Chernyakhovsky was a sombre character but, on the contrary, he was gay with that inexhaustible gaiety with which Nature endows her favourites. Even in Kursk he laughed and joked. He suddenly jumped up and began to recite: ' "Youth led us on a sabre campaign . . ." ' He smiled: 'When you begin to think about it, it seems silly, yet it's not really silly at all, it's more intelligent than most history courses . . . They say Bagritsky loved birds. But you know, an old man in Uman told me long ago that King David wrote psalms and paid homage to the frogs because they croak so wonderfully – that's poetry too'.

Throughout the war success unfailingly attended on Chernyakhovsky. Certainly he was a brilliant master of military science, but this is not enough for victory. He was bold, he did not wait for orders, and in moments of difficulty his lucky star saved him. At the beginning of the war he was in command of a tank corps, and in the spring of 1944 he was made C-in-C of the Third Byelorussian Front. He was the first to set foot on German soil. In February 1945 I was in East Prussia, in the small town of Bartenstein. Chernyakhovsky rang up Army HQ and said: 'Come along quickly if you want to be in at the finish'. Three days later he was killed.

Later I met other generals at the Supreme Soviet, at receptions, at reviews. Some died in their beds, some retired on a pension, some are still on the active list. But Chernyakhovsky has remained young in my memory; to the accompaniment of guns he is reciting romantic poetry or making his keen and caustic comments.

Let me return to March 1943. There was a long drawn out lull (the battles of the Kursk bulge flared up four months later). The press was full of lists of those who had been decorated, of photographs showing new epaulets and Orders, of articles on the traditions of the Guards and congratulatory telegrams. On my way to Moscow I spent the night in a peasant's house near Yefremov. A soldier was sitting on the stove. He had taken off his boots and was muttering: 'March, march! . . . we'll wear our legs off to the knee. I got a letter yesterday, my God, what a letter!' I fell asleep without hearing what the letter was about. But who of us in those days did not write or receive such letters?

13

I MADE friends with Konstantin Alexandrovich Umansky at the beginning of 1942. He lived in the Moskva Hotel as I did and we met practically every day (or rather every night: I returned late from *Red Star*, at two and sometimes at three in the morning. Umansky would be coming home from the Foreign Office at the same hour: Stalin liked working at night and the responsible members of the staff knew that he might ring up to ask for material or information). In June 1943 Umansky left for Mexico and I never saw him again. Eighteen months do not seem a long time but the years were difficult ones and, although salt was issued on ration cards, I can say that we had eaten the traditional *pood* together.

I have paused to wonder why, voluntarily or involuntarily, I say so little about the politicians whom I met; after all, I lived in an epoch when politics entered into the lives of everyone, and my feelings were far more roused by the news than by books or pictures. I think it is because I did not intimately know the various people with whom life brought me into contact. Much is determined by one's profession if it is a chosen rather than an imposed or a chance one. Of course I have my own element, my own predilections, my own craft; but by the very character of their work writers are seldom narrow professionals: they must be able to understand the spiritual world of different kinds of people. Captain Dreyfus was a narrow-minded specialist: he never really understood why the 'civilian' Zola had taken up the cudgels on his behalf. Mikhailovsky could not understand Chekhov, but Chekhov understood the *Narodniki* and the liberals perfectly.

I became friendly with Umansky because he was unlike the majority of the people in his circle. He seldom talked about his past: the times were not exactly favourable to reminiscence. And yet our paths had occasionally crossed and we had probably run into each other, though time had erased the memory of brief encounters. The diplomats in Washington could hardly know that the councillor and later ambassador at the Soviet Embassy, who astonished everyone by his youth and political maturity, had written a book in German in 1920, not on the Versailles Treaty nor on the diplomatic blockade, but on paintings by those artists who had made their mark in the early years of the Revolution, including Lentulov, Konchalovsky, Sarian, Rozanova, Malevich and Chagall. Umansky was then eighteen. His book, *New Russian Art*, was put out by a leading Berlin publisher. Umansky was enthusiastic about Constructivism, and I feel sure that in the days when Lissitsky and I published the journal *Object* I must have met the young enthusiast. Later he was TASS correspondent in various capitals of western Europe for many years, and it is most unlikely that I should not have come across him. Again, when I began to work for *Izvestia* he was in charge of the press department of the Foreign Office and was a friend of Koltsov, so I must certainly have met him: in Kuibyshev during the autumn of 1941 his face had struck me as familiar.

Naturally we often talked about Roosevelt, Churchill, the American isolationists and the Second Front, but we also touched on many other subjects. Apart from his job, Umansky loved painting and music, and he was interested in everything: Shostakovich's symphonies, Rachmaninov's concertos, Griboyedov's Moscow, the Pompeii paintings, and the first murmur of cybernetics. In his room on the fourth floor of the Moskva I met Admiral Isakov, the writer Yevgeny Petrov, the diplomat Stein, the actor Mikhoëls, the pilot Chukhonivsky. Umansky talked differently to different people, not out of courtesy but because he wanted to learn, to acquaint himself with every facet of life.

People say that erudition is largely a matter of memory. In the west there is a craze for competitions in which questions are shot at people before an audience: when was Pépin le Bref born? What where the the subjects of Plato's *Dialogues*? What are the tensorial quaternions of a vector? And so on. The exceptional winners receive large prizes while the losers retire to the accompaniment of laughter. Those who give correct replies to all the questions must obviously have an extraordinary automatic memory, but it does not mean that they are what is called scholarly. Umansky had an extraordinary memory but it retained only the things that roused his interest; what he carried in his head was not a catalogue but a volume. He spoke excellent English, French and German; when he was presenting his credentials to the President of the Republic of Mexico he said: 'In six months' time I shall expect to speak Spanish', and kept his word, impressing the Mexicans by his mastery of the language. Naturally a knowledge of the country's language is necessary for diplomatic work. (Though at the end of the forties men who did not speak the language of the country to which they were accredited were appointed as ambassadors, no doubt in the belief that the less they talked to foreigners the better.) But Umansky picked up languages quickly not out of devotion to duty but because he wanted to be able to talk freely to people like Pablo Neruda, Jean-Richard Bloch, Anna Seghers, and to read Paul Valéry, Brecht and Machado in the original.

He hated the atmosphere of red tape, but only too often had to breathe, or rather, to stifle in it. Sometimes he would lose patience and say: 'I'm in trouble again: I suggested changing the methods of work and got rapped over the knuckles' ... 'The things they fear above all else are "innovations", initiative.' He told me that in America he had tried to change the type of information put out for abroad but nothing had come of it. 'We don't understand what things we're entitled to be proud of; we conceal the best things we have, we're as arrogant as clumsy adolescents and at the same time we're afraid that some foreigner will nose out that there are no washing-machines in Mirgorod'.

Of the Americans he said: 'Gifted children. At times they're touching and at times intolerable. Europe's ruined, and after the victory the Americans will do the ordering about. He who pays the piper calls the tune. Of course the ordinary American doesn't like Hitler: why burn something if you can buy it? That's the way he reasons. But racialism doesn't make him angry. Don't judge American politics by Roosevelt, he's head and shoulders above his party'.

One day he said to me: 'My boss is annoyed because I don't like the houses in Gorky Street – I *ought* to like them'. On another occasion we talked about Picasso (Umansky admired him very much), and he said: 'I happened to mention his name once and was shouted down: he was a charlatan, was pulling the leg of the capitalists, was making a living out of sensationalism. Read Shakespeare in English to comrades like that and they'll say: "Gibberish! That's not poetry, it's just a jumble of words". You remember what Stalin had to say about Shostakovich's opera? And then there's Zhdanov. And *their* taste is compulsory for everybody else'.

I happen to have preserved several of Umansky's letters from Mexico City. In one of them he refers to the new Mexican ambassador in Moscow, Narcisso Bassols, and says: 'It is worth your while to devote some time to him and not let him go sour in the atmosphere of the diplomatic corps and the foreign correspondents. I am perfectly sure that if you talk to him about Latin-American and other topics you will feel the same genuine pleasure as I did in the delightful native country of your Julio Jurenito'. In another letter he writes: 'I am sending you the *catalogue raisonné* put out for the recent exhibition here of Picasso's work. By the way, the American customs held up his paintings for several months on their way from the US in the suspicion that they might contain something in the nature of a secret code'.

I always felt that Umansky had been born under a lucky star. It was a quite exceptional thing for a man of thirty-seven to be appointed to the most responsible post of ambassador to Washington. He spent the bitterest years, from 1936 to 1940, in America. This, perhaps, was what saved him. For his successor as head of the press department, E. A. Gnedin, an intelligent and well-informed man, whose collected pamphlets had been published, was imprisoned. Umansky came back to Moscow only after the temporary thaw had set in. He remained unscathed and was sent to Mexico. He was very pleased by the appointment: a new world, a new people – he had endless intellectual curiosity. There he would be able to show some initiative. (In fact, he spent eighteen months in Mexico, and the Mexicans are unanimous in their opinion that he achieved a great deal, was extremely popular and that politicians lent an ear to his views.)

Then suddenly everything changed: the star vanished from the sky. In June 1943 Umansky's life was broken by a tragic and senseless event. He had a daughter, Nina, a very young girl still at school. She was to accompany her parents to Mexico. A young boy, her schoolfellow, fell in love with her; when he heard that she was going away, he had a stormy meeting with her at the end of which he shot her and then himself. Umansky adored his daughter; she was the only bond that kept the family together. (I knew that there was a great love in his life and that in 1943 he was going through the same torments as those described by Chekhov in his story *The Lady with the Dog*.) And then suddenly this tragedy.

I shall never forget the night when Umansky came to see me. He was hardly able to speak and sat with bowed head, his face in his hands.

A few days later he left for Mexico. His wife, Rosa Mikhailovna, who left with him, was in a state of semi-coma.

A year later Umansky wrote to me: 'The terrible sorrow that has struck me has greatly sapped my strength. R.M. is an invalid, and we are in a far worse condition than when I said good-bye to you. You were, as usual, very wise and gave me some good advice which I, unfortunately, did not follow'. On re-reading this letter now I vainly try to recall what advice I could have given to a man overcome by grief. I suppose I tried to console him, to instil some hope in him, but I cannot remember.

In January 1945 the plane was taking off at Mexico City airfield. Those who had come to see the Umanskys off witnessed the catastrophe, in which Umansky died at the age of forty-two.

At a memorial meeting held in Mexico City, speeches were made not only by politicians and diplomats but also by the best known Mexican writer, Alfonso Reyes, and the actress Dolores del Rio; a Mexican poetess wrote an *Ode to Konstantin Umansky*. Evidently there, too, artists recognized him as one of themselves.

Perhaps one ought to say that Umansky, like others, died at the right time? It sounds like blasphemy, but though I can imagine him in 1962, I somehow cannot see him in 1952. He was too young to belong to the galaxy of Soviet diplomats known as 'Litvinov men', but in character he certainly belonged to it. Some of them disappeared as early as 1937, and those who had the luck to survive were dismissed, like Umansky's closest friend B. E. Stein, or, like E. V. Rubinin, were sent to distant parts by Beria. At receptions in Mexico City Umansky was obliged to wear the newly introduced uniform. I cannot visualize him in it. Still less can I visualize him in 1949, at the time of the struggle against cosmopolitanism. But really there is no point in trying to guess what would have happened to him: Fate took a hand – whether it was an accident or sabotage – the engine cut out and so did Umansky's life which he had loved so well.

14

WE SPEAK of *deep* night, *deep* autumn; when I think back to the year 1943 I feel like saying: deep war. Peace had been put out of mind by then and was as yet unimaginable. In that year everything changed: the liberation of our country from the invaders began. Early in July the Germans tried to pass over to the offensive in the Kursk bulge. First they were halted and then thrown back. A fortnight later, near Karachev, I saw a signpost: '1209 miles to Berlin'. This was in the very heart of Russia and the Germans were still holding Orel, but some ready wit had calculated the distance his battalion would still have to cover.

The reader may be surprised and even irritated by my writing so briefly about the most important years of world history in my lifetime. But I have already made it plain that I have no pretensions to be a chronicler. I interpret the title of these memoirs as meaning that men and years equal a life – my life, one of many. The years of the war were long years. Neither before nor after the war did I ever meet so many people. Sometimes in the course of a single day I would talk to dozens of people whom I had never met before, and listen in a dugout or a forest clearing to amusing stories, long narratives, outpourings of the heart. I have a clear memory of individual faces, of isolated sentences, of cottages, of ruins, but I do not remember who it was who said: 'Anger has eaten out my heart'; I do not remember where it was that one night we buried an officer who had been killed, nor who said at the time: 'He'll still be along of us when we march back into Kiev'; I do not remember in what small town, burnt to the ground, I felt a sudden pang of despair and implored a little girl with a thin pigtail not to cry or it would make me cry too. Villages destroyed by fire, shattered towns, stumps of trees, cars bogged down in green slime, field-hospitals, hastily dug graves – it all merges into one, into deep war.

If I were writing a novel or a story, my imagination would stretch to describing various people, endow them with names, set them in the Briansk forests or on the steep bank of the Desna; but I have made a vow not to invent anything in this book, even though coherent fiction might present a truer picture of life than the disjointed pages of reality. I often find myself writing more fully about people who played the part of extras than about heroes, and trivial incidents occupy more space than stirring events; but I cannot help it; I am limited by my memory, and memory has its own laws: a man does not know why he remembers one thing and forgets another. There are memoirs in which the novelist helps out the biographer by filling in gaps with entertaining stories; there are others which display the extensive reading undertaken by the author to ascertain factually the people's way of life in the years he is describing and thus give a true picture of the epoch. But I write only of the things my memory has retained.

(I still have several small wartime notebooks, but the entries are casual and meagre: was in such-and-such a place, spoke to so-and-so; lists of names – of people and villages – numbers of enemy divisions, disconnected phrases.)

In July 1943 I was near Orel. It was a wonderful summer, with frequent noisy showers. The grass was bright green and I felt that I had never seen such a profusion of flowers in the meadows. Our tanks were concealed in the forest thickets; occasionally I stumbled on disabled German tanks, the season's novelty: 'Tigers' and 'Ferdinands'. General Bagramyan's command was quartered in a camp built by the Germans, with birch-wood verandas and summerhouses. All around there were villages that had been burnt down the previous summer for their close contact with the partisans; everything was overgrown with weeds and only fresh signposts, 'Mikhailovka' or 'Butyrki', reminded one that people had once lived here. In my notebook are names: Lgovo, Kudryavets, Stayki, Boyanovichi, Penevichi, Khvastovichi.

In the autumn I went to the Ukraine: Glukhov, Klishki, Chapleyevka, Obtovo, Korop, Ponornitsa, Korobkovka, Shchors, Gorodnya, Dobryanka; to parts of Byelorussia: Markovichi, Grabovka, Vassilyevka, Gornostayevka, Terekhovka, Terekha; then again the Ukraine: Krasilovka, Kozelets, Oster, Letki, Brovary, Bogdanovichi, Semipolki; and finally the right bank of the Dnieper: Zhary, Lyutezh.

I set down these names because they sound to me like poetry: they represent the past and, to a Russian, have an unassuming beauty of their own, and they are inseparable from the self-sacrifice of the countless numbers who gave their lives to liberate old, long-cherished homesteads, warmed by the breath of generations, to which the communiqués referred as 'inhabited points'.

Near Orel the battalion commander Major Kharchenko invited me to lunch. He was a swarthy man with huge moustaches. He described how his old mother had hidden in the ruins of Stalingrad; with knowing winks he explained the forthcoming operation: 'We'll make a pincer movement, we've learnt the trick now'. Junior-Lieutenant Ionsyan said: 'The scoundrel got as far as the Caucasus, trying to force himself on my hospitality – I'm from Baku, you know. But I can say quite honestly that even then I thought nothing of him'. The tank-man Krastsov said: 'Her name's Galya. Here's her photo, nothing extraordinary about her but for me there's no one to touch her. Perhaps she's forgotten me by now, I don't know. I come from Pskov; I've heard say that she managed to get out in time, but how can I find her? I'm telling you this because you're a writer, you ought to understand. I'm no one in particular, just an ordinary fellow, a Party member, and before the war I worked in zootechnics. But now I've begun to understand a whole lot of things. I may be killed, I've been in the fighting from the start, wounded twice, but I pulled through all right. Yet somehow that's not the most important thing. I've got all sorts of ideas in my head that it'd sound funny to say: as though I was Pushkin or Yessenin, not just Ivan Krastsov'.

What has become of these men? Where is the young machine-gunner Mitya Buylov? Did Lieutenant Plavnik ever come back from the war? Is the sapper Yefimov, the first to swim across the Sozh, still alive?

Near Orel I met General Fedyunkin. I do not know what became of him in later life. In Brovary, Vassily Grossman and I spent half the night with General Martirosyan. He impressed us by his humanity, his kindness, the real and outstanding nobility of his thoughts and feelings. We were returning in the dark; the sands along the Dnieper looked like snow in the beam of the headlights. Brilliant Very lights hung in the sky. Grossman said: 'You jog along and then come across a man like that'. I never met General Martirosyan again. In peacetime you meet the same people day after day and know nothing about them: everyone has his own job, his own home, his own little world. But in war everything is shaken up: people open their hearts to you, you meet a man one day and immediately lose sight of him again.

Sometimes I receive unexpected letters from veterans of the front whom I had met or with whom I corresponded during the war. In August 1942, at the request of the Komsomol tank-men, the Commander of the First Battalion of the Fourth Guards Brigade, Colonel Bibikov, made me an 'honorary Red Army man' in one of the crews. This was the beginning of my friendship with the Tatsin tank-men, and in particular with Sergeant Ivan Chmil and Lieutenant Alexander Barenboym. I met the Tatsins in Byelorussia, visited the Corps Commander General Burdeiny who introduced me to many of his men; members of the Tatsin crew came to see me in Moscow. I have kept a few of their letters. In 1942 Chmil wrote: 'I am fairly young, having been born in 1918. I come from the glorious and beloved Poltava region with its white cottages and green gardens. Death looked me more than once in the eyes but I did not feel fear. When you think about it, you feel pain: how happily and gaily we used to live! I had four little sisters, all younger than myself. I had a father and a mother. I had a girl I loved'. Ivan fought to the very end, was shell-shocked eight times and had to fight his way out of burning tanks on many occasions; in short, he experienced great sufferings. After the war he married, studied at a technical institute, and now has a job in the finance department of the municipal administration of Shyaulyay; his wife, Antonina Vassilyevna, works at an epidemiological centre. They have three children: Igor, Victor and Natasha. In 1956 he wrote to me: 'Yes, no one wants to live through the horrors of the war again; we have settled down, built everything up again, have got families and grown accustomed to a peaceful, happy life. Igor is already in the first form. And yet there are dark forces in the world. Is it possible that I shall have to take my place again at the controls of a T-34?'

Alexander Barenboym works in Odessa. One day I had a letter from him asking me to intervene for a young man, a poet, who had got into difficulties. Ivan Chmil had written to me: 'I thought you knew that Alexander Barenboym had been killed. He was a true soldier, a man worth his weight in gold. He was killed in February or March 1944 between Smolensk and Orsha'. I wrote to Chmil that Barenboym was alive, gave him his address and soon received a letter: 'Sasha was the most popular and most admired man in our corps, everybody loved him. What happened was a miracle: he was gravely wounded at the time and almost gave up the ghost. He survived but as he did not return to our unit we thought he had been killed'. I find it difficult to account for the joy that Ivan Chmil's and Alexander Barenboym's letters give me; I saw them very seldom, yet their fate touches me far more deeply than that of many people whom I met only too often.

I was also very pleased to get a letter from the sniper Gavriil Nikiforovich Khandogin with whom I corresponded during the war. Formerly he had been a trapper in the Siberian *taiga*. Now he works in the building trade as a sawyer. 'My wounded leg has started to give me trouble. But I must work. I have four mouths to feed. At first after the war I was still able to go into the *taiga* to hunt bears. I shot sables and squirrels too, but now I cannot. Besides, I lost my gun – given me as a present – in the river and barely managed to save myself. I should very much like to meet you in peaceful surroundings, at home, among the family. I wish you would come and visit me.'

Let me go back to the year 1943. It was a warm autumn, with mushrooms and threads of gossamer in the woods, and a clear, remote sky. Everything seemed to cry out for peace, for enjoyment of all beauty. But one was forced to see terrible things. In Byelorussia the Germans systematically burnt down villages and killed the cattle as they retreated. Along the roadside lay dead cows with swollen bellies. The smell of burning hung in the air.

In the village of Bogdanovichi only one old man remained. He was sitting in the sun. I tried to talk to him but he did not answer. On the ground lay loaves of bread and a piece of bacon, evidently left by the soldiers. The old man sat staring vacantly.

In Kozelets a woman said: 'How old was Shura? Twelve. She was Lusha's youngest. Lusha was shot and Shura begged the German: "Uncle, don't kill me! I want to live. I'd rather be sent to Germany". At first he let her go, even gave her some sausage, but after that he could not help himself, he shot her too'. In little Kozelets the Nazis shot eight hundred and sixty people.

Near Tripolye, on the road to Obukhov, I saw a steep bank and a small placard which read: 'Here on 2nd July 1943 the German executioners tortured to death and shot seven hundred people – old men, women, mothers with their children, including Malya Bilykh and her five children and sixty-five-year-old mother, and Dunya Gorbatha and her two sons'.

An inhabitant of Piryatin, Chepurenko, told me how he had been forced to dig a pit. The Nazis killed six hundred Jews. Chepurenko suddenly heard his name called. Among the corpses lay Ruderman, a lorry driver from the foundry; his face was covered with blood, one eye had been gouged out. 'Finish me off,' he pleaded. 'They buried them alive, the earth heaved,' said one woman.

I saw a traitor village headman. He was perfectly composed. It was his fault that a woman and her baby had been murdered. He said: 'There's no reason for people to get excited. They said to me themselves: "You've got to be headman". What wrong have I done? I only reported on people's characters. I never laid a finger on anyone'.

There were no horses. The ploughing was done by cows. Near Vassilyevka a cow was dragging logs. A collective farm woman lamented: 'She's gone blind, poor thing. She can't stand it any more. She trudges along but she can't see. I'm worn out too. I look but I can't see. How can people live like this?' The cow had very clear, calm eyes and a large bald patch on its back.

'It'll be easier now, our side's getting the upper hand,' an old man philosophized: 'Raspberries at Intercession[1], that's a good sign'. On the right bank of the Dnieper a peasant woman was making the sign of the cross over the soldiers, over lorries and tanks: 'Five hours I've been standing here and still they come and come. The Germans said the Russians hadn't got anything'.

I sat at night by the Sozh. The Germans were bombing the bridge, there were eight direct hits. The sappers never stopped working. Medical orderlies carried off the wounded and killed. Everything looked quite simple and ordinary, the men working away with axes, saws and hammers. I thought of the pontoon builders on the Ebro, where there had been a lot of animation, singing and laughter. Apparently this was in the nature of the Spanish people. The Russians love the theatre but in real life they cannot bear anything theatrical; they are not convinced by an orator who speaks too eloquently, they are ashamed of displaying emotion; even death they conceive in a workaday spirit. The sappers talked about their work, saying that barrels were the best for the bridge, that the water was cold, that they had to get on with hammering in the piles 'and here the German was interfering, getting in the way'.

In Chernigov it was quiet. Horse-chestnuts lay scattered on the ground, looking like burnished pebbles, and I remembered how as a

---

[1] 14th October.

child in Kiev I used to play with these 'pebbles'. On a ruined house a memorial tablet still remained: this had been the Tsargrad Hotel where Pushkin had stayed and Shevchenko had lived. My thoughts turned to the beauty of old churches, to peace. Suddenly an air-raid began. A little girl was killed.

In Vassilyevka thirty peasant homes out of six hundred remained standing. The peasants had hidden in the woods. The fascists caught thirty-seven people and killed them; they killed a very old man, S. K. Polonsky, and a thirteen-year-old boy, Adam Filimonov. The wife of one of the murdered men said: 'Write that we shan't be able to go on living, our hearts can't stand it'. The 'torch-bearers' burnt one village after another, spreading straw and drenching it with petrol; they did not do the burning in the heat of anger, but in a businesslike fashion, carrying out orders. They burnt down Terekhovka. The collective farm women caught one of these torch-bearers who had burrowed into a haystack and killed him with their pitchforks.

A list of people shot was found in the possession of a headman; among the names were Muzalevskaya, Rimma Nikolayevna, aged three, and Davydov, Viktor Mikhailovich, aged one.

A traitor was hanged. His hanged body looked very long, the wind whipped his beard. A woman darted up, clutched at the beard trying to pull it out, and suddenly screamed. I can still hear that scream. In Koryuchkovo the priest went out to the Germans carrying a cross, begging them to spare the village. They shot him and his wife.

Here is another story recorded in my notebook as I heard it: 'Of course she was a stranger, some said she was a Jewess, others that she was friendly with the partisans, anyway the Germans led her out into the square. And she had a baby, she tried to hide it. She was shot, of course, but the baby was alive, crawling about. We said to them: "Give us the child". Then a German, quite a young one, caught it up and banged its head against a stone'.

The Germans had not had time to burn down Glukhov or Kozelets when they were retreating; they set them on fire later, from the air.

I was overjoyed when I came across some village that had miraculously escaped destruction. I remember the seventy-year-old collective farmer Yillistratov who was busy building a cottage. His house had been burnt down, I asked him if he did not find the job a bit too much for him. He smiled: 'What of it? I'll get it done. It's not for myself.

It's time for me to die. But we've got soldiers' widows here. Their husbands have been killed and they've got to live somewhere'.

The sand gleamed white. The press photographer Knorring was taking pictures of the pontoons, while in the water soldiers were snorting with pleasure: 'That's what I've been waiting for – there's no water like Dnieper water'. In the evening I was told that Knorring had been killed: we had just driven away from the bank when the bridges were bombed.

I am afraid that these disconnected pictures will not convey very much to the reader. Older people have trodden the path of the war, they saw these things and remember them. But the young know about it only from a handful of novels. However, I am not trying to recreate an image of the war. In 1943 I attended two or three meetings of Moscow writers. In those days 'monumental canvases' were demanded: art was to overawe by its size. Some five years later the building of skyscrapers began; during the war there was no question of building, yet writers were supposed to create literary skyscrapers as a matter of urgency. Many writers looked glum and kept silent.

It seemed to me in those years that what was needed was not to create literature but to save it: save the language, save the people, save the land. I continued to carry out my thankless task: every day I wrote several articles. According to a note in my little book, I wrote eight articles for publication abroad, six for Moscow papers and seventeen for the front-line news-sheets in October alone. I could not abstain from writing; soldiers came asking: 'Why is there nothing about Osipov? When the ferry sank he came to the rescue'. 'Write about Hakimov, his family will be able to read it.' 'Comrade Ilya, tell the story of the sniper Smirnov, then he can cut it out and send it to his mother.'

The enemy was still very strong. It was necessary to show that his morale was cracking, that the counter-attacks at Zhitomir were no more than an episode, that no 'Tigers' were going to save Hitler. Day in, day out I went on writing about fascist atrocities. Not only the soldiers but my conscience required it.

Yellow, crumbling newspapers. From them I can reconstruct isolated battle incidents and recall the places where I went, but they say nothing of my personal life: I wrote about what had come to dominate everybody's life by then: the people's sufferings, hatred of the fascists, courage.

I did not keep a diary, but from time to time I wrote poems, short ones, unlike my articles. In these poems I talked to myself. Until the summer of 1943 we lived in a mood of bitter fury; there was no room for meditation. Poetry became for me a diary again, as it had been in Spain. Today, setting this poem or that beside a brief entry in my notebook, or a phrase in an article, I remember what I was thinking, I remember the sorrow, the despair, the hopes.

I recall driving from Vassilyevka to Terekhovka. The ruins of the log-houses were still smouldering; a woman was wandering about. We called to her but she did not answer. Later we spent the night in a hut. I folded my military greatcoat under my head, it smelt of smoke. 'I shall remember as a last gift this heart-freezing fever, this night which resembles the day, and the sorrowful shadow among the ashes. The smell of burning is as acrid as unhappiness, it will never leave me, it is with me like the ashes of the villages, like the pallid sickly shadow, like the red and black sheaves of the delirious misery of typhus, like the fragment of the dead moon among the new and alien silence.'

I was on the wrong side of fifty; I involuntarily recalled the First World War, Spain. There was something unbearable in the repetitive-ness of scenes and emotions. 'Mine was a noisy age, men were swiftly extinguished, but the spring was serene and frightening by its sem-blance of happiness as silence in war is frightening. And then again the battle. And again a machine-gunner lies by a gutted dwelling. Perhaps it is still my plundered youth that is astir?'

1943 was not like 1941; little by little it all grew familiar: the shatter-ed towns, the upheaval of life, the loss of dear ones. But though one can get used to almost everything, even war, the heart is never re-conciled to the general sorrow. Which of us did not indulge in dreams of seeing something better? 'There was little reseda in life, much blood, much ash, much grief. I do not complain of my lot, but long to see, if only for one day, a day that is an ordinary day, when the darkness of the thick shade of trees means nothing more than summer, silence, sleep'.

I have already referred to the fact that, as they retreated, the Ger-mans sawed or chopped down fruit-trees; I had seen it in 1916 in Picardy and I saw it again in 1943 in the Ukraine: 'There was an hour when my heart turned to water: I saw the orchards of Glukhov and the posthumous fruit of the apple trees cut down by the foe. The leaves trembled. All was empty. We stood awhile and left. Forgive me, great art; we did not save you either'. Many years later, when he reached this octet the editor of my book tried to persuade me to alter the last line. 'Why "either"? All right, we didn't save art but we saved other things.' Yes, but we also lost a great deal. Why had I thought of art? I suppose because an apple-tree has to be planted and grafted, it does not grow wild; because I was thinking not only of the ruins of Novgorod, but also of the young poets who had died at the front, and because for me art is inseparable from true happiness, from that loftier sphere where even sorrow is luminous.

Heaven knows how we hated the war! But there was nothing else: the Fascists brought with them savagery, atrocities, the cult of violence, death. The people fought manfully, but we felt with our whole being that people are not born to blow up tanks and perish under bombs, we knew that the enemy had imposed this horrifying darkness on us. I wrote (this was soon after I had seen the gallows and the bearded traitor): 'Say, was there life here too, houses deep in foliage? Silent is the sky, silent the ashes, and silent the peaked caps of those who have been shot. Only the hanged man, stern as some grave pendulum measuring the passage of time, swings untiringly'.

My spiritual condition is reflected in a poem evidently inspired by the lamentations of the peasant woman for her cow: 'Over the potholes, among rubble and ashes, a cow drags firewood. It has gone blind. In its eyes is all our darkness. Shapes and colours have altered. Understand me, I do not regret the words, words can be replaced, I regret the towering errors of the past. There is the light of dry and sombre days, one has to live with it and it is darker than darkness'.

In Kozelets I saw a small boy playing with sand among the ruins: he was trying to mould something out of it. He was completely absorbed but every now and again gave a vague little smile. I stood for a long time beside him. I think that people never looked at children with such hungry tenderness as in the war years; they looked and could not look their fill. Perhaps it was because everybody wanted a glimpse of the future and no one had the certainty of lasting to see even the next day.

I spent a week in the gutted village of Letki. Before the war they used to make rush chairs there. The rushes whispered, but there were no people. There I remembered the little boy in Kozelets: 'There were lime-trees, people, cupolas. Rubble. Shattered glass. Cinders. But look, from out among the broken stones a babe has crept and sits, the feeble hand pressing a little pile of damp warm sand. What will he mould? What dreams? But the years look black and burnt. Evening falls. Time for us to go. A sad and passionate game'.

To return to a line quoted above: it seemed to me that I had freed myself from what I called 'towering errors'. This was yet another error. Of course there were many things I could not foresee: Hiroshima, hydrogen bombs, the fate of those many honest men about whom Solzhenitsyn has recently written, 'murderers in white coats'. But was it this that the child in Kozelets pictured when he was vaguely smiling? No, it was not he who moulded this. By now he must be twenty-two or twenty-three. He does not remember how his home was burnt down, he has not experienced the bitter post-war years. His life must be different. And there is Igor, Chmil's son, who is not yet fifteen. To push a stone up a hill just to let it roll down again is something which conscience cannot accept. And if I am told that this is the most naïve of errors I can only reply that without such errors there is no life worth living: man can part with everything except hope.

15

ON 7TH NOVEMBER 1943 the People's Commissar for Foreign Affairs gave a sumptuous reception in a great mansion in Spiridonovka; it was attended by members of the government and the diplomatic corps, as well as generals, writers, actors and journalists – in short all those whom the barber at the Writers' Club called 'aces and nobs'. After glancing round the room Peter Konchalovsky whispered to me: 'It looks like a picture by Manet'. The Soviet diplomats wore the uniforms that had recently been designed for them. The generals' chests sagged under the weight of decorations. Garreau was wildly swishing his coat-tails and after several glasses of champagne started to describe the intrigues of the British in Algeria: 'Fortunately, I managed to see Molotov at once. We know how to distinguish between true friends and false ones'. The British ambassador Clark Kerr, laying aside his usual starchiness, clinked glasses with everybody – 'To Victory' – drank vodka and soon began to look more like a Soviet writer than a British diplomat. Lozovsky embraced General Petit: 'I was a worker in France. I know your country. We shall smash them'. *'On va battre les Fritz à Minsk et à Biarritz'*. The general shed tears. Alexey Tolstoy appeared in full evening dress and with a lordly good-humoured air teased one of the American diplomats: 'Italy's a lovely country, of course, but Paris is worth a Mass'. Ivan Kozlovsky[1] sat on the floor singing romantic old songs. Margarita Aliger, throwing fearful glances at the Ethiopian Minister, aglitter with gold lace, said to me: 'Ilya Grigoryevich, do you remember 1941?' The American journalist Shapiro said: 'For the first time in eight years I feel happy in Moscow. That's what alliance means'.

The situation looked promising. During the reception a salute was fired: Kiev had been liberated. The Allies were satisfied with their Italian campaign. At the end of October the conference of the Foreign Ministers of the Soviet Union, the United States and Britain came to a close. Naturally we did not know what the Ministers had discussed

---

[1] Well-known tenor of the Bolshoi Theatre.

but the published statements stressed the power of the anti-Hitler coalition. On 6th November Stalin said that the campaign in Italy, the bombing of German towns and the supply of military equipment and raw material to the Soviet Union was after all 'something in the nature of a Second Front'.

I knew, however, that the Allies' landing in Sicily and the south of Italy was not at all what had been promised in 1942. When someone at the *Red Star* office asked whether there ought to be a geographical account of Sicily the editor said indignantly: 'Quite unnecessary'. After the announcement that the Second Front was to be postponed for another year, Litvinov was recalled from Washington and Maisky from London. At the office I read TASS telegrams not intended for publication and realized that the British were annoyed by the formation of Polish divisions in the Soviet Union, and the Americans alarmed by the mood of the Greek partisans: friendship was one thing and politics another.

The press reported that complete agreement on war aims had been reached at the Teheran meeting; on Churchill's birthday he was presented with a cake bearing sixty-nine candles: the number of his years. (Only two more candles had been added to his birthday-cake when Churchill began to prepare his Fulton speech which was to inaugurate the 'cold war'.) Naturally we could not look into the future. But I began to speculate about the kind of world it would be after victory. Until then I had not been able to let myself indulge in speculations: we lived for one thing only – to halt the enemy. But from that day in August, when the stars of the first salvo rocketed into the Moscow sky I began to look about me carefully and to reflect.

Maisky had got back from London in the summer. I was delighted with his presents of razor-blades, a notebook and a fountain pen. But what he said disturbed me. He was full of admiration for the courage the Londoners showed under heavy air-raids, but on the other hand said that the Allies felt insufficiently prepared to open a Second Front, and he added that they were not really interested in the swift defeat of Hitler because they were afraid of the Red Army. He told me that de Gaulle regarded himself as a second Joan of Arc, but that the British cold-shouldered him.

At the end of the year Mikhoëls, who had been to America with the poet Feffer, gave an account of his impressions to the writers. According to him the Americans were infected with racialism, made a cult of machinery and were not very far removed from Hitlerite ideas. Like Maisky he said that the Allies were none too pleased by the Red Army's victories.

(I have just remembered a joke made by the English correspondent Alexander Werth who sometimes came to see me. Werth was born in St Petersburg, speaks excellent Russian and is a nervous, witty man. My dog Bouzou, a Scotch terrier, had suffered shock from the blast of an explosion in the early days of the war and was mortally afraid of the victory salvoes, connecting the thunder of guns with unpleasant experiences: as soon as the radio gave the call-signal he would set up a despairing howl. Coming upon one such scene Werth said: 'Now I see that he's a true British dog: he's afraid of Soviet victories'.)

One day in November we dined at the British embassy. The ambassador, Clark Kerr, was the perfect urbane host, asking Lyuba: 'I suppose you are a Proustian?' and adding: 'I'm afraid I'm a snob'. In the meantime the councillor of the embassy, Balfour, talked politics to me, defending non-intervention in the Spanish war, vindicating Munich and finally admitting that he had a great respect for Salazar.

In December I received an invitation from the American ambassador, Averell Harriman. At the time American manners and customs were still unknown to me and I was surprised by the unpalatable food, by the free and easy ways that bordered on familiarity and by the ambassador's daughter who put her feet up on the small coffee-table. Another guest was present, a general who began by talking about literature, praising Chesterton, then told me that he was an Irishman and a Catholic, and wound up by questioning me on what are usually called 'military secrets'. I realized that the amateur of letters was an Intelligence man and immediately cut him short: 'I'm no soldier, just a writer, so let's go back to Chesterton'.

I told Lozovsky about the evening at Harriman's. 'You'd better ask permission when you're invited to embassies,' he said with a frown. 'And it's best not to frequent the Americans at all.'

I received a letter from the Vice-President of the USA, Henry Wallace, who wrote that he was learning our language and decided to address his first letter to me in Russian; he spoke of his warm feelings towards the Soviet people with such spontaneity, even childlikeness, that I was touched.

The Sovinformburo continued to insist that in my articles for the foreign press I should stress our loyalty to our Allies, but at the same time not fail to remind them that it was time to open the Second Front. I continued writing for *Red Star*, *Pravda* and front-line papers. But' somehow, it had become more difficult to work; something had changed. I experienced it at first-hand.

During the summer the Sovinformburo asked me to write a message to the American Jews about Nazi atrocities and the necessity to defeat the Third Reich as swiftly as possible. One of Shcherbakov's assistants, Kondakov, rejected my draft on the grounds that there was no need to mention the exploits of the Jews in the Red Army: 'It's bragging'. I asked for an interview with Shcherbakov who received me at the PUR. Our conversation was long and unpleasant. Shcherbakov admitted that Kondakov had been 'over-zealous' but added that, all the same, there were some things in my article that ought to be cut. I objected. Shcherbakov grew angry and switched to another subject, praising my articles but also voicing some criticisms: 'The soldiers want to hear about Suvorov while you quote Heine'. A little later I mentioned Lidin's fate: at first he had worked as a war correspondent, but for some reason he was assigned to an Army printing press and nothing of his was published. Shcherbakov replied cryptically: 'He doesn't know how to write for the people'. (Later I found out that one of Lidin's dispatches had annoyed Stalin.) Then he sneered: 'There's a lot you don't understand'. I fought back as best I could and finally said: 'It's wartime, the Germans are still strong, which means that I'll be writing for the press until you give me the same treatment as Lidin'. I got up and said good-bye. Shcherbakov suddenly smiled: 'What are you going to do after the victory?' I replied that I did not know, I had not thought about it. 'Well *I* know,' said Shcherbakov, 'I'm going to sleep for seventy-two hours without a break.' I looked at him: his face was bloated, pale, weary.

My book *One Hundred Letters*, a collection of my own articles and of letters received from men at the front, was about to come out; I believed that in these letters the soul of the people revealed itself. The book was set up, was ready for binding and then suddenly withdrawn. When I asked the reason I got no reply; finally someone on the editorial staff said: 'This isn't 1941'.

Selvinsky wrote a good poem about Russia. He had shown himself a man of courage and he was working for the front-line press, but some lines of his displeased Stalin and he was censured. *Pravda* came down on Platonov: 'Tortuosities instead of simplicity'. A meeting of writers was organized, at which Fedin's book about Gorky was condemned (unanimously, of course) and Zoshchenko and Selvinsky were also castigated. A newspaper article added an item to the list of 'wreckers'; it was devoted to Korney Chukovsky who had written the fairy tale *Barmalei* for children: 'Chukovsky's vulgar elaborations make one sick'. E. Schwarz, a writer who in my opinion possessed a wonderful gift for poetical satire, wrote a play called *The Dragon*; he was looking into the future: the knight Lancelot frees a city from a dragon, but on returning to the place some time later finds the inhabitants mourning the dragon, the 'dear little dragon' who breathed fire so that one could fry eggs without using a stove. *Literatura i Iskusstvo* (Literature and Art) wrote: 'Schwarz has produced a lampoon on the heroic struggle of the people against Nazism'. Paustovsky also got his share of abuse: in his scenario on Lermontov's life he had dared to say that the poet found the uniform of Tsar Nicholas's army burdensome. All this was reminiscent of the thirties. Yet the Germans were still in Orsha and were shelling Leningrad.

A certain Colonel Kruzhkov worked on *Red Star*. I well remember the night of 11th November 1943: State Security men came to the office, stripped the decorations off the colonel's chest and led him away. An hour later General Talensky arrived and asked Kopylyov whether Kruzhkov had read the leader. 'Kruzhkov has been arrested . . .' The editor was so upset that he could not utter a single word. (I recently met Kruzhkov who has, of course, been rehabilitated.)

The press reported favourably on the lecture of a certain historian who had glorified the *oprichnina*[1]. Eisenstein, at Stalin's demand, was working on a film about Ivan the Terrible. (The second part of the film aroused Stalin's wrath; after seeing it through he said briefly: 'Scrap it'.)

At the end of 1943 an edition of *The Fall of Paris* appeared in Magadan (in Eastern Siberia) with illustrations by an anonymous artist. I liked the drawings, certain details of which showed that the artist knew Paris. I naturally realized why his name did not appear, but wrote to the publishers expressing my admiration for the drawings in the hope that it might ease the artist's situation. A year later the

---

[1] Ivan the Terrible's household system of terrorism against the boyars for the administration of his private territory and the assertion of his rule.

wife of the artist Schreber came to see me and told me that her husband was a native of Riga, had indeed lived in Paris and studied under the poster artist Jean Colin; that in 1935 he had returned to the Soviet Union, been arrested in 1937, had worked in the mines and was now drawing posters.

Every day brought some innovation. Separate teaching for boys and girls was introduced in the ten-year schools. One educationist argued that from their tenderest years boys should be taught military science and girls needlework. (Soon after Stalin's death the segregation of boys and girls was revoked.) Uniforms were introduced for diplomats, then for the legal profession and for transport workers. A friend of mine facetiously assured us that there would soon be uniforms designed for poets, with one, two or three lyres on the epaulets according to rank. We laughed but our laughter was far from happy.

The text of the new National Anthem was published. I remembered the *Internationale* thoughtfully.

A wartime way of life had gradually evolved. Things were not easy and, in order to keep going, an unobtrusive day-to-day heroism was needed. It hurt me to watch women hauling heavy logs, building roads. Children worked in the factories and in their spare moments played like children the world over. There was only a bare sufficiency of food and people would grumble: 'Cereals haven't been issued on the ration cards again'. Speculators sold sugar at a thousand and even fifteen hundred roubles a pound. In many houses it was cold: there was only just enough heating to keep the pipes from freezing and bursting. The theatrical companies returned to Moscow and performances were well attended: people felt the need both to relax and to get warm. During the intervals they discussed the communiqués, Captain Sergeyev who had got himself a girl-friend at the front, Masha who had stopped writing to her husband and had taken up with a lame musician; they also naturally grumbled that the jam issued by the food centre was sour and that there was not going to be any butter at all.

In November Shostakovich sent me a note inviting me to hear his Seventh Symphony. I came away from the concert deeply stirred: voices of the ancient choruses of Greek tragedy had suddenly resounded. Music has one great advantage: without saying anything it can express everything.

In December Yuri Tynyanov died. He had been ill for a long time but had never ceased his work on Pushkin. During his lifetime I did not meet him often enough, or rather, when we met our conversation usually by-passed what concerned us most. And yet his *Kukhlya* and *Vazir-Mukhtar* had been events in my life. He always wrote about the past, yet what he wrote should be recognized as the intimate chronicle of a generation: it is both about the past and about ourselves. He was a mild man, good-natured even in his caustic remarks; he had the faculty of seeing and also of thinking for himself, and in the thirties that needed a high degree of spiritual vigour. Today Tynyanov is generally acknowledged as a writer of great merit, a humanist who presented Pushkin's harmony, joy and complexity in a new light. But at the time the newspapers did not so much as mention his death. His funeral was very cheap; there were pink frills on his coffin and paper flowers.

1943 saw the first clouds which, five years later, were to gather over our heads. But the enemy was still trampling our land. The people fought staunchly, and there was such strength in its heroic effort that one could live honestly and fearlessly without paying attention to certain things. I firmly believed that after victory everything would suddenly change. Today, when I look back, I have repeatedly to confess my naïvety and blindness. This is far easier to do than it was to go on having faith at the time, in face of everything. It seems that man naturally and invariably tends to mistake his desires for reality and often, like a sleep-walker, takes a step into the void, destroying himself or waking up with broken bones.

When I recall conversations at the front and at the rear, when I re-read letters, it is clear that at the time everybody expected that once victory had been won people would know real happiness. We realized, of course, that the country had been devastated, impoverished, that we would have to work hard, and we did not have fantasies about mountains of gold. But we believed that victory would bring justice, that human dignity would triumph. No one imagined that three years after the end of the war the Americans would be threatening us with the atom bomb, or that Beria would again open fire on his own people. And yet, even though we failed to foresee a great deal, I still recall the dreams of those years with tenderness as well as pride.

No matter how terrible and cruel the war was, it remains in our memories not as a plunge into the depths but as an ascent: our people soared to great heights, very great heights, and this is recorded not in the panegyrics to the 'military leader of genius', not in the huge battle-pictures, nor yet in the decorations, but in the memory of those who did not return, in the inexhaustible tears, that living water of a people's conscience.

16

TO ORDINARY mortals everything seemed to be going smoothly: fighting against the common foe was going on in all the theatres of war and the heads of governments in the anti-Hitler coalition were exchanging telegrams of congratulation. In fact, things were far from simple; a struggle was going on behind the scenes.

The Americans preferred Admiral Darlan to de Gaulle, and when the Admiral was killed they took up General Giraud. De Gaulle preferred himself to anyone else. In France his supporters did not want to come to an agreement with the partisans, the Francs-Tireurs. In Italy the Allies supported the former Viceroy of Abyssinia, Marshal Badoglio, while the partisans vowed they would hang all the Fascist leaders. The British supplied General Mihajlovic with arms, the royal government of Yugoslavia still carried on in Cairo, while the People's Liberation Army was commanded by the Communist Tito. The Greek right-wing government had moved to Cairo too, but in Greece the left-wing EAM waged war on the occupation forces. The Polish government had found refuge in London; the Soviet government had broken off diplomatic relations with it; the Union of Polish Patriots was formed; in the forests of Poland there were the right-wing detachments of the Armja Krajowa and the left-wing forces of the Gwardja Ludowa. All this was casually and sometimes only allegorically referred to in the press.

Of course I was not let into diplomatic secrets, but owing to the very character of my job I could hardly help knowing a thing or two: I was constantly invited to receptions, I had to call at various embassies, and almost every day foreign journalists came to see me. I do not intend to give the history of the relations between the Allies, and in any case I do not know it. I want only to relate certain chance encounters I had with people, and some episodes that were more entertaining than important.

One day the British ambassador asked me why I did not like the English. I protested and in a jocular vein enumerated all the things I liked about England: Magna Carta, Turner's landscapes, the green

London parks. From that day, whenever Clark Kerr introduced me to his compatriots, he invariably said: 'And this is Mr Ehrenburg who recognizes only British pipes, lawns and terriers'. Clark Kerr was a well-bred sceptic, he kept his thoughts to himself, and only once, at some boring reception after we had discussed poetry, he admitted: 'What I like about Moscow is its variety. We always like what we haven't got ourselves, don't you think?'

In October 1944 Churchill and Eden came to Moscow. I do not know what effect this trip had on Anglo-Soviet relations, but it unexpectedly proved the salvation of the old woodworker Yankelevich, whom Alexey Tolstoy called the 'pipe-master'. Yankelevich made fancy pipes and sold them to discriminating smokers. He was arrested, and I believe it was precisely for this illicit trade in pipes. Tolstoy tried to intervene on his behalf but without success. During Churchill's visit the Commissariat for Foreign Affairs decided to present him with an ancient casket that had secret compartments and an intricate lock; but it turned out to be broken and there was no one capable of repairing it. And then someone bethought himself of old Yankelevich. So he owed his thanks either to fate or to Churchill. On the other hand nothing but trouble came of the British Premier's visit to the director of the tobacco factory 'Java': it was given the emergency task of producing cigars of the finest quality. At a certain reception Churchill took one of these cigars and lit it, whereupon it hissed and threw out sparks like a victory salute. Churchill grinned. He had the face of an old bulldog and tired, even sleepy eyes occasionally lit up by a humorous twinkle. I was introduced to him. He made an effort to smile: 'My congratulations to you, my special congratulations'. What he was congratulating me on I did not know, but I smiled back and congratulated him, on what I did not know either.

A brief conversation I had with Eden was far more interesting. Eden said at once: 'I understand you aren't fond of the British?' I decided that Clark Kerr must have already told him about the lawns and the dogs, but asked him what made him think so. Eden replied: 'I was told that you were very fond of France'. This was so unexpected coming from an experienced diplomat that in my confusion it took me some moments to ask: 'But does love of France imply dislike of England?' My tone must have betrayed some irritation for Eden hastened to smile: 'I was only joking. We're all allies, of course, and personally I'm very fond of the French'.

However, others were more outspoken. Harriman, for instance, said: 'There'll be some difficulty with France: they've got more traitors there than anywhere else'. A well-known English correspondent said outright: 'We'd be better off without the French'. Wendell Willkie confided to me: 'France's role as a great power is finished for good, it's not in our interests to restore her to her former position'.

Naturally the French – the ambassador, Garreau, the councillor Schmittlein, young Gorse, General Petit – often said that they did not trust either the British or the Americans: they feared that the Western Allies would try to set a defeated Germany back on her feet. One evening we gathered at General Petit's. Thorez, Jean-Richard Bloch and Garreau were there; the last-named began to recall the past: as an officer after the First World War he had witnessed the occupation of the Rhineland; he described how the Allies admired the discipline, the organization of the Germans, how they had fallen in love with German women; no one doubted that peace was secure; but in Munich Ludendorff was already calling for revenge. And Garreau said heatedly to Thorez: 'Our only hope lies in the fact that the Russians will never allow it to happen again'.

In December 1943 I was returning from the Kharkov trial of the Germans who were convicted of the mass murder of its population. Alexey Tolstoy was sitting in my compartment. The American journalist Stevens came in. We began talking about the future. Suddenly someone banged poor Stevens on the head: it was the French journalist Champenois who was lying on the upper berth. He could not bear to listen to talk about the advantages of a 'soft peace', and in any case he had managed to prime himself with a pint of vodka.

(I had established friendly relations with Champenois. He had formerly been an Agence Havas correspondent, but when the French ambassador Gaston Bergery, who had formerly been an ultra-left, was recalled from Moscow by Vichy, Champenois stayed on writing for the French press published in London. After the war he made some attempt to go back to his own country, but it turned out that he had developed too strong an attachment to Moscow. He can drink in the Russian way and can talk half through the night, as Russians do, about everything and nothing, including nonsense and matters of the utmost importance. He is a man devoid of ambition and of practical good sense; in moments of heightened emotion he either jokes or swears, and he writes poetry exclusively for himself since he never publishes it anywhere.)

There appeared to be something that not only the Americans but also the British whom I chanced to meet failed to understand: their countries had not experienced fascist occupation. I am not speaking of politicians and diplomats – they had their own motivations – but many officers and journalists believed that the stories of Nazi atrocities were exaggerated; in their minds Hitler's army was one and the same as Kaiser Wilhelm's. That is why it was far easier to talk to people from the occupied countries.

The Norwegian ambassador, Andvord, could hardly have been an admirer of the Soviet system, but he knew the sufferings of his own country and realized that the Red Army was the only one fighting in earnest. He sometimes invited us to his house. He was an epicure and liked good French wines. We would sit by the open fire; Andvord would talk of Norway, of common friends and say: 'I hope the V-bombs will make the British see reason. They want to treat the Nazis in gentlemanly fashion, as if the whole thing were a sporting event. Only today I heard about the brutalities suffered by our students. You're right: sedatives won't help, what's needed is the scalpel'.

Among the diplomats I particularly liked René Blum; he represented the smallest country of all – Luxemburg – but he had a great heart. In 1944 at the front near Minsk a deserter came over to us. The colonel said to me: 'Fritz says he's neither a Frenchman nor a German but something like a Luxemburger'. I was taken to see the man. He was a young peasant. He asked me for some paper: 'I want to write a letter'. I thought he wanted to send news to his family and naïvely expected the letter to reach them. But what he wrote was this: 'To Her Royal Highness the Grand Duchess of Luxemburg. I beg to inform you that I have done my duty and have crossed over to the Red Army ...' When I handed the letter to René Blum he was moved to tears; he was a left-wing Socialist, but the message to the Grand Duchess affected him deeply. He had come to love our country, had learnt to speak Russian and attended lectures and talks. (I spotted him once amongst a pack of students who had crowded into the Polytechnic; he was almost crushed to death. His daughter studied at the University of Moscow. He was unassuming and courteous, and there was something about him of the past century, as there is about his native Luxemburg. A few years ago I went to see him at his home. He is chairman of the Soviet Friendship Society and speaks at meetings; everybody knows and respects him. In the evening, over a bottle of wine, we exchanged reminiscences of the war years.)

I often visited the Czech ambassador, Fierlinger. He was easy to talk to: he understood the character of Fascism. His wife, a charming, vivacious Frenchwoman, understood it too.

When Beneš came to Moscow I met him at a reception. He recalled our conversation of long ago: 'I knew then already that Czechoslovakia was doomed'. And he added: 'Our only salvation lies in a close alliance with your country. The Czechs may have different political opinions but on one point we shall be in complete agreement: the Soviet Union will not only liberate us from the Germans, it will also allow us to live without constant fear of the future'.

Yugoslavs came to see me: a commander of the partisan army, Terzic, and the sculptor Avgustincic who was working on plans for a monument and made endless drawings. I liked his work, which combined monumentality with movement, and I liked the man too: he was an artist and a fighter who always remained true to himself, surrendering nothing and living simultaneously on more than one plane. The Yugoslavs had been given several houses in Serebriany Bor. There I met partisans, both men and women. They lived in these country houses outside Moscow as in the Bosnian hills; there was the same democracy and candour. I felt happy among them.

Foreign correspondents came to see me in the hope of learning something about the military situation; sometimes I gave them German diaries and letters to read. They in their turn told me about the crooked diplomatic manoeuvres. Among the foreign correspondents were oustanding journalists such as Leland Stowe, Alexander Werth and Maurice Hindus. I have described how in the autumn of 1942 Leland Stowe accompanied me to Rzhev. He was no stranger to war: he had been in Spain and in China and had proved himself courageous and observant; he had written some very good articles. In 1946 I visited him in his bungalow near New York. The cold war had begun. There were smart little houses everywhere. Roses bloomed. People were having a good time. But Stowe was depressed. He said: 'Do you remember Rzhev? I felt more at peace there. One can live without comfort, it's far harder to live without hope'.

Of course things were not easy for the foreign correspondents: the papers contained more general articles than news; censorship was strict and journalists had to contend with their own particular adversary: the head of the Press Department. After every press conference each tried to get ahead of the others and be the first at the telegraph office. It sometimes came to blows, and on one occasion an American correspondent punctured the tyres of a rival's car.

Shapiro, the UPA correspondent, was sympathetic to us but kept grumbling: they expected sensational stuff from him, yet he was not allowed to go to the front and did not know what information he could send. And then something occurred that proved to be the last straw: Stalin replied to three questions sent to him by Henry Cassidy, the Moscow correspondent of the Associated Press. Shapiro came to see me in a great state: 'I sent a questionnaire too. Associated Press is far more right-wing than UPA. Does Stalin want to ruin me?' It was impossible to calm him down. He was impervious to the fact that Cassidy had simply been lucky because his questions arrived on the particular day when Stalin had decided to give out some information. By way of a 'consolation prize' the Press Department of the Ministry of Foreign Affairs allowed Shapiro to visit the Stalingrad front. On his return to Moscow he said to me: 'Of course what I've seen is extraordinary. I can understand a bit better now why you keep insisting on the Second Front. But from the point of view of UPA it can't compare with what Cassidy got. I still can't understand why Stalin prefers AP.' As for Cassidy, he was as pleased as Punch; he displayed to all and sundry Stalin's signature under the answers to his questions and managed to get four bottles of wine out of the Aragvi restaurant by saying: 'Stalin writes to me'.

There were also some unpleasant types among the American correspondents. I remember a breezy fellow who came to see me and put a pound of sugar on the table. Lyuba came into the room and, not knowing who my guest was, asked: 'Are you selling sugar?' I insisted on the American taking back his gift. A few days later I told the story to Alexey Tolstoy. He roared with laughter: 'He brought me some sugar too, and I, like the fool I am, was so taken aback that, you know, I accepted it. I wanted to give him something in return but I had nothing handy so I offered him a Waterman fountain pen. And he took it, the bastard'. We had a good laugh over this. (Of course we did not know at the time what the two words 'American aid' were going to mean for the whole of Europe.)

The sugar incident could be forgotten; but there were other more serious matters: the dissensions between the partners of the anti-Hitler coalition were making themselves increasingly felt. The summer of 1944 was beginning. The salvoes announcing victories had become an everyday occurrence for the Muscovites. The Allies landed in Normandy. The denouement was in sight.

On 1st July I set off for the Byelorussian front commanded by General Chernyakhovsky. Near Borisov, on the right bank of the Berezina I saw captured Frenchmen of the 'legion' organized by the traitor Doriot. All Frenchmen know the River Berezina by name: here in 1812 the Russians almost encircled Napoleon's army. Only part of it succeeded in crossing the river, thanks to the courage of the sappers commanded by General Eblé (I knew about this general because in Paris I often walked along the street named after him). The 'legionaries' got stuck on the right bank; they were despicable but pitiable mercenaries and had been hampered by their baggage: they would not part with their loot. I was asked to talk to them. One of them assured me that he had had an unfortunate love affair and had decided to die 'no matter how'; another described the privations and hardships – he had agreed 'in a moment of weakness'; a third referred to 'the mysterious workings of destiny'; a fourth kept saying 'I'm a completely civilian type; in Paris I've got a small restaurant; my customers were always satisfied. I never made a mistake in gastronomic matters. Politics is a different business altogether'. The 'legionaries' were put with the German prisoners, among whom there happened to be many Alsatians. I was later told that during the night the Alsatians beat up the 'legionaries'.

I dropped in on the airmen of the *Normandie* squadron. The French said that during the fighting for Borisov the pilot Gaston had been killed over the Berezina. For three years he had tried to get out of France to fight in the sky; he had been caught each time and finally imprisoned in the convict prison of Port-Lyautey in North Africa. When the Americans liberated him he decided to go to the Soviet Union to join the *Normandie* squadron. The battle of the Berezina had been his baptism of fire, and there he perished. I told the airmen the story of the owner of the restaurant which made them laugh; then one of them said contemptuously: 'Don't think there are many of that kidney. They're our "Vlassov men"'. I smiled: I had the firmest faith in France.

Yes, I must admit that I believed in a wonderful future; otherwise it would have been too difficult to carry on. I said to myself: things will be decided, not by the diplomats, not by the politicians, but by the peoples, for it's they who've borne the burden of suffering. And that meant that Fascism would be buried for all time.

Somewhere between Borisov and Minsk I met the foreign correspondents. They were in a happy frame of mind, both because they had seen the victory of an allied army and because they had collected interesting material for their reports. The happiest of all was the *Times* correspondent: he had taken three soldiers prisoner. The Germans had been encircled and were trying to find someone to whom they could surrender; seeing a well-dressed civilian, they decided that they could not ask for a better chance. A twelve-year-old boy called Alyosha Sverchuk did even better by bringing in fifty-two prisoners. But the *Times* correspondent was naturally in high fettle.

I must say quite candidly that while in Moscow I could be upset by telegrams from abroad, but at Minsk I gave no thought to such matters as how the Greek question would be settled, whether the Americans would recognize Tito, what Eden would say about the Poles. My one concern was to find a way into Minsk, because German divisions were still prowling everywhere.

17

I FOUND my way into Minsk on 4th July. The tank-men had broken into the town and had immediately forced on further to the west. There was still some firing in the southern districts of the town. Looking down a long street I rejoiced to see that all the houses were intact; a quarter of an hour later there was a thunder of explosions and the houses disappeared.

The sappers worked all day long removing mines; they were in time to save the big government building and a few other houses. But as I wandered about the town I saw ruins everywhere. What joy I felt at the victory! Two days before I had talked to General Chernyakhovsky who said: 'Nowadays we don't pursue the enemy, we surround him'. I knew that strong German forces had remained east of Minsk which made it difficult to approach the town: Germans would suddenly appear on the highway and open machine-gun fire. 'They're trapped in a cauldron all right,' a tank-man said, and I smiled thinking that the end of the war was now in sight. But it was distressing to see the ruins of Minsk. This was no Novgorod, no Kiev, no Leningrad; this was a town that had been burnt down and destroyed many times; it had no ancient monuments, no fine architecture, but there are times when you do not think of art. My thoughts were far from the aesthetic value of the ruined, blasted and gutted houses; they concerned the fact that people had worked, suffered, built and now there was nothing but debris and smoke-blackened rubble. The sight of wrecked homes, ravaged human dwellings, breaks your heart, and you are always deeply moved by some trifling object – an armchair with sagging springs, the discoloured patch on an exposed wall where some photograph or picture has hung for a long time, a smashed wooden horse.

(Seven or eight years later, on my way to a session of the World Peace Congress, I was stuck in Minsk: the weather was too bad for flying. P. U. Brovka rescued me by taking me to his home. He showed me the newly rebuilt town. Of course the houses were over-ornamented and hideous, like everything that was built in our country during the late forties, but I was filled with genuine admiration: people were eating, making jealous scenes, arguing, and surely over there in that flat there must be children with a wooden horse peacefully asleep.)

Wandering about ruined Minsk I suddenly thought: what luck, at least I have not come here too late. General Vadimov had never given me any freedom. On one occasion, in the early days of the war, I had accompanied him to the Briansk front; for some reason he suspected me of being foolhardy and had impressed on his subordinates the need to keep an eye on me. In the autumn of 1943 *Red Star* sent Konstantin Simonov and me to the Ukraine. I drove to the right bank of the Dnieper. The deputy editor, Colonel Karpov, sent the 13th Army Military Council member, General Kozlov, a telegram (I was recently shown a copy of it): 'You have Ilya Ehrenburg with you, for security reasons please see that he does not go any distance beyond the crossing'. But I reached Minsk at the right time; and even later I drove wherever I wanted, having managed to disappear: they did not know my whereabouts at the office, and there was no General Vadimov to organize a search as he would certainly have done.

Chernyakhovsky was right: our armies surrounded Minsk and something like a hundred thousand Germans were trapped in a cauldron. Our troops were advancing swiftly towards Baranovichi and Vilnius, while the Germans retreating from Mogilev were still hoping to break through to Minsk. They were not yet completely crushed on this front, and many divisions resisted stubbornly and attacked in an attempt to break out of the encirclement. One day I was peacefully dining with a battalion commander, a major who had formerly been a Leningrad trade union official. The battalion was resting after the fierce fighting on the Berezina, and the major talked as he plied me with captured champagne: 'You've got a wonderful knack for describing the Fritzes, you must have been observing them for a long time. But tell me, when you're writing a novel, how do you set about finding people to describe? I've often wondered how a writer knows what a man's like at heart. Does he tell you or what? Or do you just have to make it up?' I had no time to reply: the machine-guns started chattering; a German regiment trying to break through to the west had opened fire.

I drove on further west, to Rakov, to Ivenets, and on returning to Minsk heard more firing: the encircled Germans were attacking the main bakery.

I was on the Mogilev highway when it came under fire. Prisoners told us that there was a battalion in the wood and that a German general with a mortar was roaming about saying: 'I'm a German, not a louse'. A German major, who came out on to the road waving a handkerchief, said to me: 'At the present moment you may have the advantage, Germany is forced to fight on two fronts. But you must admit that the techniques of the tank break-through and encirclement are great achievements of German strategy, you're only following in our footsteps'. I replied that I was not a soldier, and that as a civilian I recognized the Germans' priority: they had started the war and had been preparing for it a long time, but that this was nothing to be proud of.

An *Oberleutnant* in the Ros cemetery at Vilnius (a clearing station for prisoners) said: 'I've been on the Eastern Front from the very beginning. In forty-one we advanced ignoring the fact that we left you behind. Now everything's changed. We tried to defend Minsk when you were already approaching Vilna. We held a few houses for three days, and now an officer of yours tells me that you're nearing the Niemen. Today it's you who're advancing as though we didn't exist'. After a pause he suddenly added: 'And I ask myself, do we really exist?' Tea-roses bloomed among the baroque cherubs and moss-grown busts. Suddenly a wild cry was heard: a wounded crow had ended its flight by flopping dead at the German officer's feet. He covered his face with his hands and sat motionless, like a statue.

I met the Tatsin tank crew near the frontier of Lithuania: they were dog tired. Colonel Lossik, the brigade commander, described the capture of Minsk: 'We didn't follow the roads, but went through trackless forests and swamps. When we broke into Minsk on the 3rd of the month there were more Germans there than our lot, but they'd panicked.'

It was very hot, there had been no rain for a long time and thick clouds of stifling dust hung over the road. Hundreds of motor vehicles, flattened and overturned, barred the way. Sergeant Belkevich said: 'I was hurrying, I had a young sister of seventeen, Tanya, who'd stayed in Minsk. They killed her literally the day before – on the 2nd – the neighbours saw it'. He wiped his face with his sleeve; sweat mingled with dust formed a mask. 'What dust!' Then he added in a low voice: 'As soon as we got into the town I asked for leave to go to our home. I ran all the way. But my sister wasn't there any more...'

There was such grief in his voice that I could not find a word to say. One grows used to anything: to sorrow, to misfortune, to loneliness, but never to someone else's grief; I felt this many a time in those years.

But the things I saw on the road from Orsha to Vilnius! The endless ruins, burnt out villages; the appalling tales I heard. In Rakov I went to see the vicar of the Catholic Cathedral, Father Hanusievicz. Old and quiet he sat among prayer-books and faded photographs. He had watched the Nazis set fire to a house. In desperation a woman had thrown her baby out of the window; a 'torch-bearer' came along, picked up the baby in a businesslike fashion, like a bit of firewood, and threw it back into the blaze. The priest shook his head: 'I could not have believed that such heartless people existed in the world. They took an old Catholic priest from Kleban, a sick man who couldn't walk, and they tortured him to death. In Dory they herded all the people into the Orthodox church and burnt them. In Peršiai they killed two Catholic priests. It is said in the Scriptures: "He discovereth deep things out of darkness, and bringeth out to light the shadow of death. He increaseth the nations, and destroyeth them: he enlargeth the nations, and straiteneth them again. He taketh away the heart of the chief of the people of the earth, and causeth them to wander in a wilderness where there is no way". I'm an old man, but how are the young ones going to live after what they've been through?'

I spent the night with the gunners. We drank inferior Hungarian rum. Everybody was indulging in dreams about the future. Suddenly Captain Sergeyev said: 'There was a letter from Yablochkin's wife who says she's got nothing to live for now: she's entirely alone, wants to say good-bye to Pasha's comrades'. Everyone fell silent and soon dropped off to sleep. But I could not sleep, so I got up, groped my way to the glimmering light and wrote down what the old priest had said.

On the next day, having gone back to Minsk and driven along the Mogilev road, I saw Trostianets. There the Nazis buried Minsk Jews and those brought from Prague. The doomed people were put into death-vans (the Nazis called the vans in which people were asphyxiated by gas *G-Wagen*; these had been improved: the bodies of the vans tipped up emptying out the corpses of the gassed; these new machines were called *G-Kippwagen*). Shortly before the rout the German command gave orders to dig up the corpses, pour petrol over them and burn them. There were charred bones all over the place. Before their hasty flight the Nazis had intended to burn the last batch of those killed; the bodies were stacked like logs. I saw charred women's bodies, a small girl, hundreds of corpses. Close by, women's handbags, children's shoes, papers lay scattered about. At the time I did not yet know about Maidanek, or Treblinka, or Auschwitz. I stood rooted to the spot; the driver called me in vain. It is impossible to write about it – there are simply no words.

Our soldiers attacking the surrounded Germans on the Mogilev highway had seen Trostianets. Nowhere, I believe, was the fighting so ferociously cruel. By the evening enemy corpses littered the highway. The heat had not abated and the stench was ghastly.

I spoke to the commander of the German infantry division, Lieutenant-General Ochsner. When he was taken prisoner he was wearing private's uniform, but an hour later he produced identification papers and demanded to be sent to an officers' camp. Unlike most other prisoners he told me that the ideas which inspired the *Wehrmacht* lived on and would sooner or later triumph. When I asked him about Trostianets he said: 'Why ask me? I didn't kill any children myself. We've lost the battle, and the defeated always get the blame. The German army has always been distinguished for its discipline, and I trained my men in the spirit of honour'. 'Then why did you change clothes?' 'I didn't want to lower the dignity of my rank – German generals do not surrender.' He smoked a cigarette with deep enjoyment and said: 'We find ourselves in the position of a small nation with two huge States, Russia and America, ranged against us. It's a duel between David and two Goliaths'. He had the dignified appearance of a professor. Later I came across his name in a list of war criminals.

Other generals behaved with more circumspection. The Corps Commander, General Hollwitzer, glanced respectfully at the young Chernyakhovsky. Chernyakhovsky said: 'You fought better at Voronezh'. 'The responsibility for what's happened is not the army's, it's Hitler's,' Hollwitzer replied. 'He wouldn't listen to experienced generals and surrounded himself with upstarts.' Hollwitzer signed an appeal which was published in the Soviet press a fortnight later: some of the German generals who found themselves in captivity declared themselves against the Führer. A short time before a group of officers in Germany had attempted to come out against Hitler; this gave the declaration of the captive generals a certain forcefulness. Of what did the generals accuse Hitler? Not of having started the war, not of grabbing one country after another, not of organizing the mass extermination of whole populations, not of creating desert zones and death camps. No, the career generals blamed Hitler for something quite different: he had fought incompetently and brought the *Wehrmacht* to defeat. The German generals suggested that the officers should remove Hitler and strive for peace before military operations reached German territory. They had nothing to say about the stacks of gassed corpses in Trostianets.

Before me now I have a copy of the West German paper *Soldaten-zeitung*. I look at the portrait of an officer in uniform: the Tank General von Saucken, holder of the Iron Cross with oak-leaves and diamonds, is celebrating his seventieth birthday. The newspaper gives his biography. During the First World War he fought in France and Russia. In 1939 he took part in the conquest of Poland, then rushed to Paris, and was later in the vicinity of Moscow and in Orel. And in July 1944 General von Saucken tried to hold Borisov. I cannot help it, I remember. I remember in ruined Borisov the corpses of Soviet prisoners of war: the Nazis murdered them two days before they evacuated the town; I remember the story of Vassily Vezelov who had miraculously managed to extricate himself from the pile of corpses; I remember Razuvayevka where the fascists killed ten thousand Jews – old men, women, infants in arms. I do not know whether the birthday hero remembers all this. In any case it is not General von Saucken who matters. The same issue of the *Soldatenzeitung* calls for the return to Germany of Silesia, Memel, Danzig and the Sudetenland. So we are to start all over again? This is something that reason and conscience repudiate.

By 3rd July the Byelorussian front was advancing so swiftly westwards that the Air Force was often hard put to it to keep up. General Glagolev, a veteran of the First World War, said: 'Don't forget the infantry. In twelve days they've covered two hundred and fifty miles. The infantry has its own motorization now: its heart. A man will fall and then get up and go on again. One of the men said to me yesterday: "We're angry". They see what the Germans have done and they're in a hurry: it's time to finish the job.'

The scenes changed yet remained the same. The people on the Lithuanian frontier spoke differently from those of the Smolensk region but they all told the same story. The ruined towns succeeded one another; the chimneys of burnt out villages stood stark and black against the skyline. I think it was in Oshmyany that I saw the tablet *'Freiheitsplatz'*. Perhaps in Krasnoye, or perhaps also in Oshmyany where an industrialist had forced pedestrians to step off the pavement, raise their arms and shout: *'Heil!'* Alexey Petrovich Malko (I took down his name) described how the Germans had burnt his daughters Lena and Glasha to death; it happened in the village of Brusy. In the fields near Smorgon the soldiers came across a small girl of four or five who told them that her name was Dora and that 'the Germans poured sand into Mama's mouth and Mama screamed'. An old Pole in Radoshkovichi told me that two years previously the Germans had burnt twelve hundred Jews to death; when a German had ordered a certain tailor to dance, he had spat and shouted: 'Get on with it, kill me, you'll get what's coming to you in good time'. I drove past a village where the houses were still standing but deserted: I do not know whether the inhabitants had been killed or driven away; possibly the people had taken to the forest.

Everything looked as it had done the year before near Glukhov and Chernigov, but the war was different. On 12th July, towards evening, I glimpsed the first houses of Vilnius; there was shooting on all sides and a major whom I did not know shouted: 'Down!' On that day our tank-men were already far ahead, halfway to Kaunas; but in the woods to the east of Minsk groups of Germans still roamed, unaware that the distance between them and the German army was far greater now than that between the Soviet tank-men and the German frontier.

Somewhere near Molodechno I spent the night at Marshal Pavel Alexandrovich Rotmistrov's quarters. He told me: 'Last summer the tanks played a different role, at that time they flushed the enemy out, but now we encircle and destroy him. In these days one can't do without technical equipment. Nor without using one's head either, naturally. Our people are intelligent but slow to get going: there's not much room for initiative. Let's hope that after the war we'll live more sensibly'. I liked the marshal: young and keen, he knew how to appraise not only military operations but many other things as well: the politics of our Allies, literature and even the various kinds of Rhine wine. I met him two or three times after the war and came to the conclusion that he was as bold in everyday civilian life as he had been on the battlefield, and that is perhaps the harder of the two.

I had never been to Vilnius before. The Germans had not had time to set fire to the town and it was extraordinary to see the houses, baroque Catholic churches, narrow old streets. Here and there a little old woman creeping out of a cellar and immediately darting back. The wounded being carried in. Prisoners being led to the Ros cemetery. There were few soldiers about, they were busy clearing the Germans out of a coppice on the outskirts. Only the day before the Germans were still holding the centre of the town, the old prison of Lukishki. Even now many of them were hiding and there was sporadic machine-gun fire.

General Krylov was sitting over a map, his eyes red from sleepless nights. On seeing me he shook his head: 'You oughtn't to be wandering about, they're shooting from windows. Of course I realize that you find it interesting, but still . . .'

At the command post I met the writer Pavlenko. I had first met him in 1926 when I was passing through Stambul and he took me to see St Sophia. We seldom ran into one another; he was an excellent raconteur and I enjoyed listening to his incredible stories but, as so often happens, we did not meet for years on end, and I never gave him a thought. Now we walked about the town together. In the main square the Germans had abandoned hundreds of motor vehicles loaded with an incredible assortment of objects: ciné-cameras, French liqueurs, detective novels, lavatory paper. At the Ostrobramsky Gate women were on their knees praying to the Virgin. We went to St Anne's Church. Pavlenko said that Napoleon had expressed regret that he could not remove this church to Paris. We made our way to the house where Mickiewicz had lived. Every few steps we came across the bodies of local inhabitants who had been killed; I remember an old man with a small pointed silver beard who looked like a scholar of the past century; by his side lay a stick with a white knob. Pavlenko examined the white knob, the statues in the church and a German radio-set with great attention; suddenly he said: 'It's raining. Let's go. I've got a bottle of French brandy'.

Later I wandered about alone. A sergeant came up to me and asked to see my papers; after reading them he broke out laughing: 'So that's who you are. I've read your articles, I don't think I've missed a single one. What I want to ask you is to tell them to make the papers print every day how many miles still to go to Germany. I keep asking and nobody really knows – some say a hundred, others say a hundred and fifty. If it can't be done in the Moscow papers, let them print it in the army sheets. I think we'll get the job done for the November celebrations. My mother's in Biysk, she writes that she's waiting from day to day, she's ill and she's afraid she won't live to see the end'.

I came across a group of Jewish partisans; they were helping to clear the Fascists out of cellars and attics. I got into conversation with two young girls – Rachel Mendelsohn and Emma Gorfinkel. They told me that they had been in the ghetto. Almost daily the Germans had sent groups of people to Ponary where they put them to death. Those who remained alive had to work; they were sent out under escort. In the ghetto itself there was a secret resistance organization; its members burnt stores, laid mines, killed Nazis. A mass escape was being organized. The leader of the organization was a Vilnius worker, the Communist Wittenberg. The Nazis found out about him and demanded that he should give himself up or they would destroy the whole ghetto. Wittenberg told his comrades: 'You'll be able to work without me. I don't want everybody killed because of me'. He was tortured to death. Five hundred of the prisoners in the ghetto managed to escape; they fought in groups called: 'For Victory', 'The Avengers', 'Death to Fascism'. Rachel and Emma had been students before the war and were greatly interested in literature. Now they held in their hands not books but grenades. They laughed gaily; I have still got a photograph of myself amongst a group of partisans.

On the morrow there was an Order of the Day announcing the liberation of Vilnius: the Germans in the copse began to surrender. I roamed about the streets again and stopped to talk to people; they looked horrifying after five days spent in cellars, often without food or even water; but everyone smiled – the worst was now behind them. There were no longer any corpses in the streets. The soldiers were removing the loot from the German cars. People said that bread would be issued.

I dined with some of the officers. Later a major took me to an abandoned flat. Everything indicated that it had not been Germans who had lived there: in a glass jar I found dried crusts of black bread and in an antique box which had, probably, housed the family jewellery there were cigarette ends. There were photographs on the wall: a group of schoolgirls, a lady in a little lace cap, a young man wearing Polish military uniform. Postcards with views of Nice lay scattered about under the table. There were French and Polish books on the shelves. The major left me a large candle and I decided to read a

French novel. After twenty or thirty pages I laid it down. What was it to me that the hero could not bring himself to leave his wife to go and live with his mistress? I tried to sleep, but sleep would not come. And suddenly I felt unutterably depressed. After all, the man in the novel was tormented by the noble emotions of love. Perhaps they had met in Nice. The hero of Chekhov's story met the lady with the dog in Yalta. They did not achieve happiness, but people were not buried alive, they were not asphyxiated in gas-vans. They did not, as now, live in constant proximity to death. The major's wife was probably waiting anxiously for a letter from him. The war was terrifying, even at this moment when victory was close at hand. Or perhaps it was precisely because victory was so close that one became a prey to thoughts, to depression?

I lifted the edge of the rug with which the major had blacked out the window. Day was breaking, the morning was overcast. Shots rang out from time to time. From the house opposite a cat ran out and gave a piercing screech. I lay down and went to sleep.

18

WHEN I got back to Moscow Jean-Richard Bloch came to see me. He was very excited over the way things were going. I told him about the Minsk cauldron, about the Vilnius fighting, about the *Normandie* airmen. He in his turn gave me his news: 'To judge by intercepted radio-messages, the partisans are beginning to occupy towns in the Dauphiné and the Limousin', and superstitiously lowering his voice he added: 'It looks as though we shall soon be able to go back to France'.

Russia had become part of Jean-Richard's world at an early age; by this I mean not only Leo Tolstoy's books which for long had been landmarks in his life, but also the message sent by French students to Russian students after 9th January 1905: it carried many signatures and the text had been drafted by a student at the Sorbonne, Jean-Richard Bloch. He had welcomed the birth of the Soviet Republic with enthusiasm. He visited our country for the first time in 1934 when he was invited to the Congress of Soviet Writers; he stayed with us for six months and later described his impressions at various meetings. His accounts were, of course, those of a favourably disposed tourist who had seen what a tourist can see in any country: the various sights, the brightest side of life.

He came to Moscow for the second time in the spring of 1941; he arrived with his wife from occupied France and spent the difficult years of the war in the Soviet Union. He came to know the Russians well and grew very fond of them. He lived through the hardships of the evacuation. Alexey Tolstoy told me that in the autumn of 1941, when he was passing through Kazan, he went to see Bloch who rented a room with a Tatar family; the room was in a basement. Jean-Richard tried to reassure his landlady whose husband was at the front: 'The Germans will soon be smashed'. 'It wasn't only his landlady he reassured,' Tolstoy added with a smile, 'he cheered me up too. I was in a desperate mood: the communiqués, the unreaped fields, the people's long faces, in fact, the misery all round, but our Frenchman calmly explained to me that Hitler was doomed as sure as two and two make four. The cold was terrible and the poor chap wasn't used to it, but there he sat smiling and drinking tea without sugar.'

Two or three times a week Bloch addressed his compatriots over the radio, talking about the valour of the Red Army and trying to put fresh heart into them. He had many friends in Moscow, too many to enumerate, but they included Lidya Bach, the Ignatyevs and Alexey Tolstoy. The Blochs never complained about anything. One day Jean-Richard fell ill; the doctor came and was appalled; I was rung up: 'It's a case of exhaustion caused by undernourishment over a long period'. If he had not caught a chill we should never have found out that the Blochs were going hungry.

His enforced separation from his country affected Jean-Richard most painfully. Today we can hear the voice of man as he circles in space. But in those days there was the crash of bombs – and silence. Bloch did not know what was happening in France. He did not know what had become of his family – his mother, his children. But he knew how to conceal his anxiety and grief better than most: others invariably saw him cheerful and active. In 1944 he reached the age of sixty, but he looked younger, perhaps because he lived in a constant state of tension. Very lean, of middle height, with sharply defined features, he resembled an old portrait of Montesquieu which used to hang in my room. His eyes always held a smile, and it was only during one of our last meetings in Paris that he allowed himself to say half in jest: 'There are times when a man has to get himself an extra pair of eyes: one pair for other people, the other for himself'.

We spent two or three hours discussing the situation at the front, then he suddenly said: 'I've had the new marriage decree translated for me'. Seeing my unhappy expression he tried to reassure me: 'There's a war on. At a time like this it's not worth bothering about'.

I knew that many things puzzled him, made him uneasy. Somewhere near Minsk I had read the decree which he had so casually mentioned; there was shooting going on everywhere, I had crammed the paper into my pocket and, like Bloch, had told myself: one mustn't think about it. The war has its own laws: as soon as a man begins to have doubts he drops out of the ranks. Of course this decree had upset me, but at the time I lived for one thing only: the smashing of the fascists; everything else was of secondary importance.

It is not by accident that I have recalled this casual phrase uttered by Bloch in August 1944: he was born a poet and a thinker, but war had too often intervened in his life, and people saw him as a soldier armed with a bayonet or with a pen.

He was only seven years older than I, but those few years made all the difference. When the First World War broke out, opening a new era, I had only just found my bearings in life. But Jean-Richard had by that time already written his excellent novel ... *Et Compagnie*, absorbed the intellectual atmosphere of the past century, acquired an individuality. At an early age he had been attracted by Socialism, and for him Socialism was not associated with *provocateurs* and disasters, or with prison, but with the noble speeches of Jaurès, with the belief in reason and progress. I went to Florence as a green youth, spiritually at sea, physically always hungry, and full of admiration for the beauty of an alien world. And in Florence lived Jean-Richard, a professor at the French Institute, the father of three children, a scholar and a humanist; he admired the art of the *quattrocento* not as a burglar who has sneaked into a rich mansion but as a lawful heir to the place.

It may be precisely for this reason that the First World War had been a catastrophe for him, a crucial test: he had to make up his mind what he ought to do. I know his self-questionings in those years not only from his correspondence with Romain Rolland but also from what he himself told me. In an earlier chapter of these memoirs I have described how Jean-Richard had had the audacity to stand up to a man whom he both loved and respected. It would be more true to say that Bloch was standing up to himself: he knew that Rolland in his distant Swiss retreat was right, but he also knew that the Germans had invaded France and that the thing to do was to fight, not to be right. And so he fought and was wounded three times: on the Marne, in the Champagne and at Verdun; the last wound was serious, for a long time it was feared that he might lose his sight. He drank the cup to the dregs. Romain Rolland loved Bloch but disapproved of his actions believing that, like many other young men, Jean-Richard was deliberately shutting his eyes to the truth. But it was not a matter of refusing to face facts, it was a recognition of those laws of war which thirty years later made Bloch say: 'At a time like this it's not worth bothering about'. On the eve of the Second World War Bloch, the editor of the Communist newspaper *Ce Soir*, wrote to Romain Rolland about Barbusse's novel *Le Feu*: 'He created a work which captures the imagination but it is not destined to endure. He contented himself with a remarkable description of scenes and profiles. But he did not show why millions of people stuck it, and that is the point'.

For Bloch, as for many of his contemporaries, the twenties and the first half of the thirties were a lull, a breathing space. History allowed the thinking reed a short time when it could not only bend but also think. During that period writers wrote. And Jean-Richard wrote novels, plays, poems. I have not the slightest intention of denying the value of his novels and plays, but in those years there were many good novels, exciting plays and beautifully written poems. There was, however, a literary genre in which Bloch attained perfection, a genre long favoured by the French: the essay.

It seems to me that other nations, more gifted in poetical moods and less carried away by the poetry of thought, regard the essay as a minor form, preferring literary criticism or creative journalism. But the French, from Montaigne to Sartre, from Stendhal to Jean-Richard Bloch, have seen in the essay a means of combining the heightened sensibility of the artist with acute reasoning. Of all the things Bloch has written I like best his *Destin du Siècle*. It came out in 1931, and it is surprising that these essays, devoted to politics as well as art, have not become outdated. On re-reading them a short time ago I realized that the problems which preoccupied Bloch thirty years ago are facing me as I write this book.

In his preface the author of *Destin du Siècle* says: 'I do not address myself to politicians. I would be wasting their time. And well they know it. I address myself to men of my own kind. To those who have a craft.

'We have a craft, they and I, and we work within this craft. At its very heart.

'My craft consists in words, in the understanding of the weight, the volume, the density of words, their manipulation, their usage, their exact application.

'And, in defiance of popular opinion, I hold it to be the best of all crafts . . .'

It might be thought that the book was entirely concerned with literary problems, but only the fewest pages are devoted to the future of the novel and of poetry. Bloch tried to define the destiny of man entering a new era. He was no detached observer; he had long since chosen his own place, for already in those days he called himself a Communist though he did not join the Party until much later. At the

147

end of the twenties he foretold the coming blackout: 'Once again the worker Caliban and the musician Marsyas are the depositories of the true spirit of civilization. May they be on guard and defend themselves well! For in this, as in other matters, we are witnessing the dawn of a second medieval age. The second wave of invasions is upon us ... These new Franks ... have already established themselves among us. It is they who control our industry, our economy, and America nourishes them tirelessly with theories, slogans and ideals'.

When he speaks of the new epoch, of what distinguishes it from the revolutionary romanticism of the past, Bloch describes twentieth-century man thus: 'The social revolution no longer appears to him as a Messianic dream, but as one of the unknown quantities in his personal equation. He sees it again as advantageous and preferable to find himself on the right side of the barricades'. He said that the characteristic thing about the man of 1930 was the exaggerated role of the individual. He traced a connection between the social problems of the century and the unprecedented cult of sports. Before Hitler's time, before much else, he gave the warning: 'Thus we are moving towards the monstrous resurrection of the caveman, covered with amulets ... but lit by electricity ... In the past I wrote of *The Heresy of the Bath-taps*. Eighteen years have passed since then. This heresy is now turning into a religion ...' And again: 'We are being led to an all-powerful police dictatorship – that is, a police of roads, of bodies and of souls'. He also spoke about the development of the exact sciences and of technology, without indignation, but without self-deception. I have recalled this book not, of course, in order to expound its contents by means of a few quotations, but because I want to show Jean-Richard Bloch as he was and as young readers do not know him.

In Bloch's life, as in the life of so many others, Spain spelt the declaration of war. This time no one called him to the colours. He was only a short time in Spain and that at the very beginning. But he realized that the breathing space was over and said that he, too, wanted to write about women, about love, to express in words, in a way in which it had never been expressed before, the song of the oriole and the soul of a dancer. He felt the need to be a simple man, simply happy among the world's bounteous gifts. But he heard the whistling of shells, the cries of the wounded, his comrades retreating under air bombardment, before tanks, and felt in his mouth the bitterness of that retreat. There was no longer any room for reflections.

From that time onwards Jean-Richard lived again like a soldier. A year later the newspaper *Ce Soir* came out in Paris; the editors were Jean-Richard Bloch and Louis Aragon. Jean-Richard wrote not about the song of the oriole but about 'non-intervention', about Munich, about cowardice, about treachery. In the autumn of 1939 the authorities stopped the publication of *Ce Soir*. A short time after, at the trial of the Communist deputies, Bloch, Langevin and Henri Wallon came out in defence of the accused. When the Germans approached Paris he tried to make his way on foot to his home in Poitiers; this is a considerable distance, and the German tanks forestalled him. He started writing for the clandestine press. At the beginning of 1941 his son Michel was arrested; the police came for Jean-Richard too, but he happened to be away from home. He went underground and in the spring of 1941 came to Moscow. I have already spoken about his years in the Soviet Union. The Blochs returned to Paris in January 1945. Jean-Richard learnt that his mother, an old woman of eighty-six, had been incinerated at Auschwitz; his daughter had been deported to Hamburg and executed there. *Ce Soir* came out again and Jean-Richard wrote articles for it. He was elected to the National Assembly. Almost every day he spoke at meetings: reaction was looming. He collected a volume of his articles—*Moscou–Paris*—corrected the proofs and, in March 1947, suddenly died.

Such a life is probably quite common for a man of the underground, a soldier, a Communist. But for a writer it is exceptional and I have already said that Jean-Richard was first and foremost an artist. In Moscow, at the First Congress of Writers, he described the calling of those who belonged to the profession which he believed to be the most admirable of all: 'A writer is not only an official extoller of *faits accomplis*. If that were the case, he would be playing a rather ridiculous role and would soon earn the ironic title of *inspecteur des travaux finis*. He would become a social parasite; there were such men at the royal courts of old, their tasks was to eulogize . . . Fortunately writers today have a different duty'. In the same speech Bloch opposed making canons of those pseudo-classical forms defined in Zhdanov's speech: 'Whatever the structure of society, there will always be artists who utilize existing forms and others who search for new ones. Among airmen there are pilots, conscientious and brave, who fly mass-produced aircraft, and there are others – test-pilots. It is inevitable and it is necessary that there should be writers for millions of readers and others for a hundred thousand readers or even for five thousand'. Bloch's ambition was to be a test-pilot, to say what had not been said before, but the war has its own laws; he wrote what had already been written about by others: that Munich was a betrayal, that one could not live under the Fascist yoke, that American gold aspired to take the place of German steel. He was a rebel, but he had to conform to military discipline. He did this with a smile, and it was only when alone that for the eyes of the exemplary soldier he 'substituted' his own eyes: the eyes of the doomed artist.

I cannot remember when I first met him; it must have been in 1926 or 1927. We did not meet often in those days but when we did our talks were long and open-hearted. I still have a copy of *Destin du Siècle* with Jean-Richard's dedication, from which I see that in 1932 he regarded me as his friend. With time our friendship became closer. Our common work also brought us together: the preparations for the Anti-Fascist Congress, the defence of Spain, the struggle against advancing Fascism. At the beginning of 1940 when I was ill and alone in the rue du Cotentin, the Blochs visited me and put new heart into me. And during the war, in Moscow, we often met. I remember the morning when the first news of the Paris rising reached us. I rushed off as soon as I could to the Blochs. Jean-Richard was so gripped by emotion that he was unable to utter a word and only hugged me. What was our common bond? Something about which we seldom spoke: our common destiny.

Jean-Richard wrote that it was unnecessary to say that the Soviet Union was no paradise and that this country, too, harboured men who were less than just. He was not blind. In his volume *Moscou-Paris* he included an article called *Ilya Ehrenbourg est notre ami*. I have just re-read it and found the story of an episode which I myself had forgotten. In 1944, when talking about the vandalism of the Fascists I referred to certain works of art they had destroyed and at the end mentioned Picasso's pictures, slashed by young Fascists. Bloch wrote: 'Eighty-three Russian painters of the academic school of thought signed a protest against this disgraceful coupling of the treasures of national art with "Picasso's monstrosities".' This was only a small thing but it angered Bloch. Many other things angered him. But though he was able to exercise discernment in some cases, in others he had to take things on trust. That Picasso was a great artist he recognized and nothing would have made him change his opinion.

Similarly, on one occasion he was in a tram and heard talk about 'Jews who prefer Tashkent to the front'. He quietly intervened to say that at the time of the Dreyfus trial he had been a schoolboy and had boxed the ears of future Fascists. He saw conceited bureaucrats, venial men; he told me several times that there were men fighting at the front whose families were not receiving any allowance. But how was he to know that Tukhachevsky was not a traitor but a victim? Bloch was a soldier, the army was commanded by Stalin, and a soldier could not doubt the sagacity and integrity of the Supreme Commander. He believed in the 'fifth column' story. He began writing a biography of Stalin. For he knew that the war was still being carried on. After his death *Ce Soir* continued to appear and, in February 1953, in connection with the arrest of the Moscow doctors, it published articles by Pierre Hervé (who was at that time a Communist, but a few years later began to inveigh against the 'immorality of the Communist Party'), articles which reminded one of the famous *Protocols of the Elders of Zion*, a forgery concocted by one of Hitler's forerunners. Fortunately Bloch did not live to see this.

In what did he find solace in those hours when he felt things were beyond endurance? Sometimes he wrote verse. Sometimes he translated poetry. During the First World War when he lay wounded in a field-hospital he began to translate Goethe. During the Second World War he was translating the second part of *Faust*. This tells much of the story.

Of course kindness is an innate quality and the proportion of the kind and the unkind is probably the same among people of different political convictions; but it seems to me that among the Fascists kindness was a defect, a deformity rather than a virtue. How would a 'kind' SS man feel in Auschwitz? No one is astonished to find that a capitalist who tramples on his rivals is unkind. But the words 'he was an unkind Communist' not only grate on the ear, they are an insult to one's conscience. Well, Jean-Richard Bloch was a man of exceptional kindness.

Even the most passionate opponent of determinism will not claim that man freely chooses his epoch. Jean-Richard Bloch wrote: 'This is a time for war correspondents and not for writers, for soldiers and not for historians, for action and not for meditation on actions'. These words contain more than the tragedy of Bloch; they explain and justify our generation.

19

WHAT I have set out to do in this book is to recall people whom I met in the course of my life and got to know, some better than others. But now I should like to speak of a girl whom I never met.

Soon after my return from Vilnius someone came to see me at the Moskva Hotel: Vera Vassilyevna Konstantinova, a teacher from Kashin. She told me that her daughter Ina had been a partisan and had been killed in March. She asked me to read Ina's diary. I put the school exercise-books into a desk drawer and it was several weeks before they came to mind again; there had been a good deal of journalistic work. But once I started reading the diary I could not tear myself away.

Ina began to keep her diary in 1938 when she was fourteen; she recorded her life during four years – the early morning of life. As I read I involuntarily recalled my own school years: there was a certain similarity, although in a way it was all very different; childhood was still childhood but the times had changed.

After the war I felt drawn to visit the Konstantinovs. I went to Kashin. This is a small town in the Kalinin region; it has a few factories, a large market-place, little ancient churches and small wooden houses. It was in one such house that the Konstantinovs lived; both husband and wife were teachers. Ina had not been their only child; they had another, younger daughter, Rena.

From her early childhood Ina had been an avid reader but she was also full of fun and was fond of games, dancing and skating; she loved puppies and kittens and enjoyed gardening. She was not particularly brilliant at school and was rather ashamed of her low marks ('mathematics poison my existence'), and tried to make up for them. There was nothing morbid or exuberantly emotional, nothing exceptional about her nature.

She had a childhood friend, Lusya, with whom she shared all her secrets, and when Lusya and her parents moved to Magadan, Ina had no one in whom to confide. But this did not make her withdraw into herself; she had many other friends and always found something likable in each one of them. When she was moved up from form 8A to B she made friends at once with Tanya and Lena. In the Children's Centre where she often went she made friends with Valya Ambrazhunas and Olya Rumanova. 'I have been lucky on the whole with people this year. Maxim and Fedor, Alionka and Tanya Volkova are wonderful, charming and good. Such a pity that Lusya has gone away!' 'Lidochka Kozhina is a darling. The ideal girl. Beautiful, clever, good at school-work, a first-rate companion.' 'Made friends with Clara Kalinina.' When the war broke out Ina volunteered for the Auxiliary Medical Service and worked in the hospital. 'Zaslavsky, from Rostov, young, wounded in the leg, shoulder and head. He is a nice chap and a patriot.' New pupils had come to the school: 'Zhenya Nikiforov from Moscow and Rem Menshikov from Leningrad. Splendid, lovable chaps'. 'I think Sasha Kulikov will stay here. That would be marvellous! I find him a very nice boy, intelligent and well-read.' In November 1941 came the evacuation. Ina found herself in a strange town, at a strange school; but two months later she was already feeling sad at parting from her new friends – Lyuda, Gerka, Galya, Vovka. In June 1942 she joined the partisans and was sent behind the enemy lines. Here is what she says about her first partisan leader: 'What wonderful people chance brings my way! He is intelligent, understanding, sensitive'. And this about Commissar Abramov: 'An extraordinarily interesting personality, so highly educated and also . . . sensitive (this is my special expression, I know what I mean by it)'. Here are her comrades in the partisan group: 'Grisha Shevachov. Tall, thin, a boy of the Jewish type, a nice chap. Igor Glinsky. Awfully nice boy with an exceptional sense of humour. Clever, well-read. Makasha Berezkin. Charming! Always gay, always smiling. Never refuses any job'. Then she writes to her sister: 'Zoya was my best friend. A wonderful girl. She died like a heroine. A true heroine. Many splendid people have died. Those whom I regarded as closest to me are Zoya, Brigade-Commander Arbuzov, the radio-operator Genka, Igor Glinsky and Grisha Sheva-chov. And now the only one left is Igor.' In the detachment she met Vadik Nikonenok who was fifteen. When the girls asked Ina with surprise: 'But what do you find to talk to him about?' she replied: 'Well, he's so interesting'.

She had a happy disposition and was prone to giggle, like most girls. 'Fedya German had two gorgeous inkstains on his cheek. When I noticed them, I could not contain myself, I laughed till I almost cried. And then all at once the teacher asked me to repeat the lesson. I did not even know how to begin. Somehow or other with a lot of prompting I managed to get it out and was given a "good". But halfway through I just could not help myself and gave a loud snort of laughter. It was very embarrassing'. 'Tonight at the Pioneers' evening to celebrate the 35th anniversary of some strike or other, the first item was a girl who danced in silk trousers. Then a 10th form pupil sat on a table and went through it. After that someone from outside broke a window-pane and Pitanov tried to catch the culprit through the window. We laughed like mad'.

Ina read a lot and quite indiscriminately. At the age of fifteen she writes: 'Took out Schiller's *Letters on the Aesthetic Education of Humanity*. It is a pity that there are some things in them that I do not understand. I must read Kant, Hegel, and other philosophers and then come back to this book'. She does not seem to have had much enthusiasm for philosophy. Like many girls of her age she admired *Martin Eden* and wept over *The Gadfly*. The most widely differing authors appealed to her: Mamin-Sibiryak and Gaidar, Spielhagen and Yuri Herman, Verbitskaya and André Gide. She loved poetry. At sixteen she liked Nadson and rejected Mayakovsky, whom she knew only from school anthologies. Later she came to know and to admire Mayakovsky and hung up his portrait in her room. She found Heine so good that he reconciled her to the German language. She often recited Blok's poems and discovered some of his early verses in old copies of a popular illustrated weekly.

In the Moscow art gallery she saw pictures by old Italian masters. 'The pictures by modern painters, in which the faces look exactly like tomatoes and whose subjects are as monotonous as sand-dunes, can never be called artistic paintings. They are daubs. Modern sculpture in which beauty is replaced by dynamics and "expressiveness" cannot be counted among noble works of art. There will never be anything to compare with the Gioconda, or the frescoes by Italian masters. No one will ever write a *Divine Comedy* or an *Anna Karenina*. The world is losing the best thing of all – beauty'.

At sixteen she blamed this on popular taste. A year later she wrote above this sentence: 'Not really true', and over her condemnation of Mayakovsky: 'Wrong!'

But her love of beauty remained, and Ina never thought better of that.

Girls often dream of becoming actresses or writers. Ina's ambition was to study at the Law Institute. Later, when she became a partisan, she changed her mind and in 1944 asked her mother to send an application to the Aircraft Construction Institute. I cannot see her either as a prosecutor or an aircraft designer, but it is a good sign that she was not attracted by either the School of Drama or the Literary Institute, although she naturally took part in school plays and, when in love, wrote poetry.

She fell in love often, passionately, believing each time that 'this is real love'. At fifteen she fell in love with a schoolfellow Lyovushka: 'I have to make a tremendous effort not to sit on a bench from where I can see him. I feast my eyes only when he passes along the corridor. But if I catch him looking at me I put on a disdainful expression. Why? Are these unconsciously the same tactics as Julien Sorel's? It cannot be! After all, what he did was out of pride, whereas I am in love'.

Lyovushka left. Ina missed him terribly. 'Mama says that I am not really in love with him but with an ideal of my own creation. I do not believe it. It is not as though I could not see his faults, I know all his worst failings, and yet I love him. I love everything about him, even his faults.' Three months passed, and Ina was asking herself with dismay: 'I cannot understand it: can one really fall in love several times and each time as deeply? The only difference seems to be in the way one loves. I liked to feel Lyovushka close to me, I wanted to hold his hands, to kiss him. But with this one . . . No, it is quite different. I want above all to be friends with him, to know that he loves me'. According to her own account this one, Nikolay, was indifferent to her. 'I danced with him! Suddenly he came up to me and asked me and we danced together. I felt very flustered, could not keep in step, babbled something about not dancing very well and all that. However, I try to behave as if I were not interested in him, and I think successfully'.

Ina learnt the meaning of jealousy: 'Again he saw her home!' She was annoyed with herself: 'When one loves one must have one's pride, and if he loves another I do not want to be a part owner'. But soon she realized that not everything in life is dictated by reason: 'Evidently this feeling is stronger than pride or self-esteem. And how can these two feelings coexist with love? They cannot, ever'.

In 1940 she made friends with two pupils at the Children's Centre, Maxim Pirushko and Fedya German. 'They told me about how their parents had been arrested, and so calmly that you might have thought it had happened to someone else. Maxim's father was arrested first, then his mother was taken off a train. He could not even say goodbye to her. In Fedya's case it was his mother who was arrested first and then his father. Now both mothers are in Karaganda, and where the fathers are no one knows. It appears that, like us, when they have something special to talk about, when they are feeling strongly about something, they go off where no one will disturb them and talk it over'. In 1937 Ina was thirteen: no misfortune befell her parents, so hers was a sheltered girlhood, while for Maxim and Fedya the arrest of innocent people was nothing out of the ordinary, it was part of everyday life. One can easily imagine how this distressed Ina, who hated injustice above all else. Fedya became her best friend. She often went to the Children's Centre. Fedya showed her photographs of his father, his mother, his sister. 'Yesterday they broke the most unwelcome news to me: an order has come from the Ministry saying that pupils of the Children's Centre over the age of fourteen are to be sent to technical schools. This means that they will soon be leaving'. Some time later she records: 'Yesterday there was an evening at the Children's Centre to celebrate Constitution Day. It is a real treat for me to go there. It is the only place where I feel happy and gay. I danced a bit. But most of the time I sat in a corner with Fedya and we talked. He seemed sad somehow. He said it was because he kept thinking about the days three years ago, when his parents had been arrested. Our *tête à tête* was noticed by the teachers and today Mama spoke to me about it. I think it is just friendship, nothing more. But this friendship is very dear to me and irreplaceable'. 'Fedya has just told me that on 19th March his Mama died. My God, how terribly sad it is and how difficult to bear!'

What impresses me in Ina's diary is her high moral standard, her honesty and straightforwardness. When she was only in the 7th form she had hated 'toadies'. She was a Komsomol, a member of the Council of the *Osoaviakhim* (Society for Air and Chemical Defence). In the autumn of 1940 she writes: 'It is in a bad, dark, uncertain time I have started this exercise-book. We live like this today, but we do not know how things will be tomorrow'. Ina was extremely sensitive to anything that struck her as false; her diary contains reflections on the discrepancy between the many difficulties produced by the approach of war and the insincere, rose-coloured speeches made at meetings in Kashin. 'But these are lies! Lusya is not here and there is no one I can talk it over with.' At sixteen she was capable of thinking for herself, of facing truth, and three years later she died fighting for the truth.

Ina's diary contains a lot of that ordinary stuff which can be found in all diaries kept by girls of her age; but there are also some much less common things in it. Perhaps her appreciation of art and poetry lent her a heightened spiritual sensibility? At fourteen she writes: 'The evening is serene and mild, not at all like a January evening. Everything looks particularly beautiful, everything is bathed in a milky pink light. The sun will soon be setting. Everything ought to seem luminous and pleasant, but it does not. On the contrary, a strange melancholy rises. Why? There seem to be no tangible reasons, but— It is just this "but" that is the trouble. Without it, things are much easier for people. Take Lisa or Nyuru for instance; they live in the real, actual world, but I cannot. Dreams, imagination mean much more to me. It is not my fault that instead of living in peculiarly romantic surroundings, such as Italy or even the Far East, I live in a poky little town where nothing happens'. Six months later she returns again to reflect about her own nature: 'I have got a double soul. The first "I" appears in the evening. This "I" lives only in the future, in dreams. This soul, melancholy and full of yearning, leaves me sometimes, and then I become an ordinary girl of the present. At those times I am interested in the topics of the day. It is going to be difficult for me to live with such contradictory tendencies in my soul. It is like being two different people'.

Thoughts about death came to Ina for the first time after reading Leonid Andreyev's *Seven That Were Hanged*: 'How grim to feel the inevitability, the closeness of death! I tried to imagine myself in their place but it was no use. At times I felt that I would calmly await the end and not even think about it, and at others I thought I would be appealing to someone, flinging myself about aimlessly'.

A teacher committed suicide in Kashin. Ina was deeply shaken although she had not known the man: 'How awful! I have just heard that V. V. Zhigarev, a teacher at the Technical School, has poisoned himself. Was there no other way out for him? Evidently not. How terrible to realize the hopelessness of the situation, to see death as inevitable and close'.

'The moon— The snow— And quiet. Like in a fairy-tale. Some

time, on a night like this, I shall go into the forest. And the fairy-tale will begin. Those things over which we shed tears, over which we rejoice, how trivial they all are! How poor and prosaic our life is. There is only one real event in the life of each one of us, one thing that deserves to be revered: death, the step into the unknown and the non-existent'.

The May of 1941 was a happy month in Ina's life: 'I happened to sit down next to Misha Ushakov and we quite casually fell into conversation. And . . . and I am, as they say, head over ears! . . . How is it possible to express all the feelings suddenly born at such moments?' 'He sometimes seems positively strange, but I love this strangeness in him too. Misha and I sat side by side all the time. The others called us bride and bridegroom and cried: "It's bitter!"[1] So we kissed again'. 'How wonderful it is to be alive when, behind you, you have sixteen years of life and nine classes, a bright sun and good marks, a great friendship and a radiant love, while ahead . . . while ahead – there is life!' Misha read Fofanov's poem to her: 'All melts away, the hopes and years. And the memory of what was once dear will thaw like the ice of awakening nature, and will depart never to return'. But these melancholy lines could hardly trouble seventeen-year-olds in love.

22nd June 1941. 'Only yesterday everything was calm and quiet, and now . . . Dear God!'

Air-raids, parting from friends, anxiety about Moscow, about the Motherland. 'Even the air seems different. What is going to happen? To go to the front – this is my dearest ambition. To smash the Fascists!' There are no heroics in Ina's diary. She loved and trusted people, and this helped her to live through the ordeals: 'No, with such people our country will never be lost, it cannot be lost'.

She did not see the war in a romantic light at all; when two wounded men died in the hospital where she was working, she wrote: 'For what did they give their lives? For what do hundreds of thousands of other young, brave men lose their lives? Who can answer this question?'

On returning from evacuation to Kashin, Ina learnt that Misha Ushakov had died from a war wound. She realized (or perhaps persuaded herself) that Misha had been her one great, true love. She sent an application to the regional military command asking to be sent to

---

[1] Old Russian custom for wedding guests to raise their glasses and cry: 'It's bitter!' at which the bridal couple kiss 'to sweeten it'.

the front and stating that she had had hospital training and was 'not a bad shot'. For a long time there was no answer. She continued going to school, falling in love, weeping for Misha privately, and asked herself: 'When will this hateful war end?' She sought distraction: 'We sometimes dance to the gramophone. Mama says this is frivolous, she cannot understand how we can even think of enjoying ourselves at such a time. But the truth is that one wants to forget all the horrors, if only for a moment. And we have so little fun that it ought not to upset anyone. Besides, it will soon come to an end.'

The fun did indeed soon come to an end: in June 1942 Ina was sent behind the enemy lines. She left without saying anything to her parents and wrote to them from Kalinin: 'I know it was a beastly thing to do to you but it was better like that. I could not have borne Mama's tears'.

She fought well, as those of her comrades who survived can tell; she did reconnoitring, took part in skirmishes with punitive detachments and went on 'assignments': blowing up bridges, attacking military stores. I shall not enlarge on her valour in fighting: in those days heroism was an everyday event in the lives of many. It is to lay bare the sources of this heroism that I have copied out these extracts from her schoolgirl's journal. The high standard she set for herself, her straightforwardness, her honesty predetermined a great deal.

One day Ina was sent scouting to pick up information about a German garrison. On her way back she was stopped by the Nazis. The officer hit her in the face, then burnt her hand with his cigar. Ina remained silent. Six months before the war she had had a tooth out: 'I cried so much that I myself do not know when and how it all ended. It seemed to me that if the pain were to get worse by even the tiniest fraction I should go mad'. But when the Nazi tortured her she kept silent: 'I thought about only one thing: not to show weakness'.

She wrote tender, simple letters to her mother: 'At night I sometimes wake up because I seem to see you quite plainly sitting on my bed, as you used to do at home. And I feel so happy and warm. Then I wake up completely and there is no one, it is quite empty'. 'All the time I keep remembering life at home during the past year. And I am so sad about Misha, perhaps sadder than last year because now I have come to appreciate life properly'. 'You seem to look upon me as something of a heroine. You really should not. I am just an ordinary Soviet girl'.

Alexander Pavlovich, Ina's father, was sent behind the enemy rear. He met Ina and said that when he had called her a little girl she protested: 'Papa, I'm not a little girl any longer, I'm a scout in the 2nd Kalinin Partisan Brigade'. However, when she learnt that there were sweets in her father's haversack, she said: 'Oh, do give me one'.

The partisan remained true to herself. In a letter to her schoolfriend Lena she said: 'I fell madly in love with a comrade, and he, too, loved me. Then he was killed. I thought I would go mad. You know what I am like'.

There is one particular entry in her diary which, if I were to omit it, would leave Ina's image incomplete. As I have said, she took part in the fighting and had no qualms about using her tommy-gun. Here is how she recorded in her diary the shooting of a traitor village headman: 'He bore himself with fortitude. Did not utter a word. Only the tips of his fingers trembled slightly. And he died quietly. It was Zoyka who shot him. Her hand never trembled. Good for her! But I felt eerie, somehow; I felt awful'.

On the night of 4th March 1944 several partisans were asleep in a forest dugout. Before daybreak the sentry woke them up: 'The Germans are here!' Ina realized that not all of them would be able to get away. She shouted to her comrades: 'Run for it!' and, dropping to one knee, opened fire with her tommy-gun. She died in that snowy forest, under the stars of which she had written three years before. She was not yet twenty.

Shortly after reading Ina's diary I wrote about her. After the war the diary was published in a slightly edited form: the heroine was not allowed to speak about the seamy side of life, though it is precisely that which demonstrated her loyalty, her moral courage. In that, as in much else, she was, to use her own words, 'an ordinary Soviet girl': before the war many things aroused her indignation, but in the hour of need she went to defend the Soviet land.

I gave Ina's diary to Elsa Triolet who translated it into French. Translations appeared in other countries too.

In 1958 Ina's mother was killed in a car accident. But her father still lives in the same small wooden house with Rena and a grandson who is now of an age to go to school. I saw the father not so long ago, and naturally we spoke about Ina. It seems to me that I know her better than I do some people with whom I have lived for years, and this not only because she reveals herself so completely in her diary but also because this girl, whom I came to know only after her death, is spiritually my kin. In the old days men discovered continents and islands, soon they will probably be discovering planets, but for a writer the discovery of the human heart has been, and always will be, the most important discovery of all. That is why I have included the story of Ina Konstantinova in a book about my own life: at that difficult time when the war crushed out all that we usually call human, I found in Ina a reaffirmation of many truths.

I believe that Ina's short life-story helps to explain why the Soviet people stood the ordeal and won the victory. It discloses the spirit of a generation which was mown down like young corn, before it had ripened. At the same time, however strange it may seem, when speaking about some aspects of Ina's spiritual life I am saying something about myself as well.

20

THIS IS how a *Red Star* correspondent described me in 1944: 'A completely civilian type with a baggy brown overcoat, civilian fur cap and a cigar appeared at the front, travelling in a mud-splashed jeep. He walked unhurriedly from one to another of the front-line positions, rather round-shouldered, speaking in a low voice and not making the slightest attempt to conceal the fact that he was a completely civilian type'.

When, at the end of January, I told General Talensky that I wanted to go to East Prussia, he smiled: 'Then you'll have to wear uniform, or else, heaven forbid, you may be mistaken for a Fritz'. I had no military rank, and the new officer's greatcoat without epaulets must have looked even more ridiculous on me than the baggy brown overcoat. However, this occurred to me only when the Germans persistently called me '*Herr Kommissar*'.

Our troops were swiftly advancing to the west, leaving behind them islands of encircled Nazis who were still holding out. In the town of Bartenstein the houses were still burning; the German positions were close by. There I met General Chanchibadze who said with a smile: 'This isn't Rzhev'. He told me that the soldiers were in a fury of impatience to push ahead, and complained of the shortage of ammunition. (The Germans held out in that particular cauldron for another two months.) When I arrived in Elbing street-fighting was still going on. At times the enemy retreated in haste, at others he resisted desperately. Mines had been laid everywhere: in school buildings, in peasants' barns, in bootshops. The General shouted into the telephone: 'Listen, give us a little more fire – the devil's hitting back'. A soldier was talking about a comrade: 'He said "the Fritzes are finished", but before the end of the day I lugged him to the field-hospital and they took one look at him and said: "Too late"'.

Everyone realized that things were drawing to an end but no man was sure that he would live to see it. At the beginning of February the weather changed sharply: spring came early, it was warm in the sun, snowdrops and purple crocuses flowered in the neglected gardens. The nearness of the end made death seem more than ever stupid and frightening.

The thought that we were moving into the heart of Germany made my head swim. I had written so much about it when the Nazis were on the Volga, and now I was driving along a good smooth road bordered by lime-trees; I saw an old castle, a town hall, shops with German signboards, and could hardly believe it: was it possible that we were in Germany? Once I came across my old friends, the Tatsin tank-men. For a long time we did nothing but smile and repeat senselessly: 'Well, so here we are ...'

Almost everyone had his own personal sorrow: his two brothers killed, his house burnt, his sisters deported to Germany, his mother killed in Poltava, his whole family tortured to death in Gomel – hatred was still hot, it had not had time to abate. My God, if we had come face to face with Hitler or Himmler, the Ministers, the Gestapo men, the executioners at that time ...! But it was carts creaking piteously on the roads, old German women rushing about distractedly, crying children who had lost their mothers, and pity welled up in my heart. I remembered, of course, that the Germans had had no pity for my people, I remembered everything, but Fascism, the Reich, Germany were one thing, and the old man in a silly Tyrolean hat with a little feather, running along the shell-pitted street and waving a strip torn off a sheet, was another.

In Rastenburg I saw a Red Army man furiously plunging his bayonet into the wax model of a girl that stood in the window of a gutted shop. The doll face smirked coquettishly while he stabbed and stabbed. 'Stop it!' I shouted at him. 'The Germans are looking on.' 'The bastards!' he yelled back. 'They tortured my wife to death.' He was a Byelorussian.

In Rastenburg Major Rosenfeld had been appointed Commandant. The Nazis had wiped out his family, yet he did all he could to protect the population of the town. He put me up for the night. In the house, which had belonged to a wealthy fascist, there was a snapshot on the wall: the owner's daughter presenting a bunch of flowers to Hitler. Local inhabitants told us that the Führer had stayed in this house when he came to East Prussia. Major Rosenfeld was very unhappy at having been separated from his regiment but went on working almost twenty-four hours on end. I was with him when a small girl whose parents had been killed was brought in. The major looked at the child kindly and sadly, perhaps thinking of his own small daughter. He had probably many a time repeated to himself the words about 'sacred vengeance', but here, in Rastenburg, he realized that this was an empty abstraction and that the wound in his heart would never heal.

Here, too, the joy of victory was mixed with that sadness which inevitably overtakes one at the sight of war, not war as shown in a painting of battle-scenes or on the screen, but war under your very nose: the destroyed houses, the down from featherbeds, the refugees, the bundles, the unmilked cows; and a human being's long-drawn ear-splitting shriek goes on sounding in your ears.

Some towns had been shattered by artillery fire; in Kreuzburg only the prison remained standing; among the ruins of Wehlau I did not find a single German – everyone had fled. Other towns escaped destruction; in Rastenburg the inhabitants were clearing the streets of smashed furniture and broken carts. In Elbing sixty thousand people, a third of the population, had remained.

For a very long time East Prussia has been regarded as the most reactionary part of Germany. There was little industry here, few workers; the well-to-do peasants had voted for Hindenburg, and later shouted '*Heil Hitler!*' The landowners were true diehards who regarded any liberal measure as an outrage to their family honour. In the towns there were merchants, civil servants and lawyers, doctors, notaries, men of liberal professions not easily classifiable as intelligentsia. The houses were clean, well-appointed, with petty bourgeois comfort: antlers in the dining-room, embroidered samplers with the maxim that 'Order in the house means order in the State' or 'Work and you will have sweet dreams'. Stoneware jars, inscribed salt, pepper, thyme and coffee stood in the kitchens. There would be a few books on a shelf: the Bible, Uhland's poems, sometimes an inherited volume of Goethe, and a dozen modern publications: *Mein Kampf*, *The Polish Campaign*, *Race Hygiene*, *Our Loyal Prussia*. In such towns as Rastenburg, Lötzen and Tapiau there were no public libraries. In Bartenstein I was told that the museum building was still intact. I warned the Commandant: 'You must post sentries at once'. I went into the museum and was appalled: apart from some stuffed animals the exhibits were all of one kind: a huge portrait of Hindenburg, a map of the 1914 military campaigns, war trophies – a Russian officer's epaulets, photographs of the ruins of Warsaw – and portraits of local benefactors.

Our soldiers examined the furniture. One, I remember, grinned: 'It wouldn't be too bad to live in a den like this'. Another swore: 'They lived well, the bastards. Why did they have to come nosing into our country? Look, those are our towels', and he pointed at the embroidered Ukrainian towels in the well-equipped kitchen.

I was dining in Elbing with the Corps Commander, General Anissimov, when a lieutenant came hurrying in: 'Beg to report'. He said that some thirty or forty men had been discovered in a cellar and refused to come out, shouting that they were hall-porters and claiming immunity. The misunderstanding was soon cleared up: a man was brought to the General who introduced himself as 'Karl Brandenburg, Vice-Consul of Switzerland'.[1] It appeared that quite a few Swiss lived in Elbing where they had established themselves as expert cheese-makers. The general gave orders to supply the hungry vice-consul with food and drink and then to fetch all the Swiss citizens out of the cellar. I was surprised to see that the safe-conduct which the neutral cheese-maker produced was written in Russian and had been issued by the Swiss government in 1944. 'In Berne they foresaw events,' the vice-consul explained, and added with a faint smile: 'In Berne, but not in Elbing'.

The Vicar-General complained to me that under Hitler the Germans had lost their faith (two pastors said the same thing). But to me it seemed that they had simply changed the object of worship. The infallibility of the Pope ceased to mean much to the Catholics, but to make up for this they put their faith in the infallibility of the Führer. The Red Army's invasion of East Prussia took the population by surprise: they had believed in Hitler and his henchmen, while only at the beginning of January Gauleiter Erich Koch had declared: 'The Russians will never break into the heart of East Prussia – in four months we have dug trenches and ditches to a total length of 13,000 miles'. The figure was reassuring. In Liebstadt I found an uncompleted 'certificate of Aryan descent': on 12th January a certain Scheller, who intended to get married, had begun to fill in a form about his forbears but had not had time to produce the necessary information about one of his grandfathers for on 26th January Russian tanks had entered Liebstadt.

In 1944 I often asked myself what would happen when the Red

[1] The Russian word for hall-porter is *shveytsar*.

Army entered Germany. After all, Hitler had succeeded in persuading not only isolated fanatics but the majority of his compatriots that they were a chosen people, that plutocrats and Communists, having made common cause, were depriving the gifted and industrious Germans of living space and that Germany was vested with the great mission of establishing a New Order in Europe. I remembered certain conversations I had had with prisoners of war, diaries that shocked not only by the cruelty of the entries but by the cult of force, of death, of a mixture of vulgar Nietzscheism and a revival of superstition. I expected the population to offer desperate resistance to the Red Army. Everywhere I saw inscriptions written on the eve of the arrival of our troops: curses, calls to fight, 'Rastenburg will always be German!' 'Elbing does not surrender!' 'The citizens of Tapiau remember Hindenburg. Death to the Russians!' I came across a leaflet which, for no reason I could see, mentioned the tradition of the Werewolf. I asked the captain, whose job it was to do propaganda among the enemy troops and who had a good knowledge of German, what was meant by 'werewolf'. 'It's the name of some general,' he replied. 'I believe he fought in Libya.' I thought I had better check this and looked up the word in a dictionary. This is what it said: 'According to old German legends the werewolf possesses supernatural strength, he is clad in a wolf's skin, lives in oak-forests and attacks human beings, destroying every living thing'. In Rastenburg I found an exercise-book in which some boy had written: 'I swear to be a Werewolf and to kill the Russians!' Yet in this same town of Rastenburg not only the boys and old men, but also those of call-up age who had stayed there, behaved like exemplary schoolchildren. The Nazis had manufactured small daggers with 'All for Germany' inscribed on the blade. The instructions said that these daggers would serve the Germans to fight the Red invaders. I picked one up and used it as a tin-opener. And I never heard of any Red Army man being stabbed. It was all talk, Goebbels' fantasies, sinister Nazi romanticism. Besides harmless old men and boys among the civilian population there were also, naturally, wolves but, unlike the legendary werewolves, they preferred, for the time being, to hide themselves under sheep's clothing and carry out conscientiously every order issued by the Soviet Commandant.

I went to dozens of towns, talked to people in all walks of life: doctors, lawyers, teachers, peasants, innkeepers, tailors, shopkeepers, mechanics, brewers, jewellers, agronomists, pastors, even a genealogist.

I tried to find out from a Catholic priest, from a professor of Marburg University, from old men and schoolboys what they thought about the notion of a 'master race', about the conquest of India, about Hitler's personality, about the Auschwitz incinerators. The reply was always the same: 'We are not responsible'. One man said that he had never taken any interest in politics, that the war was a calamity, that only the SS was behind Hitler; another assured me that at the last elections in 1933 he had voted for the Social-Democrats; a third swore that he was in touch with his brother-in-law, a Communist who lived in Hanover and was a member of a clandestine organization there. Near Elbing, in the village of Hohenwald, a German raised his clenched fist to greet the *Herr Kommissar*: '*Rot Front!*' There was an album in his house containing snapshots of Russians being hanged, with a placard by the gallows which said in large lettering: 'I tried to set fire to the sawmill, I was an accomplice of the partisans'; and of Jewish women with stars on their breasts, in a railway coach, waiting to be shot. The discovery of this album did not by any means disconcert the bogus *Rot Fronter*; he went on describing how he had opposed the Nazis: 'These photographs were left here by some stormtrooper who probably came to see my brother. My brother was a very naïve man; he was killed on the Eastern Front; for my part, I fought in France and Italy, I've never been to Russia. You can take my word for it – at heart I'm a Communist'.

No doubt among the hundreds of people to whom I talked there were some who were sincere, but it was impossible to distinguish these from the others – they all said the same things. I smiled politely in reply. Perhaps the one who appeared to me the most sincere was an elderly German who was returning from the west to Preussisch-Eylau and who said: '*Herr Stalin hat gesiegt, ich geh' nach Haus''*.

Those I talked to at first said that they knew nothing about Auschwitz, about the 'torch-bearers', the villages set on fire, the mass murder of the Jews; later, however, when they realized that they were not immediately threatened, they went so far as to admit that men coming home on leave had told them quite a lot, and they laid the blame on Hitler, the SS and the Gestapo.

The Third Reich, which until recently had seemed so stable, collapsed overnight, and everything (temporarily at least) was shoved out of sight, buried in holes: the crude Nietzscheism, the talk about the superiority of the Germans and Germany's historic mission. The only things in evidence were the desire of the population to save their property and their habit of carrying out orders punctiliously. Everybody greeted me respectfully with attempts to smile. In the region of the Masurian lakes my car was bogged down; Germans appeared from somewhere, got the car out and vied with one another to tell me the best road to take. In Elbing shooting was still going on, but a respectable, well-fed townsman was already showing initiative: he brought out a step-ladder and moved the hour-hand of his large clock two hours forward: 'It keeps perfect time. It is now twelve minutes past three, Moscow time'.

The commandants of towns were selected from among army officers, and they were not, of course, particularly well qualified for this type of job. A stereotyped notice setting out the regulations would be pasted on the walls. One of our commandants said with a laugh: 'Before I'd read what was written myself they'd already studied the regulations from A to Z: what was allowed and what forbidden. Before an hour had gone by they started coming: one wanted to know whether he could climb on to the roof to repair a hole, another where he was to take a Russian worker – a woman – who had fallen ill, a third came to inform against a neighbour'.

In Elbing I saw an unusual queue: thousands of the town's inhabitants were eagerly waiting to get inside the prison. Picking out the most peaceable-looking one I asked him: 'Why do you stand out here in the cold? Show me round the town, you probably know the districts where they're still shooting'. At first he lamented over the loss of his place in the queue and explained that the prison was now the safest place: the Russians were bound to post a guard there and one would be able to wait in safety until things calmed down; my promise to bring him back to the prison at the end of the day slightly reassured him. He was a tram-driver. I did not ask him about Hitler; I knew what his answer would be. He told me that his house had been burnt down, he had barely had time to escape just as he was. We were passing a ready-made clothing shop; overcoats, raincoats and suits lay strewn about. I told the man to help himself to an overcoat, but the idea frightened him: 'Oh no, *Herr Kommissar*, those are Russian spoils of war'. I suggested giving him a written permit. After some thought he asked: 'But have you got a seal? Without a seal it wouldn't be a proper document, and no one would take my word for it'.

In Rastenburg I was taken round by the boy Vassya whom the Germans had deported from Grodno. He told me that he had been working in the house of a rich German, he had had a label tied round his neck and everyone had shouted at him. Now he walked at my side and the Germans we met greeted him with a polite 'Guten Tag, Herr Vassya'.

Later on a great deal was written in the West German press about so-called 'Russian atrocities' in an attempt to explain the servile behaviour of the population by their understandable terror. To tell the truth, I had feared that after the crimes the invaders had perpetrated in our country, our Red Army men might try to settle accounts. In dozens of articles I kept on saying that we should not and, indeed, could not exact vengeance, for we were Soviet people, not Fascists. Patrols protected the population. There were, of course, cases of violence, of looting: in every army there are criminals, hooligans and drunkards, but our officers took measures against excesses. It is not in the brutality of our soldiers that the explanation of the civilian population's submissiveness must be sought, but in its own moral confusion: the dream had crumbled, discipline had gone by the board, and people who were accustomed to march at the word of command rushed about like a flock of terrified sheep. I rejoiced at the victory, at the approaching end of the war. But it was depressing to look about me, and I do not know what affected me most: the ruins of towns, the snowstorm of feathers on the roads, or the meekness, the submissiveness of the local people. In those days I had the feeling that a complicity in crime existed between the brutal SS men and placid Frau Müller from Rastenburg who had never killed anyone but had merely taken on a cheap servant – Nastya from Orel.

The smiles of the Rastenburg or Elbing citizens aroused in me neither wicked glee nor commiseration, rather a mixture of disgust and pity, and this sometimes poisoned the great happiness I felt at the sight of our soldiers who had fought their way from the Volga to the estuary of the Vistula. It was a relief to talk to the liberated people: Soviet girls, citizens and soldiers of countries enslaved by Hitler. In Bartenstein I was lucky enough to witness an unusual meeting: one of our soldiers, a native of Smolensk, discovered his sister with her two children aged eleven and nine among the liberated Soviet women. Until quite recently this woman had been digging the trenches of which Erich Koch had boasted. She wept and was unable to say anything but 'Vassya! Vassenka!' While the elder boy admiringly examined the two medals on Uncle Vassya's chest.

What an extraordinary variety of people it fell to my lot to meet! Among the liberated were nationals of many different countries and professions: French prisoners of war, Belgians, Yugoslavs, Englishmen, even a few Americans, a student from Athens, some Dutch actors, a Czech professor, an Australian farmer, Polish girls, priests and the crew of a Norwegian ship. They all shouted and joked, hardly knowing how to express their joy.

The Frenchmen got hold of German bicycles and pedalled away – to the east! – in a hurry to get home. There would always be someone among them who was a good cook; so, having killed a sheep, they organized a feast to which they invited our men, and they laughed and joked until even the stolid Englishmen joined in.

All had learnt a smattering of German while in captivity; a Belgian described his experiences to a Czech, while Yugoslavs and Englishmen discussed what was to be done with Germany now. Agreement was far easier to reach here than at the Yalta or Potsdam conferences: people understood one another.

In Elbing, in the barracks where prisoners of war had been kept, I saw regulations printed in ten different languages. In the region of the Masurian lakes the French had to fell trees and build military fortifications. On von Dienhoff's estate Frenchmen, Russians and Poles had worked, a hundred and five men in all. The railwayman Chudovsky from Dniepropetrovsk had made friends with a Moroccan and had taught him some Russian. In small, utterly provincial Bartenstein every family with three children or more had been allotted a servant – a Russian or a Pole. One farmer's wife told me that she lived modestly, and had only one Ukrainian woman and an Italian man working for her; she paid sixty marks to the *Arbeitsamt* for them. Today this is common knowledge, but at the time it came as a shock: the slavery of the Hellenic age had been revived, but instead of Euripides there was Baldur von Schirach, and in place of the Acropolis, Auschwitz.

A Frenchman, an army surgeon, told me that not far from their camp was another for Russian prisoners of war. When a typhus epidemic broke out the Nazi doctor said: 'No use treating them, they'll die anyhow'. Every day they would bury the dead. The Frenchman said: 'I saw that along with the dead they were burying people who were still alive. I can't think of it without a feeling of horror'.

In the kitchen of a house in Bartenstein our sappers found an exercise-book in which a Russian girl had kept a diary. I took it away with me. The entries were very simple, and for that reason had the ring of truth: '26th September. Took advantage of that woman being out and got Moscow on the radio. Kharkov is ours! After that I cried with joy for the rest of the day. I tell myself: you silly fool, it is our side that is winning, and there you are crying and crying. I thought of Petya. Where is he now, is he alive? I know I shall not live to see victory. But I know for certain now that our people will win ... 11th November. My birthday. I think of how Tanya and Ninochka used to come, and we drank tea and ate cakes and talked about books. Tanya would sing the praises of her beloved I. all the time. How could I ever have dreamt that I would have to empty that woman's chamber-pots and suffer spiteful remarks'.

I do not know the girl's name, I do not know whether she lived to see victory or what eventually happened to her, but I could not feel anything except deep admiration for the men who were in actual fact setting human souls free, and it was unbearably sad to recall those who had died in the Kiev encirclement, at Rzhev and on the Volga.

I stopped for the night in Guttstadt, intending to push on in the morning. The Divisional Commander tried his best to persuade me to stay a little longer and have lunch with him. He said that I ought not to miss seeing the ancient monastery. What I saw was not the monastery but its ruins: it had been heavily shelled. The ground was littered with books, small books bound in leather or vellum; I had seen such books in other towns: prayer-books, psalters, Bibles, works of Fathers of the Church. I was on the point of going when, I hardly know why, I bent down and picked up a small volume. I was thunder-struck: it was a first edition of Ronsard's poems published in Paris in the 1570s. Another volume, a third, a fourth ... The poems of one of Ronsard's friends, Remy Belleau. A small volume of Lucian's works in a French translation. (I later gave the Lucian to Suritz but still treasure the Ronsard and the Belleau.) On the title-page of each was a note: bought by so-and-so at such-and-such a place. In the sixteenth century friars who were too fond of wine and women used to be sent to distant monasteries at the farthest borders of the Catholic world. It may safely be assumed that a man who had a taste for Ronsard's poems and Lucian's satires was no ascetic. In all probability the erring friar had died in obscure Guttstadt and his books had become part of the monastery library. The Germans did not realize what kind of books they were, no one ever opened them, and so, miraculously, they had been preserved.

In the car I looked at the volume of Ronsard and was dumbfounded again: it fell open precisely at the poem extracts from which I had quoted in *The Fall of Paris* where Jeannette reads to Desser.

> *Mais, souffrant doucement le joug de ton empire,*
> *Tant soit-il rigoureux*
> *Dans les Champs Elysez une mesme navire*
> *Nous passera tous deux. . . .*

It was all so incongruous : rubble, tanks, a field-hospital – and Ronsard, love and Elysian fields, not the Champs Elysées of Paris, but those of which Pushkin wrote: 'And Jenny will not forsake Edmund even in the heavens'.

On my way back to Moscow, in Vilnius a fortnight later, I described the episode of the Swiss vice-consul to Y. I. Paleckis. We laughed over it and said to each other: 'The end's in sight now'.

Later I drove through the ruins of Minsk. Again the familiar road: the villages destroyed by fire, Borisov, the tannery where the Nazis did their killing. Snow still charitably blanketed the scorched and pitted earth, the rusty barbed wire, the empty shell-cases, the bones.

I thought suddenly: here is victory, why is sorrow mingled with rejoicing? It was not like that before. Evidently the end now in sight allowed one to pause for thought. I recalled Ronsard's little volumes. In Paris, in 1940, I had written: 'More than once in those noisy, morbid years, in the din of war, amid the poverty of nature, I re-read the poems of Ronsard'. My short poem had ended with the words: 'How simple it all is! How unattainable! Beloved, even to breathe is criminal'. Memory brought back the five years that had passed since that spring: the losses, the grief, the hopes. It seemed that now the time was near when one would be able to breathe, when all the loved ones would sleep without anxiety for the slender thread of human life. Perhaps other things would come within our grasp: joy, snowdrops, art? My thoughts were no longer about Rastenburg or Elbing, I was thinking about life.

21

FOUR YEARS ago I said at the beginning of my memoirs: 'I think it would be premature to publish certain chapters because they deal with people who are still living or events which do not yet belong to history'. I have omitted much of what I went through in the war years, and I shall now pass on to the last weeks of the war.

Around Königsberg, at the approaches to Berlin and in Hungary bloody battles were being fought. Almost every night victory salutes roared out in Moscow; they were of three categories, the first of twenty-four salvoes from three hundred and twenty-four guns, the second of twenty from two hundred and twenty-four guns and the third of twelve from one hundred and twenty-four guns. The Muscovites had grown used to them; there were nights when the sky would be lit up three or four times with the blaze of rockets. 'What's the salute for?' a girl would ask her friend in the foyer of a theatre, and the other would reply: 'Just a small one for some Hungarian town'. But even if the people had by now become accustomed to victories, they still awaited passionately, agonizingly, Victory itself. They waited for a letter from someone dear at the front, they went through even greater torments of anxiety than in the preceding years. That last quarter of an hour which seems an eternity was at hand.

In March General Talensky left *Red Star*. I did not find things easy with the new editor but derived some comfort from the thought that my newspaper work was coming to an end and that soon I should be able to get down to writing a book. Meanwhile I went on producing articles for *Red Star*, for *Pravda* and for the weekly *War and the Working Class*.

As early as 1944 I received a letter from England from a certain Lady Gibb. Prompted by religious feelings she urged me to leave retribution for the crimes of the Fascists to God and not to appeal to feelings of revenge. I published this letter in *Red Star* together with my reply in which I said that the feeling of revenge was alien to me, that the Red Army men, when they captured the towns of Transylvania, where there were many German families, did not murder

173

the unarmed people, and that what we wanted was justice, the eradication of Fascism and genuine peace, but we could not leave it to the Almighty to bring the Nazi criminals to justice. I reminded her that the blind politicians who had delivered Czechoslovakia into the hands of the Fascist executioners had been acclaimed 'angels of peace' when in reality they had been nothing more than foolish schemers and scheming fools.

Many letters reached me from the front expressing indignation at Lady Gibb's appeal. (I believe the lady herself received an even greater number of letters; I was later told that the postmen in the small town where she lived were overwhelmed by the avalanche of Russian letters.) Meanwhile Lady Gibb found herself in the limelight; it was, of course not she herself who mattered, for the struggle was now beginning between those who had decided to destroy Fascism and yesterday's 'men of Munich', the advocates of a 'soft peace'. Those who protested against the decisions of the Yalta conference to bring the war criminals to trial, disarm Germany and force the Germans to take part in the reconstruction of the towns they had destroyed were not kindhearted Christians but thoroughly cynical politicians. However paradoxical it may sound, as early as the end of 1944, when the Germans were counter-attacking in Alsace and the Ardennes, there were Americans and Englishmen interested in Germany retaining some part of her military force 'as a bulwark against Communism'.

Brailsford, the author of a book published in England in 1944, suggested that the Germans should be helped to rebuild their towns in the first place, that all demands for reparations should be relinquished, that the Czechs should be made to guarantee equal rights to the Sudeten Germans and that a plebiscite should be held in Austria to decide whether she should remain part of Germany. Rather strange courses were organized in the USA: German prisoners of war were trained there to form a police force for occupied Germany; according to the American press the trainees agreed that Fascist rule should make way for a democratic regime but insisted that the Americans should finance the reconstruction of the German towns that had been destroyed by Allied bombing.

In February 1945 Hitler began hastily transferring divisions from the Western to the Eastern Front. It is easy to understand that, of two evils, the Nazis were choosing the lesser. They had had the opportunity to see for themselves that when the Allies occupied German towns they treated yesterday's Nazis leniently. In the Rhineland, more often than not, the Nazi burgomaster was allowed to remain in office. The *Daily Telegraph* criticized an English officer for allowing Italian and Russian prisoners to leave the estate of a German landowner on the grounds that such measures disrupted Germany's agricultural economy. Important industrialists in the Ruhr and representatives of the IG Farben trust were drawn into the various economic organizations set up by the Allies. A well-known American columnist published a book where for the first time he spoke of the 'Atlantic community'.

Heaven knows, I have nothing of the diplomat nor of the politician – I have always found literature more congenial and easier to understand than the complicated game of politics. The only reason why I said that certain western politicians wanted to preserve the germs of Fascism was that I remembered Spain and Munich and knew what sacrifices the victory over Hitler's Germany had entailed.

I went on saying in my articles that we had not come to Germany to seek revenge but to eradicate Fascism. Bearing in mind isolated cases of excesses committed in East Prussian towns that had aroused our general indignation, I quoted in *Red Star* a letter that I had received from an officer, V. A. Kurilko: '"... The Germans believe that we are going to perpetrate on their soil the crimes they perpetrated on ours. We shall be severe but just, and our people will never, never demean themselves in such a way".' And I went on: 'I have seen Russian soldiers rescue German children; we are not ashamed of this, we take pride in it ... The Soviet soldier will not molest a German woman ... It is not for booty, not for loot, not for women that he has come to Germany'.

The 'Cold War' was still only hatching in its top-secret incubator, and there were people in the West who said that one ought to try to understand the feelings of a people which had borne the brunt of the sacrifices. In March the *New York Herald Tribune* wrote that my recent summing-up of the military situation had been worth all the long-winded contributions of fifty congressmen, twenty commentators and a dozen political experts: that it was no armchair strategy but concrete tactics; that here was the truth of the brutal nature of the war into which the Germans had dragged the world. Nobody had wanted it. The Russians who in 1939 concluded the non-aggression pact had not wanted it. Mr Chamberlain, who went to Godesberg with his furled umbrella, had not wanted it. The Poles, the French, the British, the Americans had not wanted it, but the Germans had forced it upon them and were now reaping what they had sown. Only those who knew the nature of this war were capable, at the moment of victory, of ensuring peace to our ravaged civilization.

On 11th April *Red Star* printed my article *Enough!* which differed little from what I had written before. In describing how Mannheim surrendered to the Allies by telephone I said that the Fascists feared Soviet far more than Anglo-American occupation. *Enough!* referred to those political circles in the west which, after the First World War, had banked on the retention and encouragement of German militarism.

On 12th April Roosevelt died. This was a grievous loss. In the perspective of time we can now see that Roosevelt had belonged to that small number of American statesmen who wanted to change the climate of world affairs and retain good relations with the Soviet Union. Moscow hung out mourning banners. Everybody wondered what Truman, the new President, would do.

On 17th April I attended a dinner given in honour of Marshal Tito by the Slav Committee. G. F. Alexandrov came and sat down next to me. He asked me if I was not very tired and complimented me on my journalism. On unfolding *Pravda* the next morning I saw a large headline: 'COMRADE EHRENBURG OVERSIMPLIFIES'. The article was signed by Alexandrov. (I naturally realized at once that he was not writing on his own initiative and that the reason why he had not said anything about it to me the night before was the embarrassment he must have felt; it would also explain why he had praised my articles.)

Alexandrov took me to task for not differentiating between the Germans, for saying that there was no one in Germany to capitulate and that all Germans were equally responsible for the criminal war, and, finally, for explaining the transfer of German divisions from the west to the east by the Germans' fear of the Red Army, whereas in fact this move was a provocation, a manoeuvre of Hitler's, an attempt to sow mistrust among the members of the anti-Hitler coalition.

Of course I should not record any of this if I were writing the history of the epoch, but it is a book about my own life that I am writing and I cannot pass over in silence an incident which caused me many painful hours.

I had once again shown myself naïve although I was fifty-four years old: I cannot plead youth or inexperience as an excuse. Apparently this kind of naïvety is inherent in my nature. I realized the reasons for Alexandrov's article: it was necessary to try to break down the Germans' resistance by promising immunity to the rank and file of those who carried out Hitler's orders, and it was necessary to remind the Allies of the importance we attached to unity within the coalition. I accepted both the one and the other; like everybody else I wanted the last act of the tragedy to be played out without needless sacrifices and the approaching end of the war to bring genuine peace. What upset me was something else: why were ideas attributed to me that I did not hold, why was it found necessary to make accusations against me in order to reassure the Germans? Now, when the bitterness of those days has long been forgotten, I see that there was a certain logic in the manoeuvre. Goebbels had represented me as a fiend, and Alexandrov's article could have been a clever move on the chessboard. Where my naïvety came in was in refusing to see a man as a pawn.

Red Star naturally reprinted Alexandrov's article. The editor spoke to me harshly as if I were a defaulter in the army. The office was flooded with letters from the front asking why there were no articles by Ehrenburg; this fact was also commented on abroad. I was invited to write about the battles for Berlin. I knew that the editor would submit any article to the Central Committee, to Alexandrov, and I preferred to do this myself. I have kept a copy of the letter I addressed to him: '... Reading your article anybody might come to the conclusion that I have been calling for a complete annihilation of the German people. Whereas, naturally, I never issued any such call: it was German Fascist propaganda that ascribed this to me. I cannot write a single line until I have cleared up this misunderstanding, one way or the other. As you will see, I have done this not in the form of a refutation but by quoting from my previous article. It is my integrity as a writer and an internationalist, to whom the racialist theory is an abomination, that has been challenged'. I received no reply.

Only on 10th May, the day after Victory, did *Pravda* publish my article: *The Morning of Peace*. I had realized by then that I would not be allowed to justify myself and, for the benefit of those with a memory, I had inserted, without quotes, passages from my old articles in which I said that the feeling of revenge was alien to us and that the German people would find a place in the sun after it had purged itself of Fascism.

Unfortunately Alexandrov's article did not produce the desired effect on the Germans. They were demoralized long before this article appeared, but fighting-fit divisions still existed and these kept up a stubborn resistance. As for the Allies, at the first moment some of them were disturbed: were the Russians going to try to draw the Germans over to their side? But they were soon reassured, realizing that rivers of blood were not bottles of ink, and that one article would not alter the feelings of the Soviet people towards the Nazis or the German bourgeoisie's fear of Communism. No doubt the officers and men of the Allied armies had been too deeply shocked by what they had found at Ravensbrück and Buchenwald for the fascist leaders to expect mercy, but the Ruhr industrialists, the *Wehrmacht* generals, the high functionaries of the Third Reich and the more obscure Nazis, who hastily burnt their party cards, knew where they would find powerful protectors.

Perhaps Alexandrov's article produced the greatest impression on our men at the front. Never in my life have I received so many sympathetic letters. In the street complete strangers shook me by the hand (I must confess that I rather dreaded this and tried to avoid showing myself in public).

Men at the front sent me presents by way of comfort; one of these is worth a word or two. It was a somewhat damaged sporting gun which the armourers of Liège had presented to the Consul Bonaparte in the Year VII of the Republican Era, a handsome piece bearing the insignia of the Republic, a bas-relief portrait of the young Napoleon and a niellated scene of a naval engagement with the British fleet. The inscription 'Freedom of the Seas' recalled the struggle of revolutionary France against the blockade. But, much as I admired the gun, I was still more heartened by the letter from the soldiers who had found it on the road somewhere in Prussia and sent it to me. The letter was full of kind words about my articles in the difficult days and of sympathy and warmth.

When Suritz came to see me he said: 'You shouldn't worry. It's not against you, it's just in the character of the man. I recognize the hand'. By and large he proved to be right. For several weeks nothing of mine was printed, then the whole matter was forgotten, and today only the neo-Fascists of the *Soldatenzeitung* still remember Alexandrov's article.

But the problems which deeply preoccupied me during the last

178

months of the war are not, alas, outdated. When, in April 1945, the Nazis welcomed the troops of the Western Allies they knew what they were doing: what they needed was a wing under which they could find shelter, recover their breath and bide their time until they could once again emerge into the daylight and start talking about the 'Red menace', the 'defence of the west', the 'historic mission of Germany'. On my desk I have the latest newspapers: reports on the German army's manoeuvres, on the demonstrations by Sudeten Germans, on the speeches made by the Minister of War Strauss. It makes depressing reading. And memories are depressing too. One is not obliged to listen to the nursery tale about the little white bull which keeps going back to the beginning and never ends. But I am writing this book in New Jerusalem, where close by is a common grave long since overgrown with grass. It is a luminous autumn day; important-looking little boys are on their way for their first day at the newly rebuilt school. I cannot help wondering what the future holds in store for them.

22

At the end of April a Sovinformburo communiqué announced that Edouard Herriot had been liberated in a western suburb of Berlin by the forces of the First Ukrainian Front. Two days later I had a telephone call: 'Herriot wants to know whether you are in Moscow. He would like to see you'.

Herriot embraced me: '*Mon petit*, it was pretty grim'. And in his excitement, as he related what he had been through, he suddenly began to *tutoie* me.

I had first met him in the middle twenties. Later we met from time to time, though not often, at V. S. Dovgalevsky's, at the embassy, at the Palais Bourbon, in Lyons, in Marseilles at the Radical Socialist Party conference, and on two or three occasions we had lunched together. Now he talked eagerly about his experiences and I listened to him with sympathy; I felt that he was well disposed towards me, though it would have been absurd to speak of friendship: he was twenty years older than I, a fact which allowed him to call me '*mon petit*', and we lived in very different worlds; for the man who had been Premier, President of the Chamber of Deputies and Mayor of Lyons, literature was a recreation, whereas politics is for me more like military service than either a passionate interest or a profession.

He had the sort of face that is not easily forgotten; his large head, coarse hair, bulging forehead and plump cheeks were reminiscent of a work by some modern sculptor who, in modelling his clay, avoids smoothness above all. And Herriot's blue eyes had a kindly twinkle. Before the war caricaturists always depicted him with a huge paunch. He had been born in the Champagne but had lived for half a century in Lyons, famous for its excellent cooking, and had enjoyed the good food without bothering about his figure. He was much thinner now and his suit hung on him in folds. Since his arrival in Moscow, although the Germans had treated him far better than the common run of prisoners, he was always hungry. When he was invited to a VOKS (Society for Cultural Relations with Foreign Countries) reception he whispered to me: 'D'you think they'll give us something to eat?'

Smilingly he described how he was liberated by the Red Army: 'One of your officers and his men came in. I shouted "Fransuz! Edouard Herriot". And believe it or not, he knew the name. He shook hands with me, laughed and repeated "Herriot" in the Russian way'. He said that he had been aware of the panic and had realized that the end was near: that he would either be killed or set free. 'But it's a good thing that it was your people who liberated me – the whole of my political life has been bound up with the idea of Franco-Russian friendship. I don't have to tell you that. And I'm beginning to think about the biographical record: everything should be consistent'.

He dwelt at length on his experiences after the fall of France. Much of what he told me I already knew, but I was interested to hear his personal reactions. I realized that I had not been mistaken in regarding him as a most striking representative of nineteenth-century France, the France that had lasted until the First World War. It was not merely a matter of age, but of outlook, of character, of habits. As a politician he was inevitably doomed to defeat, with his outdated ideas of strategy and antiquated armaments, his old-fashioned turns of speech, but it was precisely these anachronisms that I found endearing.

I think it must have been on the following day that he was shown a war newsreel in the small VOKS auditorium. With keen pleasure he watched our tanks moving along German roads. Then there was a sequence showing corpses, the Auschwitz incinerators and the bales of women's hair ready for dispatch to Germany. I was translating: 'Six tons of women's hair', when I suddenly noticed that Herriot's eyes were closed and tears were running down his cheeks. 'I knew nothing about all that,' he said to me when we had left the hall. 'I feel that it's time for me to die – I don't understand the world any more. Do you know why I took up politics? Because of the Dreyfus affair. I was a teacher, with literary ambitions. Then suddenly the "affair" cropped up. A man had been unjustly condemned for the simple reason that he was a Jew, and the whole of France was split into two camps. I was twenty-six at the time, I shouted myself hoarse. Zola, Jaurès, Anatole France — telegrams from Leo Tolstoy, Verhaeren, Mark Twain: everybody protested. Because *one* innocent man had been sent to Devil's Island. Tell me, do *you* understand what the human race has come to? It doesn't make sense. Six tons of women's hair! I know it's those Nazis, those Germans, but they're our contemporaries, our neighbours. They produced Beethoven'.

He had no love for the Germans and said: 'What strikes me most is their perfidy. Even more than their cruelty. In a talk I had with Stresemann he lied three times in less than fifteen minutes. His main aim was to take advantage of a short breathing space and then have his revenge and restore the supremacy of "Greater Germany".' There was, however, nothing racialist or chauvinist about Herriot's dislike of the Germans: he loved classical German music and had helped anti-fascist German refugees. It might sound extraordinary, almost grotesque, that this man, who had more than once headed the government of a great twentieth-century power, should attach the utmost importance to such completely outmoded notions as 'keeping one's word' and 'saving one's honour'. 'We must pay our debts to America, we gave our word.' 'The British are allowing Germany to rearm, what has happened to their promises?' 'We have deceived the Czechs, it is a blot on the honour of France.' 'The King of the Belgians, the son of the *roi-chevalier*, has acted unworthily: he capitulated without consulting his allies.' 'We cannot lay down our arms – we are bound by our agreement with Britain.'

During the tragic days of July 1940 Herriot came out in support of the plan for the government to move to Algiers from where it could organize resistance. At the same time he revealed his weakness to the full by demanding that his own Lyons should be declared an open city. Although he alleged that Pétain was even more perfidious than the Germans, Herriot nevertheless appealed to the Marshal's sense of justice. The National Assembly was convened: the deputies were asked to renounce their mandates and bury the Republic. Herriot, who presided over the first session, said in his speech: 'Our people that is suffering a great misfortune has rallied round Marshal Pétain whose name is revered by all'. 'This was one of the worst mistakes in my life,' Herriot admitted when talking to me about those days. 'I knew, of course, that Pétain hated the Republic but I thought he had some notion of honour and would not dare to raise his hand against liberty.' He did not protest against the capitulation. He accepted the handing over of full power to Pétain. But he would not concur in the accusations levelled at those deputies who had gone to Algiers: 'They obeyed the call of duty, of honour'. The pro-fascist deputies interrupted him angrily. 'Veritable cannibals!' Herriot said recalling the scene. (This was the expression Zola had used when the aristocratic mob howled under his windows at the time of the Dreyfus trial.) At the beginning of June 1941 Herriot demanded that Pétain should protect the dignity of France: it was infamous that the Germans should deprive the deputies of Alsace and Lorraine of the right to call themselves members of the French Parliament. In August 1942, when Germany seemed invincible, when her armies had reached the Volga, the Northern Caucasus and the frontiers of Egypt, Herriot took action on three occasions: invoking the Hague Convention, he protested against the shooting of hostages by the Germans; he expressed his indignation at the persecution of French Jews; and, finally, he returned his insignia of the Légion d'Honneur after that Order had been bestowed on two traitors who had fought with the Germans in Russia. Herriot was arrested and, in the autumn of 1944, handed over to the Nazis who deported him to Germany.

Viewed as the policy of an important statesman this inconsistent behaviour seems baffling. It is true that Herriot was one of the leading Radical-Socialists: that extremely mixed, amorphous party which comprised poor peasants in the South and big businessmen, freedom-loving teachers and semi-fascists who called themselves 'Young Radicals'; nevertheless it is amazing that a man so full of contradictions, at once courageous and confused, well-informed and naïve, could ever – and that for a number of years – have headed the government of a great power. But if one remembers that Herriot's character was formed in the past century, that he was the author of books on Madame Récamier, on the philosopher Philo Judaeus of Alexandria, on the young Soviet Republic, that between two meetings of the cabinet he was able to converse with a Russian writer about Descartes or the tastes of young people in the Soviet Union, that in his mayor's parlour in Lyons he received citizens every week and listened patiently to their complaints, that he took pride in being personally acquainted, not with crowned heads or industrial magnates, but with Gorky and Einstein, then much in his life becomes clear.

After the Second World War the right wing accused Herriot of hobnobbing with the 'Reds', while the left accused him of ingratitude: 'He has forgotten how he danced with joy when Soviet soldiers liberated him'. Herriot forgot nothing, he simply remained what he had always been: inconsistent in his politics and steadfast in his loyalties. I visited him in Lyons in the spring of 1954. We talked about Soviet art among other topics. I told him that I thought it disgraceful the way the French government had treated Ulanova and the other artists of the Bolshoi ballet who had been invited for a season in Paris but on arrival had been forbidden to appear, on the pretext of the events in Indochina. Herriot listened attentively, then went to his desk and there and then wrote a formal letter to me: 'I take this opportunity of telling you how much I regret the incident concerning the ballet and how heartily I condemn it. An evil fate seems to raise every obstacle to a Franco-Russian *rapprochement* which I, as an old democrat, passionately desire. I can assure you that the majority of Frenchmen agree with me in this matter'. He handed me the letter with the words: 'You have my permission to publish it'.

Soon after, the disease from which Herriot was suffering took a turn for the worse: he was hardly able to walk. In August 1954 the National Assembly was due to ratify the European Defence Community Treaty, or, to put it bluntly, France's agreement to the remilitarization of Western Germany. Herriot attended the session; he was unable to mount the rostrum and spoke seated in a chair. He sharply criticized French foreign policy and said that the guarantee of European security lay in a Franco-Soviet understanding; he then addressed a warning to the deputies: 'Do you not realize, my dear colleagues, that you will not find peace if you go looking for it on the paths to war'.

In 1956 a delegate conference of various peace organizations was held in Lyons to discuss the dangers of the revival of German militarism. We had a meeting in Herriot's study. His health had been deteriorating with every month that passed, nevertheless he wished to welcome us. He walked with great difficulty and had to be supported. In his address he said that the struggle for peace must go on, that weapons in the hands of the Bonn government were a menace to the whole of Europe; he looked feeble and decrepit, but his eyes still held the same mild twinkle and his voice had a clear and youthful ring. I never saw him again.

In Moscow, in 1945, he expressed a wish to meet and talk to one of the men responsible for Soviet policy. Relations between the Allies were rather strained. All the people at the embassy were new. The French diplomats told Herriot that 'the Russians have been asking when you intend to leave; it is a very broad hint'. Someone was evidently anxious to sow discord between Herriot and his Soviet friends.

At the time he had no pipe tobacco. I searched about for a long time and finally managed to get hold of several packets of 'Golden Fleece', but when I tried to ring up I was told that Herriot had 'left rather suddenly'. I sent the tobacco on, in the hope that it would catch up with him *en route*, and shortly after had a letter from him saying: 'I received your tobacco in Teheran. According to my calculations it should last me to the end of my days. I am very sorry I had to leave without saying good-bye to you and that I did not have the opportunity of spending the historic Victory Day with you as a fitting end to my stay in Moscow. But at 10 p.m. I was told that I was due to leave by air at 4 a.m.'

He lived to the age of eighty-five and died a year before the end of the Fourth Republic. His likes and dislikes never changed. He did not like militarists, clericalists, Prussians, chauvinists or anti-Semites; he did not like perfidy, music-halls or strict dieting; what he liked were the traditions of the Jacobins, Lyons, Descartes, the Russians, Beethoven, eloquence, popularity and the wines of the Beaujolais.

When I saw him in 1954 he suddenly began to talk about poetry and described to me how in his young days he had met drink-sodden Verlaine who was soliciting a grant of money. 'You're fond of Villon', he said, 'but do you know the poems of Louise Labé, a sixteenth-century poetess of Lyons?' And he recited the opening lines of one of her sonnets:

> Ie vis, ie meurs: ie me brule et me noye.
> I'ay chaut estreme en endurant froidure:
> La vie m'est et trop molle et trop dure.
> I'ay grans ennuis entremeslez de ioye:
> Tout à un coup ie ris et ie larmoye,
> Et plaisir maint grief tourment i'endure: . . .[1]

It would not be inappropriate to end my recollections of Herriot with these lines. But I must pick up the thread of my narrative to repeat the fact that though on 2nd May (1945) he had said to me: 'I shall soon be clinking glasses with you, with all my Russian friends, to celebrate Victory', on the eve of that Victory Day he had been put on board a plane.

---

[1] From *Œuvres de Louise Labé*, edited by Charles Boy. (Alphonse Lemerre, Paris 1887.)

23

I HAVE a very clear memory of the last days of the war. Owing to Alexandrov's article I was unable to go to Berlin. I sat in front of my radio and tuned in to London, Paris, Brazzaville: I was waiting for the denouement.

Wars almost always begin suddenly and end slowly: the final outcome is plain but men still go on dying.

In April I had written: 'There is no one in Germany to capitulate'. The Third Reich was dying as it had lived – inhumanly. There were no Kiel sailors now, not even a Prince Max von Baden. Not a single regiment, not a single town had the spirit to rise, even at the last minute, against the Nazi leaders. Later a German said rather wittily that red curtains remained intact everywhere but there were no sheets left: white rags came creeping out of every window. The Allies were now advancing swiftly: one German town after another surrendered. But in Berlin the battle was still being fought, and the city surrendered only house by house. Veterans who remembered the Hohenzollern empire, schoolboys befuddled by cheap heroics, SS men fearing retribution fired at Soviet soldiers from windows and roofs. Meanwhile the Nazi leaders gave way to hysterics in bunkers or stealthily made their way to the west, changed their clothing and disguised themselves.

On 1st May the German radio announced that Hitler had died a hero's death in Berlin. A couple of days later London gave out the news that the Führer and Goebbels had committed suicide. Goering and Himmler had vanished. Admiral Doenitz announced that he was forming a new government; this, however, proved no easy task: there had been no Opposition in Germany for a long time past, and as for the men who only the day before had supported Hitler, they were far more eager to obtain a Swiss passport than a portfolio.

On the evening of 7th May I listened to Brazzaville: in Rheims the representatives of Doenitz and the German High Command had signed the instrument of unconditional surrender; on the Soviet side the document had been signed by Colonel – I listened to this item three times but could not distinguish the colonel's name: the announcer was incapable of pronouncing it (it turned out to be Colonel Susloparov whom I knew: he had been military attaché in France). Brazzaville also announced that 8th May had been declared a holiday. I was very excited and rang up the office; I was told that rumour should not be trusted, that this could be a provocation, an attempt to reach a separate peace, and that one way and another military operations were still in progress.

On 8th May London and Paris transmitted the joyous roar of the crowds, songs, descriptions of demonstrations, Churchill's speech. In the evening there were two salvoes: for Dresden and for several Czech towns. However, from two o'clock onwards the telephone never stopped ringing: friends and acquaintances asked: 'Have you heard anything?' or mysteriously warned me: 'Don't turn off your set'. Meanwhile Moscow radio was giving the story of the battles for Liepaja (Libau) and describing the successful launching of the new government loan and the San Francisco conference.

At long last, late at night, the news came of the surrender signed in Berlin. I believe it was 2 a.m. I looked out of the window: almost everywhere there were lights in the windows – people were staying awake.

The tenants in our house came out on to the landings, some of them scantily clad, having been wakened by their neighbours. Everyone embraced everyone else, somebody sobbed aloud. At 4 a.m. Gorky Street was thronged: people stood about outside their houses or poured along the street towards Red Square. After days of rain the sky was swept clear of clouds and the sun bathed the city in warmth.

So began the day which we had so eagerly awaited. I strode along without a thought in my head, a grain of sand caught up by the wind. It was an extraordinary day, both in its joy and in its sadness; it is difficult to describe it; nothing happened, and yet everything was full of significance: every face, every word uttered by a passer-by.

One elderly woman was showing everybody the photograph of a young man in uniform and telling them it was her son who had been killed the previous autumn; she wept and smiled. Girls, holding hands, were singing. I walked next to a woman and a small boy who kept saying: 'Ooh, there's a major, hurrah! There's a senior lieutenant, Order of the Patriotic War Second Class, hurrah!' The woman had a sweet, rather haggard face. I suddenly remembered the woman with the small boy sitting in the Strastnoy boulevard at the beginning of the war; he was being naughty, and she was crying. I felt that this was the same woman though there was probably not the slightest resemblance; it was just that the two faces merged into one. A little girl pushed a bunch of snowdrops into a sailor's hand, but when he tried to kiss her she gave a tiny hoot of laughter and ran away. 'Eternal memory to the dead,' an old man said in a loud voice. A major on crutches raised his hand to his cap in a salute while the old man explained: 'It's the wife who begged me to say it. She's in bed with a chill. Sergeant Berezovsky of the Guards. Mentioned twice by Comrade Stalin'. Someone remarked: 'Well, now he'll soon be home again'. The old man shook his head: 'He died a hero's death on 18th April. His commanding officer wrote to us. My wife said to me: "Tell people about it"'.

As I have already said, there was a great deal of sorrow: everybody was remembering the dead. I thought of Boris Lapin, and it seemed to me that on the night when we had read Hemingway's novel together he had wanted to tell me something, but we were in a hurry to finish the book and never got talking properly. It also came to me that, though we had lived at such close quarters, I never really talked to him; I mean, we talked a lot but always about something else, not about the most important things. I recalled kindly Yevgeny Petrov, his laugh and the way he had said: 'When the war's over I'll write a classical novel in seven volumes about the heroism of Commissar of State Security, third rank, Yustian Innokentyevich Prokakin-Stukal'. I remembered how he had tried to persuade me to put on warm underclothing: 'You're no chicken, and Mozhaisk is not Nice'. I recalled my comrades on *Red Star*, the young poets Mikhail Kulchitsky, Pavel Kogan, the Tatsin tank-men, Chernyakhovsky, Yuri Sevruk of *Znamya* ('Banner'), the dispatch-rider Misha who read his poems to me near Rzhev. For some reasons I kept seeing Rzhev, the rain, the two buildings – 'Colonel' and 'Lieutenant-Colonel' – as if there had been no Kastornoye, no Vilnius, no Elbing after it. It was Rzhev, always Rzhev.

That evening there could not have been a single table in our country where the people gathered round it were not conscious of an empty place. Tvardovsky later put it into words: 'To the thunder of guns, for the first time we bade farewell to all who had died in the war, the way the living say farewell to the dead'.

In Red Square the very young were enjoying themselves and their gaiety infected others. And, indeed, how could one help being happy? It was over. Soldiers were tossed into the air. One officer protested: 'Why me?' but the crowd only shouted 'Hurrah!' by way of reply. Several soldiers recognized me: 'Ehrenburg!' I was tossed in the air too, which is no fun in itself but, in addition, makes you feel embarrassed. 'Enough!' I cried, but this only acted as a challenge and they tossed me higher still.

'It's over,' I said to Lyuba, to Irina, to the Saviches, to acquaintances and to strangers. There are no words to describe how much I had come to hate war. Of all human undertakings, often cruel and senseless, it is the most damnable. There can be no justification for it, and no talk of war being part of human nature or a school of valour, no Kipling or his imitators, no idealized pictures of 'manly talks round the campfire' can cover up the horror of mass murder, the fate of uprooted generations.

In the evening Stalin's speech was broadcast. He spoke briefly and with assurance: his voice betrayed no emotion and he addressed us not as 'brothers and sisters' as he had done on 3rd July 1941, but as 'Men and Women Compatriots'. An unprecedented salute thundered out: a salvo of a thousand guns. Window-panes rattled. For my part, I thought about Stalin's speech. Its lack of warmth grieved but did not surprise me. He was the Generalissimo, the victor. What use had he for emotion? People listening to the speech shouted in reverent admiration: 'Hurrah for Stalin!' This had long ceased to astonish me; I had grown accustomed to the fact that there were the people with their joys and sorrows and somewhere above them there was Stalin. Twice a year one could see him from a distance as he stood on the tribune of the Mausoleum. He wanted the progress of humanity, he was leading the people, deciding their fate. I myself wrote about Stalin-the-Victor; I thought of the soldiers who believed in him, of the partisans and the hostages, of letters written on the eve of death that ended with the words 'Long live Stalin!' Now, as I recall the evening of 9th May, I could ascribe to myself different, far more right-headed thinking, for even at the time I had not forgotten the fate of Gorev, Stern, Smushkevich, Pavlov and I knew that they had not been traitors but men of the highest honour and integrity, I knew that their destruction, like that of other Red Army officers, engineers and members of the intelligentsia, had cost our people dear.

But in all honesty I must say that on that evening none of these things were in my thoughts. Every word spoken (or rather transmitted) by Stalin was convincing, and the salvoes of a thousand guns sounded like an 'Amen'.

On that day everyone must have felt that this was one more milestone, perhaps the most important one: something had ended, something was beginning. I realized that the new, post-war life would be hard: the country was devastated and impoverished, the war had killed off the young, the strong, probably the best; but I also knew how much our people had gained in stature. I remembered the wise and hopeful words about the future which I had more than once heard in trenches and dugouts. And if anyone had told me that evening that ahead of us lay the Leningrad case, the indictment of the doctors, in short, all that was exposed and condemned eleven years later at the XXth Party Congress, I should have taken him for a madman. No, I was no prophet.

From the middle of April I had had plenty of leisure and gave much thought to the future. At times I was gripped by anxiety. Although during the last weeks talk of dissensions between the Allies had disappeared from the columns of our press, I realized that there was no genuine agreement nor could one reasonably be expected. I was surprised at the indulgent tone in which the Americans and the British referred to Franco and Salazar. I feared that the western Allies would try their best to obtain the kind of peace that would allow the German militarists to regain a foothold within a short time. I recorded in my notebook a French broadcast: an interview with a German general who had surrendered to the Americans. He was cordially received at Supreme Command HQ. In reply to the interviewer's questions he said: 'Hitler made an unpardonable mistake in directing his blow at the west: we are paying for it now. I hope that your governments will act more reasonably, for ten years hence you will have to rely on Germany in a war against the Russians'. The commentator remarked indignantly that such statements could only provoke a contemptuous smile. I listened but I did not smile. The radio announced that the Americans were negotiating with Admiral Doenitz, who had at long last raked up enough Ministers and installed his government in the small town of Flensburg near the Danish frontier. Everybody sent congratulations to Stalin and glorified the Red Army, but in spite of that I did not feel easy.

And how would things be in our country after the war? This pre-occupied me even more. New methods of education were needed: not bullying, not dinning things in, not 'campaigns', but inspiration. The young should be inspired with the principles of humanity, with confidence, with the fire that does not allow of indifference to the fate of a comrade or a neighbour. Above all, what would Stalin do now? In March Irina went on behalf of *Red Star* to Odessa from where the British, French and Belgians liberated by the Red Army were being repatriated by sea. While she was there a troopship arrived bringing our prisoners of war, among whom were men who had escaped and joined the ranks of the French partisans. Irina told me that they were received like criminals, isolated and, it was rumoured, were to be sent to labour camps. There were moments when I asked myself whether 1937 would now be repeated. Once again logic misled me: in 1937 fear of fascist Germany had caused the fire to be directed at our own people. But now Fascism had been defeated. The Red Army had shown its strength. The people had endured too much. The past could not repeat itself. And so, once again, I mistook my wishes for reality and logic for a compulsory subject in the school of History.

The reason why I record all this is that I want to understand myself what made me write, late on the evening of that extraordinary day, the poem entitled *Victory*. It is not long and I quote it in its entirety: 'A poet spoke of them in bygone times: they awaited one another for many a long day, and when they met they did not recognize one another in the heavens which know no sorrow. Not in paradise, but on this vast tract of earth, where at every step there is sorrow, sorrow, sorrow, I awaited her, as one waits only when one loves; I knew her as one knows only oneself; I knew her in blood, in mud, in grief. The hour struck. The war ended. I made my way home. She came towards me, and we did not recognize each other'.

Fadeyev once asked me when I had written this poem. I said it was on Victory Day. He was surprised: 'Why?' I had honestly to admit that I did not know. And even now, when I recall that day, I still do not understand why I saw the long-awaited victory in that way. No doubt it is in the very nature of poetry to sharpen and deepen perception; I was not trying to be logical in my poem, I was not trying to comfort myself, I was only expressing the bewilderment, the anxiety that lurked somewhere deep inside me.

I have done my best to reconstruct that distant day as exactly as possible. After re-reading what I have just written I feel some doubts: I may have given the impression that all I did was to ruminate, to nurse misgivings, whereas in fact I rejoiced with everybody else, exchanging smiles and congratulations. Victory! I recalled the nights in Madrid, the SS men in the streets of Paris. Kiev. Dear God, what joy! When all was said and done, a new epoch was beginning. Our people had shown its strength: ill prepared, taken unawares, it had not surrendered, it had stood to the death at the gates of Moscow, on the Volga, it had turned to face the invader and struck him down. I was reminded of a phrase in an article in the *Christian Science Monitor*: 'Perhaps the coming era will be known as the Russian Century'.

But it is not with speculations about the future that I want to end my description of 9th May: it was a day which drew people closer together, and this manifested itself not merely in strangers embracing in the street, but in smiles, in glances, in a kind of haze of fellow-feeling, of tenderness, which on that night enveloped the whole city.

The last day of the war. Never had I felt such a bond with other people as during the war years. Some writers produced fine novels, stories and poems at the time. But what have I to show for those years? Thousands of articles, all very much alike – which only an over-conscientious historian will bring himself to read some day – and a few dozen short poems. But those years remain precious to me above all others: with everybody else I grieved, I despaired, I hated, I loved. I got to know people better than I might have done in many long decades, and also grew to love them better, for there had been so much unhappiness, so much spiritual strength, so many partings and such steadfastness.

I thought about all this, too, in the night when the blaze of the rockets had faded out, the songs had died down, and women wept into their pillows for fear of waking their neighbours: I thought about grief, about courage, about love and about loyalty.

INDEX